The Immortal

The Immortal

*True Accounts of the
250-Year-Old Man, Li Qingyun*

By Yang Sen

Translated by Stuart Alve Olson

Valley Spirit Arts
Phoenix, Arizona

Translated from the Chinese Edition
An Authentic and True Record of a 250-Year-Old Man
(二百五十歲人瑞實記, *Er Bai Wu Shi Sui Ren Rui Shi Ji*)
By Yang Sen (楊森著, Yang Sen Zhe)
Zhongwai Library Series 3
(中外文庫之三, Zhong Wai Wen Ku Zhi San)

Editors: Wang Chengsheng (王成聖), Li Huan (李寰)

Contributors: Zhang Qichang (張其昌), Yan Lingfeng (嚴靈峯)
        Liu Guiyun (劉桂雲), Wang Liankui (王聯奎)
Zhongwai Library series 3 copyright reserved
An Authentic and True Record of a 250-Year-Old Man
Author: Yang Sen
Editors: Li Huan and Wang Chengsheng
Publisher: Zhong Wai Publishing House. No. 7-2, sec. 3 Xinsheng S.
Rd., Taipei City 106, Taiwan (R.O.C.)
Published By: *Zhong Wai Magazine*
No. 7-2, sec. 3 Xinsheng S. Rd., Taipei City 106, Taiwan (R.O.C.)
    1st edition: Republic of China year 59 (1970) July.
    2nd edition: Republic of China year 65 (1976) May.
Government Information Office, Republic of China (Taiwan)
enrollment No. 138

English Translation Edition

Library of Congress Control Number: 2014946206
ISBN-13: 978-1-889633-34-3
ISBN-10: 1-889633-34-8

Book and cover design by Patrick Gross.
www.valleyspiritarts.com

Daoist Immortal Li Qingyun
(1678–1933)

General Yang Sen
(February 20, 1884, to May 15, 1977)
In 1927, General Yang Sen brought Li Qingyun to Wanxian.
The above photo was taken when Yang Sen was eighty-four years old.

Yang Sen was born in Guang'an, Sichuan province, on February 20, 1884. When he was twenty, he joined the military in Sichuan, and at age forty became its governor (1924 through 1926). In 1925, he was appointed as the military governor, and then in 1933 was the commanding general of the 20th Army Corps and the 27th Army Corps, Beiyang Army unit. From 1938 until 1945, he took on the additional tasks of being the Deputy Commander of the 6th and 9th war areas, and then in 1945 until 1948 was the chairman of the government of Guizhou province.

Despite being a provincial warlord, he served as a general for President Chiang Kai-shek—honorably serving the Chinese nationalist government until the defeat of the Kuomingtang, called the Chinese Civil War. He continued his military and political service of the Republic of China (Taiwan) under President Chiang Kai-shek, concluding in seventy-three years of service.

In 1949, he left mainland China for Taiwan in what was called the Nationalist Exodus. In Taiwan, 1950, he held the post of the Republic of China's (Taiwan) Committee Chairman at the Olympic Games in Mexico and was the flag bearer during the opening ceremonies. He was an avid mountaineer and Chairman of the Taiwan Mountain Climbing Association.

Yang Sen reportedly had eleven wives, many concubines, and numerous children. According to Master T.T. Liang (1900–2002), Yang Sen had nearly three hundred concubines, many of whom he never met (as these arrangements were of political favoritism). While living in Taiwan he followed Li Qingyun's teachings, began writing articles on Li Qingyun, and compiled the book *An Authentic and True Record of a 250-Year-Old Man* (二百五十歲人瑞實記, *Er Bai Wu Shi Sui Ren Rui Shi Ji*). Yang Sen became a Daoist master in his own right with many students until the end of his life on May 15, 1977.

Military photograph of Yang Sen.

Acknowledgments

This book has been a work in progress for more than thirty years and many people have given their suggestions and help during this time. Foremost, I offer deep gratitude to Master T.T. Liang for not only presenting Yang Sen's Chinese text to me, but for all his help and encouragement in getting this book completed in English.

In the early years of translating this work, Dr. Neil Nathan, Dr. Stuart Zimmerman (the Elder), Vern Peterson, and Dr. Koon Yuipoon all offered invaluable advice and support. Dr. Teresa Chen and her daughter Julia helped me really progress with the translation and research work.

Thanks to my good friend and student, Dan Kelly, for all his support and encouragement; Bryant Seals, who provided much-needed Chinese connections for helping complete the work; Genny Cheng, without whom I could not have finished the translation; and to Prof. Dave Capco, who has always encouraged, advised, supported, and pushed me to complete these projects.

To my longtime student, friend, and editor Patrick D. Gross for working so hard on the final edit (encouraging me to include many more helpful comments and footnotes) and for formatting the book and cover—many, many thanks. Much appreciation is given to Jenny Hsieh for her research help. To my wife, Lily, who always strives so hard on the content editing of my books, and always brings greater clarity to my work.

To all those mentioned above and to all the contributors of the original Chinese text, I bow in deep gratitude and offer my highest appreciation.

—Stuart Alve Olson

Contents

Frontispiece v

General Yang Sen vi

Acknowledgments ix

Timeline of Li Qingyun's Life and Important Events xvi

Translator's Introduction 1

Chinese-Foreign Library Preface by Wang Chengsheng 31

The Immortal Li Qingyun

Preface to *The True Story of the 250-Year-Old Man,*
Li Qingyun by Yang Sen 37

The 250-Year-Old Man Talks on His Own Experiences

by Wang Chengsheng 39

How Do You Live to be 250 Years Old? 39

His Appearance Was Very Majestic 40

Walking Lively and Refusing to Sit on a Sedan Chair
to Exercise His Muscles and Bones 42

Collected Herbs for 200 Years in Remote Mountains 47

Meeting a Daoist Master and Learning Secrets 51

Publication in the *North China Daily News* 58

The Centenarian, the 250-Year-Old Man 61

The Evidence of the 250-Year-Old Man 63

Familiar With Anecdotes Through Nine Emperors
of the Qing 66

Eat Three Qians of Gou Qi Daily 71

Pouring the Liquor of Clarified Butter Over the Head
to Increase Wisdom So Not to Arouse Affections 78

Live for a Hundred Years, But Only Today Is Today 83

250-Year-Old Man, Li Qingyun by Yang Sen 89
    Nourishing-Life Seminar in Baizhuang 89
    Li Qingyun's Background, Stories, and Footprints 93
    Speaking on the Regimes and Methods on the
        Way of Nourishing-Life 95
    Presenting Photos to Chairman Chiang Kai-shek 97
    Talking About Li Qingyun One More Time 98

Anecdotes of the 250 Years Old Man
    by Li Huan 107

**A Big Hit in the U.S. When *Zhong Wai* Published
the Article of "The 250-Year-Old Man"**
    by Zhang Qichang 111

**Do You Believe That Human Beings Can Live
for 250 Years?**
    by Yan Lingfeng 123

Replies to the Queries Regarding the 250-Year-Old Man
    by Li Huan 137

The Secrets of Li Qingyun's Immortality
Preface to *The Secrets of Li Qingyun's Immortality*
    by Yang Sen 151

Part One: The Great Dao of Long Life 155
    The Secrets of Long Life 155
    Chapter on Nourishing Life 164
    Chapter on Regulating the Mind 168
    Chapter on Purifying and Illumining 172

Chapter on Breathing 183

Responses to Lianxiazi's Questions 190

**Part Two: Discourses on the Beginning Foundations
of Long Life** 197

The Method of Tranquil Sitting 201

The Method of Circulating the Breath 203

The Method for Calming Spirit 206

The Methods of the Elemental Skills 208

The Methods of Walking, Moving, Sitting,
and Lying Down 229

A Summary of Names for Acupuncture Points
and Meridians of the Entire Body 232

The Diagram of Human Body Acupoints 245

Part Three: The Way of Achieving the Dao 247

Huainanzi 248

Laozi 250

Zhuangzi 251

Guanyinzi 257

Zihuazi 265

Yangzi 265

Xuanzhenzi 270

Lumenzi 272

Nanshanzi 273

Hengtongzi 273

Fangshuzi 274

Linchuanzi 276

Yinguangzi 278

Ranghuizi 278

Yangmingzi 279

Qianmingzi 280

Mingliaozi 281
Fuyuanzi 281
Laozi 282
Guanyinzi 285
Tanzi 288
Canzi 290
Benjizi 293
Chongxinzi 295
Longanzi 298
Huizhongzi 299
Kuangzi 302
Huzi 304

Part Four: Chapters on the Nature of Mind 307
The True Nature Dwells in the Constant
    by Zhuangzi 307
The Indignant Mind Is Not Benevolence or Righteousness
    by Zhuangzi 308
Benevolence and Righteousness Falsely Wandering
    in the Mind by Zhuangzi 309
Obtaining Perfection in Heaven by Guanyinzi 310
The Human Mind Is Like Water in a Dish by Xunzi 312
Those With a Virtuous Mind, Master the Mind
    by Guanyinzi 312
The Mind Has a Great Constant by Guanyinzi 313
Detaining the Mind by Guanyinzi 314
My Mind Creates the Transformation and Circulation
    by Guanyinzi 315
The Mind Is Affected So Easily [No author listed] 316
Doing Good or Bad Cannot Be Forced by Zihuazi 317
The Snobbish and Confused Mind by Zihuazi 319
The Highest Spirit of the Human Mind by Yangzi 320

Great People Are Not Robbers of Life by Tanzi 321

Conceal the Qi and Accumulate Essence by Tanzi 321

Forget Form, Seek Nature by Tanzi 322

The Harmony of Nature by Liuzi 323

Nature Has Its Own Preferences by Liuzi 324

Remove Sense-Desires and Nourish Nature by Liuzi 327

Mind and Body Were Originally Ultimate Void
    by Xuanzhenzi 328

Cultivating Nature and Penetrating the True
    by Tianyinzi 328

Lessen Desires and Nourish the Mind by Zhuzi 329

Do Not Forget to Study the Correct by Chengzi 330

Honor Your Mind By Renewing It Each Day
    by Zhangzi 331

The Mind Methods of Sages and Worthies by Zhenzi 333

The Source Is the Original Body by Zhangzi 335

Clean Water as an Allegory for Nature by Wuzi 335

A Discourse on the Movement and Tranquility of Mind
    by Haiqiongzi 336

The Perfect Human Mind by Zhuzi 338

Self-Nature Is Difficult to Clarify by Zhuzi 338

The Delirious and Insane Mind by Yangmingzi 339

Guard Your Mind Cautiously by Yangmingzi 339

Preserve the Origin, Revert to the Origin
    [No author listed] 340

The Peacefulness and Purity of the Heavenly Sovereign
    by Xinxinzi 340

The True Mind Acts on All Things by Tianhuzi 341

Everything in Nature Is Good by Fuyuanzi 342

Dao Mind, Human Mind by Feixiuzi 342

Shut Off the External, Hold Fast the Internal
    by Bidongzi 343

My Mind Can Work in the Myriad of Things
  by Guanyinzi 343
Realizing the Dream of Life and Death
  [No author listed, from the *Zhuangzi*] 345
The Wanderings of a True Person
  [No author listed, from the *Huainanzi*] 347
Wang Liang Asked the Shadow by Yingzhenzi 349
Obtaining Mind in the Foremost Pavilion
  [No author listed] 351

**Part Five: A Record of Quotations from the Old Man,
Qingyun** 355

Appendix

Questions About Li Qingyun's Age
  by Yan Lingfeng 385
I Had Seen Li Qingyun
  by Liu Guiyun 387
I Had Seen Li Qingyun, Too
  by Wang Liankui 389

Afterword by Stuart Alve Olson 393

Timeline of Li Qingyun's Life and Important Events

During the Life of Li Qingyun

1678[1]   Age 1   Li is born in Qijiang County, Sichuan. Family moves to Tiaodengchang, Kaixian, Sichuan.

1681   Age 4   Li begins his private tutorial learning.

1690   Age 13   Li leaves Sichuan with three elder herb gatherers (according to Yang Sen).

1727   Age 50   Meets elder, introduced to Gou Qi.

1728[2]   Age 51   Serves as a tactical and topography advisor in the army of General Yu Zhongqi.

---

[1]   According to *The New York Times* and *Time* magazine, Dean Wu Chung-chien of the Department of Education at Minkuo University, China, discovered records of Li Qingyun having been honored on his 100th, 150th, and 200th birthdays, and that this would put his date of birth as 1677. However, Li Qingyun said he was born in the 17th Year of the Kangxi (康熙) reign, which was 1678. This date makes sense if taking into account that the Chinese traditionally considered a newborn as already being one years old, counting the time of the pregnancy. This timeline, then, works from the assumption that Li was born in 1678, but counts his age as being one years old so that the dates match those of the Imperial Government documents.

[2]   According to Master Liang from conversations he had with Yang Sen and Xiong Yanghe, Li Qingyun's knowledge of mountain terrains earned him positions beyond just a common fighting soldier.

1755	Age 78	Li engages in the battle at Golden River, leaves army afterward and goes to White Snow Mountain to gather herbs.
1777	Age 100	Receives birthday wishes from Imperial Government.
1790	Age 113	Li Bao is born (possible son of Li Qingyun).
1806	Age 129	Li meets his Daoist teacher, Xu Jing, in Kongtong Mountains. Other reports say he was 139.
1807	Age 130	Begins teaching at Mt. Emei, Sichuan, for next one hundred years.
1827	Age 150	Receives birthday wishes from Imperial Government.
1877	Age 200	Receives birthday wishes from Imperial Government.
1908	Age 231	Master Yang Hexuan publishes *The Secrets of Li Qingyun's Immortality* (alleged copyright date according to Master Liang).
1912	Age 235	Li moves back to Chenjiachang.
1914	Age 237	Zhang and Zhou visit with Li.
1920	Age 243	Xiong Yanghe visits Li and writes article about him for a Nanjing University paper.
1923	Age 246	Wu Peifu first visits Li in Chenjiachang.
1924	Age 247	September 8, *Time* magazine cover and article on Wu Peifu.
1926	Age 249	Gui Yunjin visits Li in Chenjiachang. Li meets with Yinshizi (Prof. Jiang Weiqiao). Li goes to Beijing and stays with Wu Peifu and teaches at Beijing University Meditation Society.
1927	Age 250	February, Li is invited to Wanxian by Yang Sen and Gui Yunjin.

		March, photographs are taken of Li

		March, photographs are taken of Li at Yang Sen's residence.
		April, Li leaves Wanxian for Chenjiachang.
1928	Age 251	June 5, *North China Daily News* article.
		June 6, *Shanghai Declaration News* article
		June 8, *Letters From Readers*.
1929	Age 252	October, Prof. Wu Chungchien discovers Imperial Government records of Li.
		October 29, *Time* magazine article on Prof. Wu Chungchien's findings.
1930	Age 253	April 15, Chiang Kai-shek receives photo and news of Li Qingyun.
		Chiang Kai-shek invites Li to Nanjing.
		Yang Sen's envoy to Chenjiachang is told of Li passing away.
1933	Age 256	May 5, Li's death announced in Beijing.
		May 6, *The New York Times* announces Li's passing.
		May 15, *Time* magazine announces Li's passing.

After the Death of Li Qingyun

1949	Yang Sen escapes to Taiwan.
1965	Articles on Li Qingyun in *Zhong Wai Magazine* by Wang Chengsheng.
1969	Zhang Qichang writes article on Li Qingyun from New York.
1970	First Chinese Edition of Yang Sen's book is published.
1972	Yang Sen posts two more articles on Li Qingyun in *Zhong Wai Magazine*.
1974	*Taoist Health Exercise Book* by Da Liu is published.

1976	Second Chinese Edition of Yang Sen's book is released.
1977	Yang Sen passes away.
1982	*Tao of Pooh* by Benjamin Hoff is published.
1989	*Tao of Health, Sex, and Longevity* by Daniel Reed is published.
2000	*Qigong, the Secret of Youth* by Yang Jwing-Ming is published.
2002	*Qigong Teachings of a Taoist Immortal* by Stuart Alve Olson is published.
2014	First English Edition of *The Immortal: True Accounts of the 250-Year-Old Man, Li Qingyun* by Yang Sen is published.

Introduction

...ed Li Qingyun to Wanxian, ...nd longevity. Li Qingyun was ... at the time, and his visit to ...970, Yang Sen compiled a book of ...of Li Qingyun, titled *An Authentic and ...Year-Old Man,* which I started translating ...-two years ago.[2]

...st began living with my teacher, Master T.T. ...his family in 1982, he gave me a copy of Yang Sen's ...I immediately recognized the photo of Li Qingyun fi... ...g seen it years before in Master Da Liu's *Taoist Health and Exercise Book* (Links Books, 1974).

Yang Sen's book was not just a random text that Master Liang felt I should read and study, as he was deeply connected to the work through his friendship with Yang Sen, and from

---

1   I wish to address a political issue that may arise for some readers, especially those of Chinese descent. The contents of this book concern some history revolving around the Nationalist Republican Army (NRA) and the Republic of China (ROC) government headed by Chairman Chiang Kai-shek. Many people still harbor ill feelings towards the people and events that created such political turmoil in China and Taiwan of those times. I hope, however, that these issues can be set aside, as this book is about Li Qingyun, and is not seeking to advocate any of the political agendas or glorify any of the political leaders of the period in history covered in this work.

2   My translation is from both Chinese editions, with the bulk of the work from the 1976 edition.

having heard about Li in the late 1920s and wanting to have met him then.

When Master Liang had made a return trip to Taiwan in 1970, he visited with his good friend Yang Sen, who gave him a few copies of the first edition of his recently published book. After Liang returned to America, he gave one of these copies to Master Da Liu (1904–2000). These old friends had lived together for a while in New York in the early 1960s. Master Liang had come to the United States from Taiwan in 1962 to serve as a translator at the United Nations for his teacher, Professor Cheng Manching. While briefly staying with Da Liu, he was able to meet with his old friend George Yeh, the Republic of China's ambassador, and the famous Chinese painter Zhang Qichang,[3] as well as other old acquaintances. Articles on Li Qingyun published by *Zhong Wai Magazine* were really popular with the Chinese living in New York at this time, and were the topic of many conversations.

Master Da Liu's numerous books on Daoism contain much of what he had learned from Yang Sen's book. In his *Taoist Health Exercise Book,* for example, he wrote,

I happened to read a Chinese book, *Biography of a 250-Year-Old Man* by Yang Shen [Sen][4] (Taiwan: China and Western Publishers, 1970), which inspired me to expand the manuscript into a more detailed version and append supplementary material. The

---

3   Zhang Qichang wrote "A Big Hit in the U.S. When *Zhong Wai* published the article of 'The 250-Year-Old Man.'" See page 111.

4   All text in brackets are my insertions in the translated text to clarify a person, show the original Chinese, or offer some brief comment. Footnotes serve for longer commentaries and to offer notes and insights relevant to the text.

250-year-old man was Li Ch'ing Yuen [Li Qingyun] who, besides being an expert herbalist, had been a regular practitioner of exercises similar to those described in this book.

I should point out that Li Ch'ing Yuen's longevity is recorded and authenticated: he was a legendary figure of ancient times such as the 800-year-old P'eng Tzu.[5]

I was familiar with Da Liu's works before I met Master Liang, and in many ways they helped me start along my Daoist path, so it was fascinating for me to not only learn that he and Master Liang were friends, but that Liang had given him the copy of Yang Sen's book that so influenced his work.

Yang Sen's Chinese text was difficult for me at that time, and in some ways I felt Master Liang had given me the book to frustrate me more than present me with what he called, "a treasure trove." When he gave me the book, he informed me quite sternly that it was my duty to translate this book and "make it accessible to round eyes" (Westerners), to which I na-ively and prematurely promised I would do. A few years later I

---

5   P'eng Tzu (彭祖, Peng Zu) reportedly lived for eight hundred
     years during the Yin dynasty (1900–1066 BCE). Peng Zu is con-
     sidered the Chinese Methuselah. Specific reports say he lived
     to be 777 years old, but most accounts just say 800 years old.
     Legend states that despite his old age he still had the appearance
     of a young man. His youthful look and longevity were due to his
     diet of regularly eating mica dust and powdered deer antler, as
     well as having cultivated specific sexual practices. In Daoist inter-
     nal alchemy teachings, he is credited with having introduced
     the sexual practices and teachings for the prolonging of life.

discovered he had promised Yang Sen in 1970 that he would translate the book into English. So, now, with the publication of this work, both our promises have been fulfilled.

Many years passed with little progress on the translation. My first attempts focused on the chapters I found of interest, and that I felt my Chinese skills could handle at the time, such as Li's comments on the Eight Brocades Dao Yin exercises, the section on the "Way of Longevity," and Li's personal account of gathering herbs in the mountains. Even though my book *Qigong Teachings of a Taoist Immortal: The Eight Essential Exercises of Master Li Ching-yun* was published in 2002, which includes translations from Yang Sen's book, it took me until 2014 to finally complete the whole translation.

Much of my interest in translating this book stemmed from hearing about the close friendship that Master Liang and Yang Sen shared when they were both in Taipei after the communist takeover in 1949. On more occasions than I can recount, Master Liang and I would talk about Li Qingyun and Yang Sen, so I was privileged to hear many stories about them.

Master Liang said that news of Li Qingyun spread quickly throughout much of China during the mid 1930s and early 1940s, and Yang Sen's articles during the 1960s and 70s within *Zhong Wai Magazine* on Li fueled a kind of "250-year-old man" fever. The fever rekindled in 1970 when Yang Sen released his book, which received worldwide attention among the overseas Chinese.

Master Liang said that in China after Li's stay in Wanxian, everyone was talking about him, so much so that he was considered a national treasure at the time. Li's death was even announced in *The New York Times* and *Time* magazine in 1933.

Liang always regretted that he was unable to visit Wanxian to see Li for himself. As the highest ranking Chinese official

(Chief Tide Surveyor) for British Customs, he could not break away from his duties in Shanghai helping the British prepare for what they knew would be an invasion from Japan along the eastern seaboard of China.

Turmoil in China

Eighty-six years have passed since Li's visit to Wanxian and the accounts of this event are now finally appearing in English. Some people may question why it took so long for Yang Sen to start writing about Li Qingyun, but this is understandable when you consider the times in which they were living.

Most readers will be unaware of how chaotic China was during the period of Li Qingyun's final years. Starting in 1850, the Tai Ping Rebellion against the Manchu government began and didn't completely end until 1871. More than 20 million people were killed in this civil war. The Opium Wars between China and Britain (1839–1842 and 1856–1860) marked the beginning of the end of the Qing dynasty. The real problems for China began when British and French forces attacked Beijing (to retaliate for the arrest of a British envoy and the torture and killing of a number of foreign hostages), wherein the imperial family was forced to flee to Manchuria for a time.

In 1861, Emperor Xian Feng (咸豐) passed away (suffering from dementia and depression, which he treated with alcohol and drugs). The Empress Dowager Cixi (慈禧太后) then ruled until her death in 1908, leaving China in chaos and financial ruin. During her reign, she incited the Boxer Rebellion (1898–1900) to rid the country of foreign intervention.

Before Cixi's death in 1908, she installed Puyi (溥儀), a two-year-old boy, as emperor (popularly known as the Last Emperor). Puyi was forced to abdicated his throne in 1912 after the Xinhai Revolution, effectively ending the Qing dynasty. The Republic of China (now in Taiwan) began in 1912, which experienced numerous changes of leadership and foreign intrusions. The first Sino-Japanese invasion of Manchuria took place in 1931, which had put China in a precarious situation internally as the home territories of the Manchus were now under Japanese control. Many political factions were attempting to take control of China, including Japan, the Communists under Mao Zedong, Chiang Kai-shek (National Republican Army), and foreign interests as well. To say the least, this was an extremely tumultuous time in China.

In 1937, the second Sino-Japanese war began with Japan taking over most of the eastern seaboard and northeast areas of China. This invasion lasted until 1945 when Japan surrendered to foreign allies. Four years later, Mao took over China and many Chinese fled to Taiwan (Formosa)—Yang Sen included.

This is just a brief account of how uncertain and dangerous life was in China during the time Yang Sen met with Li Qingyun, but it does help explain, in my opinion, what led Li to leave Wanxian and why he was so secretive and protective of his family and students.

Words can never describe the horrors of that period in Chinese history. My teacher (Master Liang) was imprisoned and tortured by the Japanese for having a small bag of rice hidden under his bed, but his suffering was minor compared to the millions of other atrocities that occurred. When considering this historical backdrop, it's amazing that the record of Li Qingyun survived at all.

As a general for Chiang Kai-shek, Yang Sen was constantly on the move, eventually having to flee to Taiwan in 1949 during the Nationalist Exodus. He didn't have time to collect many belongings from his different residences in China, so much of his material on Li Qingyun was lost. Furthermore, his connections with mainland China broke off completely, as associates, friends, and even some family members basically disappeared. Once in Taiwan it took several years for him to re-establish his life and to reunite with those who could collaborate with him on his book.

Li's Date of Birth and Death

The belief in whether or not Li Qingyun lived over 250 years is unimportant in many ways. Certainly, Li was vetted by some very credible, intelligent, and influential people in his time, and the evidence presented by Yang Sen and the contributors to this book strongly support this claim. Likewise, Yang Sen also included the concerns and arguments of those who did not believe Li lived for 250-plus years, as well as rebuttals to those arguments, which gave the book a good balance by addressing the issue.

Of all the issues concerning Li Qingyun, the dates of his birth and death appear to be the most debated. Li Qingyun, when talking with Yang Sen and others in Wanxian, said he was born in the early Qing (清) dynasty in the 17th year of the Kangxi (康熙) reign, which was 1678.

An abstract from an article in *Time* magazine, "Medicine: 252 Years Old," published on October 14, 1929, cites the following information about Li Qingyun's age:

> The reputable Dean Wu Chung-chieh [sic] of the department of Education at Minkuo University, China, last week announced that he had found recorded in Imperial Chinese chronicles dated 1777 the fact that one Li Ching-yung had been imperially honored for being 100 years old, that 1877 annals reported the same Li Ching-yung celebrating his 500th [sic] anniversary, that the same ancient is now 252 years old and is still living in Kai-shen, Szechwan Province.

The New York Times and *Time* magazine also reported that Li said he was born in 1736, making him 197 years old at the time of his death, but they also mention that inquiries put his birth year as 1677—with both articles citing the reports of Professor Wu Chungchien on his finding of the Imperial Government documents honoring Li on his 100th, 150th, and 200th birthdays.[6]

Although Da Liu's *Taoist Health Exercise Book* stated that *The New York Times* announced Li's death in 1930, this was incorrect, as *The New York Times* article appeared on May 6, 1933, and was sent from their correspondent in Chungking, China, on May 5, 1933. Some people have erroneously written that Li died on May 6, 1933, possibly thinking *The New York Times* announced his death on the very same day of his passing. Da Liu's report of Li passing away in 1930, however, accords with what Yang Sen and Li Huan wrote in this book.

Despite the newspaper reports, no evidence exists of the exact date Li died. If one accepts the 1677 (or 1678, if counting by traditional Chinese reckoning) date of birth and *The New York Times* announcement of his death, then Li died at the age of 256.

Li Qingyun had told his disciples that living in big cities was harmful to one's health, and he said that if he stayed in Wanxian too long it would cause his death. In 1930, Yang Sen had sent an envoy, at the request of Chairman Chiang Kaishek, to invite Li Qingyun to visit Nanjing so people there could meet a true immortal. When the envoy reached Li's home village, he was told by two of Li's disciples that their

---

6   See "Li Ching-Yun Dead; Gave His Age As 197," *The New York Times,* May 6, 1933, and "CHINA: Tortoise-Pigeon-Dog," *Time,* May 15, 1933.

teacher had died somewhere out in nature. They gave no location of a gravesite or any particulars of a funeral, just saying that he died a month earlier (in March 1930).

Based on discussions Master Liang told me he had with Yang Sen and Da Liu, Liang believed that Li may have orchestrated his death in 1930 to be free of all the attention he was receiving, as he wanted to return to his humble life. As mentioned, Chairman Chiang Kai-shek was trying to arrange for Li to come to Nanjing and be, as Yang Sen said to Liang, "put on display." So, regarding Li's actual death, little is certain. Yang Sen and Li Huan both reported that Li had passed away before Chairman Chiang Kai-shek could meet him in April 1930, but *The New York Times'* correspondent reported the death on May 5, 1933, so what information he was going on is unknown. The 1933 date is interesting, however, as this lends credence to the belief that Li hadn't passed away in 1930.

Wu Peifu Connection

Wu Peifu (吴佩孚, 1874–1939), mentioned in the 1933 *New York Times* article, was a powerful and influential scholar-warlord in China. At one point, he declared himself as the new emperor of China and was featured on the cover of *Time* magazine on September 8, 1924.

In 1926, Wu invited Li Qingyun to his residence in Beijing. Wu was intensely interested in Daoist longevity practices. The story goes that Wu Peifu had seen Li a few years earlier (possibly in 1923), but could not accept the idea that long life was obtained by just "keeping a quiet heart, sitting like a tortoise, and walking like a pigeon." So Wu invited Li to come and stay in his Beijing home so he could learn the secrets of long life from him directly.

Master Liang recalled hearing about Li Qingyun staying with Wu Peifu while stationed in Shanghai, and that it was Wu Peifu who arranged for Li to teach at Beijing University under the sponsorship of Prof. Jiang Weiqiao. The event was attended by many members of the Baoding Military Academy (where Wu Peifu studied) and members from the Dragon Gate sect of White Cloud Monastery in Beijing (with whom Wu was also well acquainted). Master Liang also remembered reading an article in a Shanghai newspaper that mentioned Li Qingyun meeting with Wu Peifu and of the findings by Prof. Wu Chungchien, saying that all this was pretty big news back then, but not as important as the political strife going on in China at the time.

Interestingly, the events of Li staying with Wu Peifu and teaching in Beijing in 1926 are not mentioned in Yang Sen's book. This is curious because it was the very next year, 1927, that Li traveled to Wanxian. Certainly, this omission was for political reasons, as Yang Sen and Wu Peifu had been contending warlords for control of the government. It is also the case, as Master Liang thought, that to mention Wu Peifu would have meant that Yang Sen was not the first (of the power elite in China) to convince Li to come to his residence.

Yinshizi Connection (Prof. Jiang Weiqiao, 蔣維喬)

In 1914, Jiang Weiqiao's book on meditation, *Yinshizi's Tranquil Sitting Methods* (因是子靜坐法, *Yin Shi Zi Jing Zuo Fa*) was published. Jiang Weiqiao was born in 1872 and passed away in 1954. Although he wrote two more books, they were actually supplements to his original work.

Jiang's book became very popular because he provided a detailed record of his meditation practice, which took an unusual approach. Instead of being a typical work about what should happen when practicing meditation, Jiang revealed only what had occurred by keeping a complete record of his practices and experiences. With the publication of this book, Jiang styled himself as Yinshizi, and it is by this name that he is most recognized in Chinese meditation circles.

In his book, Yinshizi (Jiang) mentions that he began his meditation practice at age seventeen, and then went into seclusion to practice Daoist meditation from 1903 to 1913, a ten-year vigil in Shanghai. He published his book in 1914, upon his return to Beijing. In 1917 he was appointed President of the Beijing University Meditation Society. In 1926, at age fifty-four, he returned to Shanghai, taking a post at Guan Hua University as a professor of physiology.[7]

In Wang Chengsheng's introductory section of this book, "The 250-Year-Old Man Talks on His Own Experiences," Wang mentions the following on Li Huan and his connection to a Prof. Jiang Weiqiao,

> Mr. Li Huan is very knowledgeable, and interested in many kinds of new things, he enjoys researching new things just like General Yang does. He once joined Beijing University Meditation Society in 1917. The president was Professor Jiang Weiqiao. Professor Jiang also taught Daoist practices that matched Li Qingyun's practices. So, they [Mr. Li Huan and Prof. Jiang Weiqiao] and Li Qingyun found it easy to get along with each other and had many in-depth conversations.

This is the closest Yang Sen's book comes to mentioning Li's visit to Beijing, and the wording of the text is cloaked so as

---

7   To read portions of Yinshizi's book, see *The Secrets of Chinese Meditation* by Lu Kuan Yu (Samuel Weiser, 1964).

not to reveal that Yinshizi had met with, and possibly learned from, Li Qingyun in Beijing in the years before the Wanxian event, as evidenced by the statement that Jiang's meditation methods matched those of Li Qingyun.

When Master Liang and I were talking about this section of the book, he confirmed that Li Huan had been friends with Yinshizi for many years. He also said that Li Huan was a member of the Beijing University Meditation Society and that he had attended the lectures Li Qingyun gave at Beijing University.

Lack of Family and Personal Documentation

According to those who met him, Li had an incredible memory for Chinese history and literature. Yet, when questioned about his family and personal life, he feigned a failing memory. Nowhere in the book do we find any name of a parent, past wife, or a child. Considering that he claimed over 180 descendants, it's reasonable to assume he knew at least one of their names, but he declined to name any. He only mentioned two names (and just the surnames) of two of his companions, Mr. Zhou and Mr. Zhang, with whom he had roamed the mountains gathering herbs. He revealed his teacher's name, Xu Jing, from Kongtong mountains, and a teacher by the name of Immortal Du. He also mentioned one disciple, Master Yang Hexuan, who published a book about Li Qingyun in 1908.

Master Liang said that he and Yang Sen talked about this, and that Yang confirmed that Li did not want to be asked about details concerning such personal matters, as it would have only caused others to rush to his descendants and disciples, investigating every aspect of his life and theirs. In Wanxian, Li was invited to meet with powerful figures of his day (people difficult to refuse and who could be dangerous politically). Powerful warlords and Western and Chinese correspondents were vetting him, while China was in turmoil politically. Drawing attention to his family, disciples, and acquaintances could have been very dangerous for them. Fame was not a good thing in those times and no one wanted to draw too much attention to themselves. As Master Liang said, "It was a period for keeping your head down."

It was also the case that Li found no good reason to go into such details. After all, he was a wandering Daoist, and was not looking for fame or profit from his visit to Wanxian. Yang Sen commented that Li asked for very little, and what he did ask for was primarily a food item, and not money. Li came to Wanxian to educate others about health and longevity, not to engage in any business or profitable venture. Bear in mind that Li left Wanxian because he felt it was damaging his health and said that he wished to get back to nature to wander the mountains and cross streams. This is not the intention of a profit maker.

So, for Li not to have offered personal information on his family makes sense, as he was not attempting to convince anyone of his advanced age or even of his history. Li didn't care whether people believed it or not, and he certainly was not trying to profit or benefit in any way from those who did believe it. These were things the media of his day wanted, so they could sell it and profit from his longevity.

As Master Liang told me, "Li was the end of an era of true Daoist cloud wanderers. According to Yang Sen, Li behaved as a cloud wanderer and never cheated anyone, nor wanted a following of students. He came to Wanxian because men like Yang Sen asked him to, and because a fellow villager from a good family and high rank, Adjutant General Gui Yunjin, came to him and respectfully asked him to come to Wanxian." This is all it was, nothing more.

The Family of Li

No information exists on the names of his fourteen wives (some reports allege twenty-three), even of the last one, except that, as the *New York Times* correspondent reported, she was sixty years old when she had married Li. Likewise, there is no information on the names of any of his children. Li did state, however, that on occasion he would take his sons and grandsons with him when gathering herbs, but offered no more information than that. This lack of information makes it really difficult to ascertain how involved he was with his family.

If we take literally the idea that Li lived, for the most part, away from his family, then he was an absentee husband and father for a major portion of his life. But, we also don't have enough information to accurately make this judgement. Li chose not to give any details of his family life, and as Yang Sen and Master Liang discussed, this was because he wanted to protect them. Li Huan admitted that no one really thought to ask him about it, and to ask these questions would have been very impolite by Chinese standards, so no one would have pressed the issue. Also, Li Qingyun was a product of his times and culture. He never claimed to be an immortal or a saint. Indeed his words reveal someone of high spiritual cultivation, but he was also very influenced by his cloud wandering and herb gathering lifestyle. The other unknown issue is that we really don't know for certain he was not in contact with his wives or children. The book states that he buried fourteen (or twenty-three wives), which means he had to have been with them to do so. Since he chose not to talk about his family, we cannot be certain or make the assumption that he wasn't involved in family matters.

Other Sources on Li Qingyun

I hope that from the publication of this translation of Yang Sen's book, other sources and materials on Li Qingyun are revealed, such as more of the photos from Yi Fang Studio. Information about Li Qingyun has been around for a long time, especially if you take into account the imperial records from his 100th, 150th, and 200th birthdays. Besides the newspaper articles in the 1920s through 1940s, the articles by *Zhong Wai Magazine* in the 1960s, and Yang Sen's and Da Liu's books in the 1970s, other authors have presented teachings and information on Li Qingyun.

The book *Tao of Pooh* (Dutton Books, 1982) by Benjamin Hoff, for example, gives a brief explanation of Li Qingyun in the "Bizy Backson" chapter. This is noteworthy because the *Tao of Pooh* was on the *New York Times* bestseller list for forty-nine weeks, and so lent great exposure to the person of Li Qingyun and of Daoism, comparable to the *Time* magazine and *New York Times* articles that appeared fifty years earlier.

Hoff wrote that Li gave twenty-eight lectures, three hours each day, at a Chinese university, but cites no references as to the details of these talks. These lectures Hoff is referring to are most likely the ones that Li gave at the Beijing University Meditation Society in Beijing, where Li reportedly gave talks over a one-month period. However, I saw no confirmation that Li talked for three hours a day for twenty-eight days as Hoff suggests. Also, Hoff's statement that people in that period described Li as having strong teeth and a full head of black hair contradict those who witnessed Li in Wanxian a year later, who said Li was bald and had no teeth.

Daniel Reid in his excellent work *The Tao of Health, Sex, & Longevity: A Modern Practical Guide to the Ancient Way* (Fireside

Books, 1989) provides brief biographical information on both Li Qingyun and Yang Sen.

Dr. Yang Jwing-Ming in his very informative book, *Qigong, The Secret of Youth: Da Mo's Muscle/Tendon Changing and Marrow/Brain Washing Classics* (YMAA Publication Center, 2000) also included a photograph and brief biography of Li Qingyun.

Also, as mentioned, my book *Qigong Teachings of a Taoist Immortal* focuses on Li Qingyun's Eight Diagram Active Methods (herein called *Eight Diagram Elemental Skills),* the text of which appears in this book in its original context. Nowadays these methods are referred to as the Eight Brocades Seated Qigong exercises.

In addition to these books, numerous references to the person and teachings of Li Qingyun appear on the Internet. Although visitors to these websites will find that most of the information is repetitive (and often incorrect), they do show the popularity and interest in this 250-year-old man—as well as the doubters, conspiracy theorists, rumor mongers, and myth makers.

Li as a Martial Artist

Some reports claim that Li practiced and taught Eight Diagram Palm (八卦掌, Baguazhang), a form of martial art related to Taijiquan. According to Yang Sen, Li clearly stated that he was not a "swordsman," an older term for a martial artist. This misconception may have come from his Eight Brocades exercise, which Li called the Eight Diagram Elemental (or Active) Method. Master Liang also told me that when he questioned Yang Sen on this matter, Yang was very clear that Li did not practice any type of martial art.

The rumor for this seems to start with Da Liu. *In his Taoist Exercise Book,* Liu wrote,

> At the age of one hundred and thirty while traveling in the K'ung Tung mountains, Li Ch'ing Yuen met a Taoist who was 500 years old. Li Ch'ing Yuen asked the old Taoist the secret to his longevity, and the Taoist taught him an exercise called Ba-Kua (eight trigrams) exercise, which is similar to T'ai Chi Ch'uan.

The persistent rumor is that Li learned and taught a system of Baguazhang called Nine Dragon Eight-Diagram Palms (九龍八卦掌, Jiu Long Ba Gua Zhang). Two dissimilar stories relate how Li was supposedly introduced to this martial art style. One is that a Tibetan monk, traveling in Sichuan, met up with the young Li Qingyun while gathering herbs and taught him Baguazhang. Another story is that Li learned it in his middle years from wandering Daoist monks while living and teaching in the Emei mountains.

Both of these accounts are highly improbable. In the first story, consider that Li himself said that he had left home to gather herbs with three men at the age of thirteen. He also never mentioned learning Baguazhang or any other martial art in his childhood. The second account is problematic because Baguazhang had not been introduced into the Chinese martial art world until 1875 by its attributed founder Dong Haichuan (1798–1882). Of Dong's students who went on to teach their own personal styles of Baguazhang, no records mention a style called Nine Dragons.

Still, this is really a matter of Li clearly stating that he was not a martial artist, so to either credit him with the creation of Nine Dragon Eight-Diagram Palms or to say he learned it on Emei mountain is not supported by any credible evidence or persons of that period. In the end, I think this is a matter of misinterpreting the title Li gave for his seated Eight Brocades exercises, "Ba Gua Xing Kung Fa," with that of Ba Gua Zhang. None of this implies that Nine Dragon Eight-Diagram Palms is not a credible or legitimate system of martial art. The point is that it should not be assigned as something Li created or taught. No evidence supports that claim. Like many practices coming out of Daoist traditions, they get assigned to someone of historical reputation to give more credibility to the method, and I can only assume that is what happened here.

On this subject, however, I did hear a rumor many years ago from Master Liang, which he never confirmed as anything other than hearsay. At the time of hearing this rumor, I really had little interest in the details, so this is all I can recall about it. Many years ago I asked Master Liang if he had any information about Li Qingyun practicing Taijiquan or any other martial art. His response was an emphatic "No," and that "according to Yang Sen and others in Taiwan connected to the story of Li Qingyun, Li had not practiced any form of martial art." However, he quipped that many people believed Li Bao (李寶, 1790–?, who reportedly passed away in Henan province) was a son (or grandson) of Li Qingyun, and that he was attributed with the creation of Eight Immortal Boxing (八仙拳, Ba Xian Quan).

Supposedly a Tibetan monk had gone to Mt. Emei and visited with Li Qingyun's family. The Tibetan Buddhist monk taught Li Bao a style of martial art based on quick and agile turning methods, like a butterfly fluttering about and a dragon twisting through the sky. Li Bao then styled what he learned as Eight Immortal Boxing (not to be confused with the Drunken Style of Eight Immortals Boxing made famous by martial artist and actor Jackie Chan).

I have no evidence if this rumor is based on any actual truth, and only present it here in the hopes that someone knowledgable of this person Li Bao could either substantiate the story or put the rumor to rest. Regardless of whether it's true or not, the rumor does present an interesting backdrop on Li Qingyun, by suggesting that he had his wife and family with him on Mt. Emei and that he had a son who also cultivated Daoist practices. It also provides an alternative answer to Li being a martial artist and having practiced Eight Diagram Boxing, when it could be true that it was his son who created and practiced Eight Immortals Boxing. In any event, I do not wish to just start another rumor concerning Li Qingyun. There is an abundance of those already, but this rumor, if credible, could bring further clarity to the story of Li Qingyun.

Li as a Family Lineage, Not One Person
Some people have propagated the idea that the person of Li Qingyun was entirely a hoax, that Li Qingyun was actually just a family line of a great-great grandfather, a great grandfather, a grandfather, and son (the then Li Qingyun). As difficult as Li's advanced age is to accept, this theory of it being a family lineage is not backed by any evidence. In 1928, a *New York Times* correspondent wrote that "many of the oldest men in Li's neighborhood asserted their grandfather's knew him as boys and that he was then a grown man." Yang Sen himself sent envoys to Chenjiachang to interview hundreds of people, mainly elders, who all knew of, met, and heard their grandfathers speak of Li Qingyun. Unless there was some fully organized mass conspiracy taking place by all the residents of Kai County and surrounding areas, I think it's best to accept the idea of Li Qingyun as one person, not a fabricated 200-year family lineage.

Chinese Foreign Publishers

When I finished my translation, I attempted to contact the publisher of Yang Sen's book, but it appears that Zhong Wai no longer exists. A friend of mine in Taipei went to the address listed in the book, but it's now a motorcycle repair shop. Other efforts were to no avail. I have also been unable to obtain any personal information on Wang Chengsheng (the publisher), Li Huan (editor), Liu Guiyun (contributor), Yuan Huanxian (records transcriber), or on Master Yang Hexuan (Li's disciple and compiler of Li's book). I know that information is out there, but my resources are limited, and much was lost during the Nationalist Exodus to Taiwan and the Communist takeover of China. Even the original city of Wanxian is no more, as it was torn down and rebuilt during the Three Gorges Dam project.

About This Translation

This book provides an unabridged translation of Yang Sen's work, including information from the front and back covers. I saw no good reason to reorganize the material into a more modern Westernized approach. This means, however, that much of the introductory material is repetitive, like the constant references to Li's advanced age, where he was born, and so forth. In the book's defense, a different contributor is saying this in each case, so I wanted to stay faithful to how the material appeared in the original. Additions I made to the work, besides my introduction, are contained in the footnotes and bracketed comments, and to move and add some illustrations for clarification. In some chapters, I added subtitles for certain sections. I did this because some of the subjects just ran together, making the separate subjects somewhat difficult to discern. All text in brackets are mine, and any mistakes within the translation belong solely to me.

Yang Sen's book is divided into multiple sections, with its introductory material covering a great deal of information on Li Qingyun. Six contributors present their work in the introductory section and appendix.

The largest section, titled *The Secrets of Li Qingyun's Immortality* clearly comes from the teachings of Li Qingyun as published in Master Yang Hexuan's book. Yang Sen said that book was written in classical Chinese, but later the editors punctuated it for the article in the magazine, where they first ran excerpts from it. Without having access to the original book, I can't say how much was edited and where they included their own insertions, if any, but I do think they added references to Li Qingyun as being the "250-Year-Old Man," both when mentioning Yang Hexuan's book title and in the sections that excerpt from it. Since Li lectured on these topics while in Wanxian, some of the material may be from Yang Sen's notes (as transcribed by Yuan Huanxian), so it would have been understandable for them to refer to Li as the "250-Year-Old Man" because that's how old he was when they knew him.

Liu Guiyun, who wrote the article "I Had Seen Li Qingyun," which appears in the Appendix, mailed in his copy of Yang Hexuan's book to *Zhong Wai* and he refers to it as just *The Secrets of Li Qingyun's Immortality.* So, it makes sense that the actual book did not have the "250-Year-Old Man" references in it. Especially if it was published in 1908, which is the copyright date that Master Liang had told me when it was published. Even though the book was most likely published then, this doesn't mean that Yang Hexuan didn't round up Li's age and refer to him as the "250-Year-Old Man" as well. Without having that book as a reference, though, I can only assume that Yang Sen and the editors of his book included these references to Li as the "250-Year-Old Man," as this is how they refer to him everywhere else.

Yang Sen's book, then, is a compilation of the articles written in *Zhong Wai Magazine* on his, Li Huan's and other people's recollections of meeting Li Qingyun, the text from Yang Hexuan's *The Secrets of Li Qingyun's Immortality,* and the recorded notes that Yuan Huanxian had made for Yang Sen on the Daoist practices of Li Qingyun.

Yang Sen wrote a preface to the section of this book on *The Secrets of Li Qingyun's Immortality,* and the outline for the major parts of it is as follows:

Part One, *The Great Dao of Long Life,* covers various aspects for the attainment of long life.

Part Two, *Discourses on the Beginning Foundations of Long Life,* presents the methods and practices for longevity.

Part Three, *The Way of Achieving the Dao,* contains quotes from many ancient Chinese philosophers on the subject of Dao (the Way). Many of these quotes have not appeared in English before, and they range from Daoist, Buddhist, Confucianist, and other philosophies and schools of thought.

Part Four, *Chapters on the Nature of Mind,* presents various selected chapters from the One Hundred Schools of Thought, which includes the works of many of the philosophers mentioned in Part Three. Again, many of these works have not previously appeared in English.

Part Five includes quotes directly from Li Qingyun.

Despite this brief overview of the book, with specific emphasis on *The Secrets of Li Qingyun's Immortality,* the information contained within each part is really extensive, and almost overwhelming. It dawned on me many years ago that it would take many books to explain the contents of this book. Beyond this, the work is presented in colloquial language. It was not compiled to be an academic work, rather a living record and story of Li Qingyun. At times the book brings out interesting historical facts, and other times relates profound philosophy. In my opinion, there has never been a book in English (or Chinese) on the subject of Chinese longevity, philosophy, and methods of practice that contains such a vast array of materials. Without question, it is one of the most informative pieces on the attainment of health and longevity yet to be presented to an English reading audience. The contributors to this work should be applauded for what was certainly a great effort and accomplishment in compiling the personal conversations, history, evidentiary material, and stories on the life of Li Qingyun. Because of Yang Sen the record of this incredible immortal will be with us for a very long time, as the old adage states, "Books are the essence of immortality," and so Li Qingyun's immortality has now been even further augmented.

Li Qingyun was obviously a very intelligent man. His ability to address the deeper aspects of Daoist, Buddhist, Confucianist, and Physicianist theories is remarkable. I can think of no other work, in English or Chinese, that covers such ground with such clarity. I think anyone who has an interest in these subjects will find this book truly informative and quite interesting. I certainly did, and I have read hundreds of books on Chinese philosophy and practices, and none compare with this work. A great deal of credit must go to Yang Sen, his contributors, and publisher. They did an excellent job of capturing Li's lectures and discussions, as well as the research they completed. More astonishing is that they did this while keeping most of the book in a novel-like form, rather than retreating into a dry research-based account of Li's life, which would have been far easier to produce, but much less interesting and informative.

The Issue of Immortality

In my book *Being Daoist* (Valley Spirit Arts, 2014) I devoted a chapter to the subject of immortality and noted a research paper on a remarkable species of jellyfish. It bears worth repeating here as it goes to both the existence of a living species having physical immortality and to Daoism's early recognition of the immortal jellyfish:

> Physical immortality shouldn't be dismissed as impossible. A species of jellyfish, Turritopsis nutricula, has been proven to be biologically capable of immortality. [8] This jellyfish can revert to its earlier polyp stage, effectively restarting its lifecycle and reversing the aging process.
>
> Theoretically, Turritopsis can repeat this process indefinitely. Interestingly, "The Sleeping Immortal" poem by Zhang Sanfeng (Song dynasty, 1200 CE) mentions a Jellyfish Method:
>
> > The Sleeping Dragon [9] once rose up and ascended into Heaven. It was he who transmitted this Jellyfish Method.

Calling this transmission the Jellyfish Method is fascinating because it not only shows that Daoists equated jellyfish with immortality centuries ago, but that they

---

[8] Piraino, Stefano, et al. "Reversing the Life Cycle: Medusae Transforming into Polyps and Cell Transdifferentiation in Turritopsis nutricula (Cnidaria, Hydrozoa)," *The Biological Bulletin* 190 (June, 1996): 302–312.

[9] *The Sleeping Dragon* is a moniker for Zhang Guolao (張果老), one of the Eight Immortals.

knew this long before modern scientists discovered the ability of the Turritopsis species.

Aside from the above reference to the Jellyfish Method of Daoism, the long life of Li Qingyun is obviously an anomaly. A question that often gets raised is "If Li Qingyun lived to be 250 years old, why have we not seen other people accomplish this feat?"

This question cannot be answered, in part because we do not have records of every human being who ever lived and the ages of their death. So we cannot say others did not reach his age or beyond, even though Daoist works mention numerous adept cultivators who did accomplish extraordinary life spans. After all the work I put into this book, and from my many conversations with Master Liang and the other extraordinary teachers I have learned from and met over the past forty years, I sincerely believe that Li Qingyun did not lie about his age, and that he was able to live as long as he did because of the following reasons:

1. He started traveling in the mountains at a young age with three accomplished herb gatherers who knew how to live in harmony with nature, which is where he acquired the foundation of his longevity.

2. During his life, he never ingested manufactured pharmaceuticals, or ate processed foods with preservatives (he ate completely organic).

3. He lived a life free of stresses, maintaining a calm and easygoing state of mind.

4. He practiced exercises, internal and external, to keep his body healthy and his mind sound.

5. He lived in nature almost his entire life, drinking fresh water from streams, walking everywhere, and eating the freshest of herbs and plants.

6. He obviously knew meditation and internal alchemy techniques, but these practices came later in his life (after meeting his teacher in the Kongtong Mountains).

So, I feel that the first five points on Li's life developed his longevity, and then his later practices maintained it. Just from his lifestyle alone, how could a person not live longer than most? I think that once people finish reading this material, many of the doubts will be answered. However, even knowing how it can be done, how many of us could possibly imitate the lifestyle or inhabit the environment in which Li had lived? Infinitesimally few.

In a humorous admonishment Master Liang once said to a group of students, "If you're going to lay around on the sofa all night watching movies, drinking beer, and eating pizza, don't expect to live as long as Li Qingyun, nor should you think you're smart enough not to believe he lived to 250 years of age. Armchair strategists are the worst kind of strategists."

Needless to say, Liang was a believer in Li Qingyun and his advanced age, but he also thought that much more research could have been done, especially at Mt. Emei where Li claimed to have lived and taught for nearly one hundred years. Surely with over one hundred students living there with him, there would be some record of his entourage?

Originally, Mt. Emei was mostly inhabited by Daoists in the third century BCE, but by the sixth century CE it was predominately Buddhist. During Li's time on Mt. Emei there were an estimated seventy Buddhist temples and monasteries. Master Liang felt that there must have been records of Li in one or more of those temples. Adding that Li was on Mt. Emei when the Imperial Government sent both greetings for his 150th and

200th birthdays, so obviously the imperials knew where he was, and therefore many temples there would have known as well. Unfortunately, neither Yang Sen nor his contributors were able to look into these records as there was simply too much going on with the Civil War taking place. After the war ended in 1949, there would have been little incentive for the Communist regime to do the research.

Besides the tantalizing notion of someone in our recent times living to 250 years of age, this book goes well beyond the story of Li Qingyun. It has great historical value, especially for Westerners who are unfamiliar with much of Chinese history. It also explains incredible health therapies and provides information on what is now called Medical Qigong. Much is explained about Daoism on meditation, breathing, qigong exercise, food, sex, and philosophy for Daoist living. Another true gem of this book is the philosophical teachings, as much of this material, to my knowledge, has never been presented in English. The book is also a kind of "who's who" of Chinese philosophy. These are not just statements to glorify the book. From my more than forty years of studying and practicing these subjects, I can honestly say I have never come across such an abundance of insights that this material provides, nor that are expressed with such clarity.

My hope for this book is that it stimulates further research on Li Qingyun, that it inspires readers to undertake the practices to increase their own health and longevity, and that it brings about a new light on the value of life itself. I say this last statement because in our present era we put more attention on the material aspects of life, and not enough on the spiritual or naturalist way of living—one of the most important messages Li Qingyun left behind.

We may not reach the age of 250 by following Li's advice, but as Master Liang said, "If practicing these methods brings you one extra day on this beautiful earth, it is worth the effort."

—Stuart Alve Olson

二百五十歲人瑞實記

楊森著

An Authentic and True Record
of a 250-Year-Old Man

By Yang Sen

Chinese-Foreign Library Preface

By Wang Chengsheng (王成聖)

Knowledge is authority, knowledge is power, knowledge is fortune, and knowledge brings happiness and prosperity. The Chinese-Foreign [中外, Zhong Wai] Publishing Company addresses the needs of readers around the world. We select and publish valuable books with high readability from reputable and honorable authors. We named this book series, "Zhongwai Library."

Chinese traditionally believe writing and publishing books is a sacred business and books are to be preserved and to be handed down to posterity. Formerly, people were hesitant to write and publish books. However, after the invention of printing, newspaper publishing has become very popular and the mass medias are booming. Learning new knowledge and information has become one of the musts for modern living. Reading is as important as air, food, and water. Thus, reading good books improves oneself [and] we urge good writers to write and publish more books. That is the main purpose of publishing "Zhongwai Library." We want their wisdom to shine everywhere in the world, so it can last forever.

Undeniably, a publisher is a bridge between writers and readers, and also acts as an intermediary for both parties. It appears that when a writer finishes a good book, they can't find a publisher to publish the book. When a reader knows a good book will be published, the book title and the author are most likely what they care about. They do not need to consider who the publisher is. However, every writer who has dealt with a publisher or readers who have spent money on books would like to know if the same book was published by two different publishers. This makes a big difference. A good publisher not only helps writers to publish, but also helps readers to screen good materials. The results show very clearly that a good publisher knows how to choose excellent books to publish and also knows how to edit and proofread, how to typeset, how to bind the books, and how to publish them. With well-educated and knowledgeable staff, all this can be done.

China pays a great deal of attention to typography in the world, at least it was the first country to take typography seriously. The oldest typographic books in the world were first published in the last years of the Tang dynasty [around 900 CE] and flourished in Song dynasty [960–1279 CE]. In the "Biography of Cuiyi" [崔頤] in the *Histories of the Song* [宋史, *Song Shi*], one finds a discussion and criticism about typography. The *Histories of the Song* [dynasty] says, "At the beginning of the Xianping years [咸平, 998 to 1003 CE] there was a scholar, Liu Keming [劉可名], who criticized the books published of his time for having typographical errors." This meant the same book, because of different editing, copying, printing, and binding, etc., would then make it a different book. After a thousand years, if readers nowadays can not tell the pros and cons of different editions, doesn't this seem ironic?

Zhong Wai Publishing Company set long-term development plans to prepare good books one after another. But before we provide them to vast numbers of readers, we must emphasize, the staff at Zhong Wai Publishing Company are all serious readers who love to read and treasure books, and everyone tries their best to build this publishing business. Before starting the publishing company we all spent several decades reading good books, some with bad typography, which made us feel helpless and disappointed. So we decided to publish good books that are well written, edited, packaged, and precisely proofread, to comply with the needs of the readers. Moreover, we would keep prices low and simplify the purchasing procedure. We would maintain very sincere and honest attitudes to serve our writers and readers. When Zhongwai Publishing Company published "Zhongwai Library," our business policies guided us to consider issues carefully and be self-vigilant to provide the best service to our numerous readers in the world.

In the Republic of China 61st year [1972], March, *Zhong Wai Magazine* is in its sixth year of publication [started in 1966].

Sincerely,
Wang Chengsheng

The Immortal Li Qingyun

Preface to the True Story of the 250-Year-Old Man, Li Qingyun

Sichuan[1] has high mountains and long rivers. Sichuan is also rich in natural resources, with fertile soil and good water, enriched produce, and peaceful and happy people, so there are a good number of long living elders there. When I was young, I researched the Sichuan history. Some examples [of long lived people] were in Jintang [金堂] county, such as a man named Eight Hundred Li [李八百, Li Babai]. On Nourishing Village Mountain [育城山, Yu Cheng Shan] in Guan County [灌縣, Guanxian] there is a village of elders with many people who are over one hundred years of age. In Fuling [浮陵], Zhou Huang's [周惶] father married and had a newborn when Huang was 120 years old, but I had doubted it.

In 1927, I was garrisoned in Wan County [萬縣, Wanxian]. The Adjutant General Gui Yunjin [桂雲津], from Kai County [開縣, Kaixian], talked about a man named Li Qingyun living in the village of Chenjiachang [陳家場] in Kai County who was 250 years old, still healthy, and in a good shape. I told [Gui Yunjin] to invite Li Qingyun to Wan County, and [when he did visit] I stayed with him for many days and verified all kind of details about him, so I knew the stories about him were not fake. I believe human life can be prolonged. People believed the stories of Eight Hundred Li, but no one knows him, so it seems like a fiction.

In 1930, Mr. Li Huan [李寰] was promoted in Nanjing [南京] and had the opportunity to meet National Government

---

1   Sichuan (四川) is a province in southwest China.

President Chiang Kai-Shek.[2] I asked Li Huan to deliver Li Qingyun's photo along with wishes for the president to have a long life, and prosperity for the nation. President Chiang Kai-Shek was very happy and wanted to invite Li Qingyun to come to Nanjing and let the Chinese and foreign people get to know him. Unfortunately, I could not make this happen. But at that time, the incredible stories about Li had been published in *North China Daily News* in Shanghai.

After I moved to Taiwan, people often asked me about the stories of Li Qingyun. I wrote an article to answer questions in detail, and chose to publish this in *Zhong Wai Magazine*. The stories spread even to America. After hearing the story, many people became very interested and wanted to know more about the details.

Now, Mr. Wang Chengsheng, with particular use of his related information about Li, printed and published this book, *An Authentic and True Record of a 250-Year-Old Man*. He asked me to write this preface, and I roughly describe the story from beginning to the end to make a simple start.

March 29, 1970
Yang Sen, Guang'an

---

[2] Chiang Kai-Shek (蔣中正), October 31, 1887, to April 5, 1975.

The 250-Year-Old Man Talks on His Own Experiences

How Do You Live to Be 250 Years Old?

By Wang Chengsheng

General Yang Sen, when he was eighty-eight years old, had posted two articles about "The 250-Year-Old Man, Li Qingyun" in *Zhong Wai Magazine*. It's been three years since he published the articles, and people are still wondering whether the stories about Li Qingyun are true or not? It is still a very hot topic. People from all over the world are interested and still discussing this. Many of them wrote letters to consult with General Yang Sen and so this issue is still rapidly expanding. General Yang Sen spent days and nights answering these questions. So I made a decision, and asked General Yang Sen to see if he would do an interview about this matter to clear up all the questions and doubts. In addition, we also interviewed Mr. Li Huan, who was General Yang Sen's Secretary-General, and many other old leaders from Sichuan province who have good reputations. It took quite some time for the interviews and research, and finally we obtained the most complete records, and organized them into articles to help answer the thousands of readers' questions.

This long article includes three parts:
1. The details about General Yang Sen's invitation to Li Qingyun to visit Wanxian.
2. The evidence of Li Qingyun proving he was indeed 250 years old.

3. Conversations with Li Qingyun by General Yang and
    Mr. Li Huan about the ways to maintain good health.

Although it may sound a little highbrow, it is easy to follow and also practical and logical. For those people who are interested in living a prolonged healthy life and away from diseases, these are very good references.

His Appearance Was Very Majestic

In 1927, General Yang Sen served in the National Revolutionary Army as the commander of the 20th Corps, garrisoned in Wanxian. One day, General Yang chatted with Adjutant General Gui Yunjin. They talked about that in Mr. Gui's hometown, Chenjiachang in Kaixian, there was an extraordinary man named Li Qingyun. He was born in Kangxi 17th year [1678] and he is still alive now [in 1927]. By Chinese algorithm, he was exactly 250 years old.[1]

At that time, General Yang could not believe this and said, "How could this be possible!"

"This is real!" Gui Yunjin loudly exclaimed and said, "I have heard about Li Qingyun since I was a kid. My grandparents had told me. My great grandparents all saw him before. During that time, he was more than one hundred years old, but he looked full of energy and walking as fast as a young man, from then until now, it is also more than a hundred years."

General Yang remained dubious about it and said, "This is a story elders use to trick kids."

---

[1] Although Li Qingyun was born in 1678, the Chinese count a newborn as being one years old. So by "Chinese algorithm" he was 250 years old in 1927.

"No, it's not," Gui Yunjin denied directly. "I have seen Li Qingyun many times. He originally came from Qijiang [綦江], but I do not know how long he has lived in Chenjiachang. He comes and goes, and nobody knows about where he is or when he [will appear]. He had a house in Chenjiachang, but he usually went to other provinces that were far away from here, and would go into the mountains to collect herbs, leaving for long periods. Only since 1912 did he stop those long trips, and now carries his own water, cooks, lights his own fire wood, and does laundry all by himself. The neighbors felt he was pretty old, and respected him as an immortal, so they voluntarily offered him groceries such as cooking oil, salt, wood, and rice. They also took turns to help him with cooking, doing laundry, and fixing his house. Li Qingyun was always very grateful about this and usually offered some herbs to these people in return, and practiced medicine in the village for free. His medicines are very effective and he can cure some hard to treat diseases."

General Yang listened to his lifelike story and it seemed realistic, and so was curious and asked, "Is this person still alive?" Gui Yunjin answered quite assuredly, "He is still alive. I visited my parents last year and stopped by to visit him also."

"OK!" General Yang seemed very pleased and said, "You go back to Chenjiachang tomorrow, and tell Mr. Li Qingyun I would like to invite him to Wanxian as my guest and I will be very thankful if he can come, please."

General Yang then reminded Gui Yunjin, if Li Qingyun is really 250 years old he is not only a centenarian but also a living wonder of our age. General Yang directed to Gui Yunjin that he must serve Mr. Li very well on the way back to Wanxian. In Sichuan, people usually use simple human-powered bamboo litters as transportation in remote mountain areas, which are made by two solid bamboo poles and bamboo stalks weaved into a backrest chair. General Yang, afraid that these litters were not stable enough, ordered Gui Yunjin to prepare a four-person carrying sedan chair to welcome Mr. Li.

Kaixian is a small county with the radius about three kilometers to the north of Wanxian. Between Kaixian and Wanxian is the Iron Phoenix Mountain [鐵鳳山, Tie Feng Shan], and the village of Chenjiachang, located in the foothills of Iron Phoenix Mountain, is very close to Wanxian. At that time, this was also the 20th Corps' administrative region.

On the second day, when Gui Yunjin set out to welcome Li Qingyun, General Yang told him, "When you join up with Mr. Li, bring him to the Commerce Port Bureau's dormitory. I will ask the clerk, Mr. Li Dingyu [李定宇] to entertain Mr. Li Qingyun, and prepare a special room for him to stay in."

Later that day, Gui Yunjin brought the 250-year-old man Li Qingyun to Commerce Port Bureau of Wanxian, bringing him to a special room there. General Yang was very happy when he knew Mr. Li had arrived, then he went to meet Mr. Li Qingyun by riding on a horse. In the special room, he met the centenarian, he noticed he was over six feet tall and very strong, his waist and back were straightened up, and his chest muscles were particularly well-developed. He looked very majestic.

Walking Lively and Refusing to Sit on a Sedan Chair to Exercise His Muscles and Bones

At that time, General Yang looked at Gui Yunjin, who obviously was out of breath and looking exhausted. General Yang was astonished and asked him, "What did you do? Why are you so tired?"

Gui Yunjin forced a smile and said, "It's about thirty to thirty-five kilometers. I was walking as fast as running. I was utterly exhausted coming the way back. It was like a race."

General Yang stared at Gui Yunjin and asked, "Don't tell me Mr. Li did not sit on the sedan chair and he also walked?"

"That's right!" said Gui Yunjin, feeling frustrated. "Mr. Li had said it is only thirty to thirty-five kilometers, It's a good walk for exercising muscles and bones, and so he refused to sit on the sedan chair. I had no choice but to follow him. Ah! I don't think he is old, he was walking so fast it was if he was flying and I could not catch him when we were on the way here."

General Yang looked at Li Qingyun, seeing he smiled and didn't show a hint that he had just finished a thirty kilometer walk. At that time, General Yang knew this 250-year-old man's physical health was better than a middle aged man, and assumed he must have learned kung fu.

In a very short time, all the social circles in Wanxian knew that General Yang invited the 250-year-old man and that he was staying in quarters at the Commerce Port Bureau. The crowds admired the centenarian, and they came from everywhere just to see this old man face to face. They thought the centenarian was an auspicious sign of the age and a spectacle rarely seen in one's lifetime. Tens of thousands of people crowded around the Commerce Port Bureau, a mass of spectators came to welcome Li Qingyun. Nothing like this ever happened in Wanxian before.

Gui Yunjin introduced Li Qingyun, and General Yang stepped forward to greet and do salutations with him, and in the meantime he observed him carefully. This 250-year-old man was bald. There was no hair on his head, but he still had a few short mustache hairs above his lips and under his jaw. His complexion looked florid, just like a healthy middle aged man. All of this teeth were gone, lips deflated, but both cheeks were still plump. He had a wide forehead, straight nose, round face, and big ears, which were different than ordinary people. He had three distinctive features. First, he had piercing eyes, bright and sharp like lighting. Second, his voice was loud and full of energy right out of his Elixir Field.[2] Third was that his left [little finger] fingernail was curly and had layer upon layer, shaped like a small pagoda. The length of the fingernail pagoda was about nine to ten inches long, further evidence showing his old age. His dress was no different than ordinary elders except that it was loose. He wore a blue robe, a pair of black socks, and straw sandals. Sichuan people normally do not wear socks when wearing straw sandals, so maybe it was because he wanted to show his respect in being an honored guest of General Yang, or it was just that he was too old to stand the cold without wearing the socks.

Li Qingyun could still see and hear very well. From his words, people could tell he was educated. He was not shy at all and looked very confident and comfortable. However, he was humble in the way he talked. Li noticed that General Yang was staring at his nine- to ten-inch-long fingernails,[3] so he then took out a small wooden box from his pocket. He opened the

---

2   *Elixir Field* (丹田, Dan Tian) is an area (Qi center) behind the navel in the abdomen.

3   According to Medicine.net, fingernails grow approximately .012 inches per month. So in one year a nail could be 1.44 inches long. Therefore, to have ten nails around ten inches in length would constitute between seventy to one hundred years of life. In Li's case, no one knew when he started collecting his long nails, nor if he was able to save them all. From what people saw in the box of Li's collected nails, and the one growing on his little finger back then, this could easily add up to over one hundred years. This estimate is conservative, however, as the nails were "curly and had layer upon layer," so they would have been much longer than ten inches if straightened out.

box and showed it to General Yang. There were more than ten of these fingernails in the box. Most were nine to ten inches long and some were longer than thirteen inches. Li Qingyun smiled and said, "These fingernails grew and shed naturally. I was unaware that I collected so many fingernails."

That night, General Yang hosted a dinner for Li Qingyun in the Commerce Port Bureau's special room. Li did not drink wine, he did not smoke, and did not eat meat nor fish. He explained in a self-mocking tone, "In the recent two hundred years, I usually stayed in the mountains to collect herbs. I eat vegetables and fruits, but I can no longer stand to eat too much meat and fish."[4]

However, he still ate a few slivers of lean meat that night. He ate three big bowls of rice. Everyone noticed when he was eating, he chewed slowly and took time to enjoy his food. It seemed everything he ate was delicious.

General Yang asked him, "Mr. Li, what kind of food do you like? Just go ahead and let me know. I will assign someone to buy it for you."

"I usually only eat vegetables, fruits, and rice," he replied smiling, "If I can have some rice cakes, that would be terrific."

---

[4] Yang Sen commented that Li ate meat periodically when he had studied with him, but would finely sliver the meat so that it was used more as a seasoning, and that he could not stand eating whole pieces of meat. The reason for this, as Yang Sen explained to Master Liang, was that meat takes a long time to process and digest in moving through the intestines. If meat is to be eaten, it should be consumed last, with all the vegetables and softer foods eaten first. Otherwise the soft food sits behind the meat in the intestines and so will ferment and turn toxic.

General Yang asked someone to get rice cakes right away. The elder man then also ate a few pieces of the rice cakes.

General Yang eagerly wanted to know Li Qingyun's real age and background, so he asked him, "Mr. Li, do you still remember what year and date you were born?"

Li Qingyun, who was in a very good humor, approached General Yang's ear to whisper and replied, "I usually do not talk about my age with other people. But I was born in Kangxi in the 17th year [1678 CE]. I don't remember the month and date."

People incited him to talk about his lifetime stories. Li Qingyun started to talk slowly and deliberately, and he seemed very interested in talking. According to his statements, his ancestors came from Guizhou [贵州] province, then they moved to one of the lofty mountain ranges on the west side of Qijiang city [綦江城], Sichuan, and its neighboring Guizhou. When he was a kid, his family's financial situation was not bad, so he had been to school for a few years and was able to read and write.

When he was thirteen years old, he met three elder herb collectors. Now according to a rumor they came from Eternal White Mountain [長白山, Chang Bai Shan] in Jilin [吉林] province. These three elders were all over sixty years of age. When they passed by Li Qingyun's house, they took a break and had a small talk with him. They heard Li Qingyun liked climbing over mountains and ridges, to go sightseeing everywhere, was not afraid of wild beasts, and had great courage. So they joked with him and said, "It would be good if you came with us to collect herbs. You can also go everywhere and have a lot of fun."

Collected Herbs for Two Hundred Years in Remote Mountains

So it was from these two incentives that the young Li Qingyun decided to follow the three elders to collect herbs. Of these three "old" friends of two hundred years ago, Li Qingyun only remembered one man's last name,[5] Zhang [張], who came from Dragon-Tiger Mountain [龍虎山, Longhu Shan] in Guixi [貴溪] county, Jiangxi province [江西], the other two friends came from Jilin province in northeast China.

Since then, he followed these three elders. They collected herbs for a living, going back and forth between mountains and rivers. He visited Xikang [西康, eastern Tibetan region], Xizang [西藏, Tibet], Yindu [印度, India], Xinjiang [新疆], Gansu [甘肅], Qinghai [青海], and Shanxi [陝西], then he traveled throughout Henan [何南], Shandong [山東], Jiangsu [江蘇], Anhui [安徽], Hubei [湖北], and Hunan [湖南], etc. When he came back to Sichuan, he was already 139 years old. The time was the 21st Year of Jia Qing [1816].[6]

Li Qingyun said, "We collected herbs in barren hills and remote mountains where we could not see any sign of human habitation in the radius of hundreds of miles. We walked on foot and never rested throughout the year. Nature is our best company and the ground was our bed and sofa. We lived the wildlife with no issues to worry about.

"We had to endure weather and hardships from mother nature, and also had to fight with ferocious beasts and snakes;

---

5   Yang Sen wrote that Li mentioned two of their names: Zhou and Zhang.

6   See note 1 in Yang Sen's "Preface to *The Secrets of Li Qingyun's Immortality,*" where it's mentioned that Li was actually 129 years old at this time.

therefore, we were all trained by nature, with a strong body and never got sick.

"Because most of the time we were in savage and remote areas, there were no villages, so we did not eat common or cooked food. Sometimes we were short on rations, and it was hard to get wild vegetables and fruits. The only way we could allay our hunger was using the herbs we collected."

On this point, General Yang noticed and asked him in detail what kind of herbs did he usually use to substitute his rations, and had he ever eaten an elixir of immortality?

Li Qingyun shook his head and said, "I've never eaten nor found out about an elixir of immortality. We used herbs to allay our hunger, and these were usually He Shou Wu[7] and Huang Jing.[8] There was also Baiji,[9] which is best if eaten right after being picked, and eaten raw. Chew it slowly. This is the best way to maintain good nutrition."

After that, Yang Sen referred to the book *The Origins of Plants* [本草, *Bencao*]. He Shou Wu and Huang Jing really can prolong life, allay hunger, reduce weight, and improve energy, but Baiji only can treat wounds and lung bleeding. So according to Li Qingyun, Baiji being "nourishing," could just be his own experience, and still needs scientific evidence to prove it.

Li Qingyun still remembered clearly about his days of collecting herbs and would like to go back if he could. He said every time they went into mountains to collect herbs, they always could find rare herbs and fruits. When he would go, he

---

[7] *He Shou Wu* (何首烏), Chinese Knotweed, Fallopia multiflora.

[8] *Huang Jing* (黃精), Polygonatum.

[9] *Baiji* (白芨), Bletilla striata.

only brought a small hoe, a drug back sack, and a few rations with him.

About a month in the mountains, the back sack would be full of herbs and more. Until he could not carry any more on his shoulders and back, he would then go to the market of some village on his way back, and sell the herbs at a low price. Even at the lowest price, he could get enough money to buy at least three months of food supply.

If there was still some money left, he would donate it to poor people and elders. Other people collect money; he collected herbs. Some people wonder why he was so generous, and asked him, "You are just an herbalist collecting herbs, and you risk your life and go into remote mountains for those rare herbs to make money. Why are you giving the money away like it's nothing?"

Li Qingyun said, as he always replied, "For more than two hundred years, I collected herbs for a living. I have never needed money, and there are so many herbs in the mountains. When I carried it back, the sack was very heavy and it makes me so tired. It would be better to unload and sell the herbs quickly, so my shoulders would feel relaxed. Since I don't need that much money, I give it to those who do need it."

[It is said], "Shen Nong[10] tasted hundreds of different herbs." Li Qingyun collected herbs for more than two hundred years, and he might have tasted thousands of herbs? Therefore, he was very familiar with herbs' medicinal properties, and knew how to practice medicine. When patients had difficult to treat symptoms and critical ills that other doctors could not cure, he

---

10   Shen Nong (神農) was one of the first three mythical emperors of China, living some five thousand years ago. He is also called the Divine Farmer and Emperor of the Five Grains.

always could take some special herbs from his drug sack, and more than 90 percent of the time, cure the patient right away. Patients often appreciated him very much for saving their lives, which he took very lightly. Some would give him money and gifts to show their gratefulness. He declined to accept. When people asked him why, he would respond, "The purpose of practicing medicine is to save people. How can I take money for saving people's lives?"

Li Qingyun said he had married, and had fourteen wives because they could not live as long as him. So after one died, he married another. His wives were all from his hometown of Qijiang. Whenever he left, he would return home every few years. People asked him how many descendants did he have? He smiled and said, "Too many, I can't remember.[11] For those still alive, they are my grandsons and younger generations. I haven't been back for many years. We are not in contact with each other any more. I have heard that the total count of my descendants is more than one hundred eighty. They all live around Qijiang and Guizhou. Their lives are pretty good."

Another interesting question was, until now, how many generations are living under one roof? To this question, Li

---

11   This is an interesting and revealing conversation. At first it seemed curious to me why Li Qingyun could remember with such clarity different times and events in his life, but not recall any names of his family. Li was definitely an absentee father and husband, which would have caused some dissension within the several families he created. Chinese culture during his time, however, was purely patriarchal and any of his wives would have had no say in his wanderings for years at a time. Nevertheless, I also believe, as Master Liang suggested, that Li kept silent about giving out family information because he didn't want Yang Sen or others delving into his personal life or searching out any of his family.

Qingyun replied very quickly, and said, "The youngest one is my twelfth generation, but I don't even know any of their names. It can be said that there are twelve generations living under one roof, but this is not really true, because a few generations are all gone."

"Do they all know about you?" Li Qingyun smiled and said, "Most of them do not know about me. I also cannot recognize them. We have been separated for too long."

He spent most of his long lifetime collecting herbs. There was only a short time when he followed Yue Zhongqi in military service. [12] When asked about Yue Zhongqi and in what dynasty and what battles he had fought in, Li Qingyun explained tirelessly and was very familiar with all of this.

Meeting a Daoist Master and Learning Secrets

Li Qingyun entered another stage of life when he was 139 [or 129] years old. Because in this year, he went to Gansu [甘肅] to collect herbs, in the Western Grotto Mountains [崆峒山, Kong Dong Shan] in Pingliang [平涼] county, where he met a Daoist priest who was much older than him. [13] Li Qingyun asked him about what his "methods of longevity" were?

---

[12] Yue Zhongqi (岳鍾琪, 1686–1762 CE) was a military commander and governor of Sichuan during the Qing dynasty. He was a descendant of the famous General Yue Fei of sixth century CE.

[13] In his *Taoist Health Exercise Book,* Master Da Liu states that Li met this Daoist priest in 1808 when he was 130 years old. Li claimed the priest was born in 1270 CE. So, from this account, the Daoist priest was 538 years old when Li Qingyun met him.

The old priest laughed and said, "Why are you asking this? Didn't you get it already? Ginseng [人參], Lingzhi [苓芝],[14] and Hui [蕙][15] are the medicines of longevity. The mountains and wilderness are places of longevity where Non-Action, Clarity, and Tranquility[16] can occur. These are the tips of longevity. Now, you have it all already, so why are you still asking about this?"

The Daoist priest could not bear Li Qingyun's repeated requests, so he finally taught him some mnemonic chants about Daoist practice and the techniques of longevity. After he learned these secrets from the Daoist priest, Li accepted three to five apprentices, traveled to Mt. Emei [峨嵋山] and built huts in which to reside, and he then started teaching the "Ways of Longevity."

On Mt. Emei, he practiced the secrets and techniques learned from his Daoist master. Meanwhile, he taught his followers, and according to Li Qingyun, after a few years, he taught what he had learned about cultivating refinement.[17]

---

14   *Lingzhi* is thought to be either the fungus growing on the roots of fir-trees (ling) and is sometimes called, "China Root," or a fungus growing on a purplish stalk of an iris plant (zhi). Both are said to bequeath longevity and immortality. In Latin, the term for Lingzhi is *Ganoderma lucidum.*

15   *Hui* is a unique stalk of the orchid plant that produces nine blossoms on one stalk. The Latin term is *Cymbidium taber.*

16   These words form a special Daoist phrase, Qing Jing Wu Wei (清靜無為), referring to the three ultimate objectives a Daoist seeks to achieve: "Clarity, Tranquility, and Non-Action."

17   *Xiu lian,* 修煉, *refinement,* a Daoist term used to describe internal alchemy practices.

He could eat two to three catties[18] of rice for a meal, and still could eat more. On the other hand, he could fast for as long as three to four months and did not feel hunger.[19]

Quoted from the *Historical Records of the Feudal Houses and Honorable Families* [史記留候世家, *Shi Ji Liu Hou Shi Jia*]:

Learning the techniques of Dao Yin [導引][20] will lighten the body.

After Li Qingyun knew the techniques of Dao Yin, his perceptiveness, physical and mental health were much better than before. At that time, he was 140 years old already, but people who had seen him all said, he looked just like a forty-year-old man.

He lived on Mt. Emei for about one hundred years, and gained more and more followers, usually around one hundred students. Li Qingyun's apprentices were all elders who had baby faces and gray hairs, most of them were over one hundred years old. After these years [living on Mt. Emei], towards the end of the Qing dynasty and the succession of the Republic of

---

18   A catty equals 1⅓ lb.

19   A reference to Li's ability to live off "Wind and Dew." *Wind* is an aphorism for the breath, and *Dew* refers to the saliva.

20   *Dao Yin* literally means "to lead and guide" the internal energy of Qi. Dao Yin is the practice of the *Eight Brocades* exercises (八段錦, Ba Duan Jin) and the *Wind and Dew* exercises (風露, Feng Lu), which are more formally referred to as *Tu Na* (吐納), methods of respiration and swallowing saliva. Within Wind and Dew are the techniques of *Opening the Three Passes* (開三關, Kai San Guan) and *Refining the Jade Secretions* (練玉液, Lian Yu Yi). All these are exercises designed to replenish the Three Treasures (三寶, San Bao) of Jing, Qi, and Shen (see note 24, p. 56).

China [1912], Li Qingyun thought he was getting very old and so moved back to Chenjiachang in Kai County.[21]

The most annoying thing for Li Qingyun was to live in the city, the environment is noisy and too many social interactions. Many people had said previously they did not believe he was actually 250 years old. He always replied with no indignation, "Do I need to lie? Believe it or not! There is no benefit to me if you believe it, and I don't feel any pain if you don't believe it. But let me tell you, in my lifetime, I have never lied and never cheated."

When Li Qingyun came to visit, General Yang did not want to trouble him too much. He asked Mr. Li Huan to be very careful and let Li Qingyun decide with whom he would meet and whom he didn't want to see. Nobody was to be allowed to bother him. But When Li Qingyun arrived in Wanxian, everyone knew about it already, and so everyone wanted to see him and talk to him. General Yang assigned his adjutant to lead bodyguards to protect him. It was a tough task to keep so many visitors away and countless invitations were denied.

The owner of the Yi Fang [異芳] Photo Studio in Wanxian sent a request to see if they could take some photographs of Li Qingyun. General Yang thought it was a good idea to take a few photographs and enlarge them, to display them in the photo studio for anyone who wanted to see what a centenarian looked like. People could then just go to the studio to take a look. Unexpectedly, the owner of the photo studio made a small fortune because of these pictures. They took pictures of Li Qingyun in a sitting posture, standing posture, the whole body, and half-length

---

21   According to Yang Sen, Li moved back to Chenjiachang because he thought it was getting too dangerous politically and also because he wanted to be left alone.

photos of Li Qingyun. When they displayed these photos in the studio's window, people clustered around the studio and the street was packed with visitors. So many people wanted to pay money to buy Li Qingyun's photos. We also heard there were overseas Chinese who wrote letters requesting to buy pictures. This is why the owner of the photo studio made so much money. Li Qingyun's photos became widespread, and General Yang believed that even after forty-two years, many people still treasured Li Qingyun's photographs.

Mr. Li Huan is very knowledgeable, and interested in many kinds of new things, he enjoys researching new things just like General Yang does. He once joined Beijing University Meditation Society in 1917. The president was Professor Jiang Weiqiao [蔣維喬]. Professor Jiang also taught Daoist practices that matched Li Qingyun's practices. So, they [Mr. Li Huan and Prof. Jiang Weiqiao] and Li Qingyun found it easy to get along with each other and had many in-depth conversations. According to Mr. Li Huan, Li Qingyun told him:

> The method of the Dao is in the "naturally-just-so"[22] Dao reverts to the Before Heaven. If we want to live longer, we should turn Acquired Breathing into Innate Breathing,[23] change our shallow lung breathing to deep lower Dan-Tian breathing. The breath should be as soft and smooth as possible, just like an infant.

---

22   *Naturally-just-so* (自 然, Zi Ran) is a Daoist term that refers to the spontaneous workings of nature and all phenomena.

23   *Before Heaven* (先 天, Xian Tian) refers to prenatal conditions and Innate Breathing. This term applies to aspects that are inherited, natural, and innate to our being. *After Heaven* (後 天, Hou Tian) refers to postnatal conditions that can be developed from our own efforts, such as Acquired Breathing.

Breathing should be long and smooth, following the nature [of the breath] and not forcing anything. If you learn all this, then you have mastered breathing.

Li Qingyun also said,
The Deer nourishes its Essence, Turtles nourish their Qi, and Cranes nourish their Spirit. If a human being could learn the manners of achieving longevity from animals and birds to preserve the Essence, Qi, and Spirit,[24] it will bring about longevity and eliminate diseases.

Mr. Li Huan thought these words from Li Qingyun sounded very reasonable, but the most important thing was to put all this into practice. Mr. Li Huan had secretly observed Li Qingyun's way of practicing Dao Yin and thought Li's method of Dao Yin was just *Chui* [吹, Blowing and Puffing Breath], *Xu* [呴, Yawning and Roaring Breath], *Hu* [呼, Exhaling and Exasperating the

---

24   *Essence, Vitality,* and *Spirit* are the Three Treasures (三 寶, San Bao) of Daoist Nourishing-Life (養 生) regimes and Internal Alchemy (內 丹, Nei Dan) practices. *Jing* (精, essence) generally means the physical body of a human being. More specifically, the term is used in the context of bodily fluids—namely, saliva, blood, marrow, and sexual secretions. *Qi* (氣, vital-life) energy is the energy of the body that both heats and animates it, and is also the breath. In Daoism, two ideograms are used for Qi: 氣 and 炁. The first indicates a vaporous heat, and the second a formless heat. *Shen* (神, spirit) is what gives the human body its mental functions: mind (心, xin), consciousness and awareness (覺, Jue), and mind-intention, or will (意, yi). Briefly stated, the object of internal alchemy is to cultivate the "Acquired" (After Heaven) aspects of these Three Treasures to restore and join the conditions of the "Innate" (Before Heaven) aspects.

Breath], and *Xi* [吸, Inhaling and Absorbing the Breath], which are basic expressions of "exhaling out the dirty air of the body and inhaling fresh air, as well as stretching the body like a climbing bear and a bird stretching its legs." But he thought [Li Qingyun] had not mastered these methods,[25] thus he considered the reasons for Li Qingyun living to 250 years old might not be entirely from practicing these particular Daoist skills [功夫, Gong Fu].

On another note, three years after Yang Sen found out about the centenarian Li Qingyun, the National Revolutionary Army [NRA] was wrapping up a victory of a Northern Expedition. The Nationalist Government of the Republic of China [ROC] made Nanjing [南京] the capital. The entire country was then unified under the flag of blue sky, white sun, and red earth. Centenarians are symbols of auspiciousness and witness the national prosperity and rejuvenation. So, Yang Sen had asked Mr. Li Huan, who at the time was General Yang's representative stationed in Nanjing, to submit Li Qingyun's photograph to Chairman Chiang Kai-shek. In 1930, April 15 at 10:00 a.m., Mr. Li Huan presented the photo to Chairman Chiang, and when he saw the photo, he felt delighted and he inquired on many things about Li Qingyun. He then asked Mr. Li Huan to notify General Yang to try and escort Li Qingyun to Nanjing, so admirers from all over the world could pay tribute to our centenarian, and so he could also learn his methods and secrets of longevity. Regrettably, Li Qingyun had seemed not to have the good fortune to meet the head of the

---

25   Master Liang said that Li Huan's statement that Li Qingyun "had not mastered these methods" was somewhat prejudicial and probably motivated by Li Huan preferring teachings he received from Yinshizi.

country. When the telegraph arrived, he had already went back to Chenjiachang in Kai County and died a natural and sudden death.

Publication in the *North China Daily News*

Some remaining evidence could prove Li Qingyun lived for around 250 years. The delegate of the National Assembly, Mr. Li Huan, collected this evidence. One such piece of evidence was a photo of Li Qingyun, the second was that the *North China Daily News* published an article in Shanghai on June 5, 1928. Below is the original text: [26]

**The North China Daily News
Shanghai
5th June 1928.
250 Years Old.**

---

[26]   This newspaper article was originally printed in English, so it is reproduced here just as it appeared in Yang Sen's book—with all spelling and punctuation retained.

And still doing well: wonder man of Szechuan!

The accompanying portrait, taken in the spring of last year, is that of Mr. Li Ching-yun, an old and respected recident of Shangchun Village, Kaihsien a place to the north of Wanhsien, Szechuan.

Born in the 17 year of reign of Kang Hsi, on the second Emperor of the Manchu dynasty, Mr. Li is now in his 250th. Inspite of this years, he is young and vigorous in spirit and he is physically strong. His facial appearance is no different from others who are two centuries his junior.

A native of Ching-an he has travelled very widely and every where he goes, the people welcome him. Numerous military and civil leaders have conferred honours and presents upon him.

When he was only a few years old, he could read and write and upon arriving at the age of 10, he had travelled throughout Shensi, Kansu, Sinkiang, Manchuria, Tibet, Annam and Siam gathering medical herb. This continued to be his trade until he was 100 years old. After that, there were a number of his friends who were even older than himself.

Mr. Li has many disciples, all of whom are old men. Some of the oldest men in the district say that their grandfathers knew him. His disciples, when questioned, say that Mr. Li has taught them to "Keep a quiet heart.

Sit like a tortoise. Walk sprightly like a pigeon. Sleep like a dog," the teachings of longevity of Wang Lao [27] have been burnt but Mr. Li still lives and his teachings may lead to many others learning to live long lives.

[Publication in the *Shanghai Declaration News*]
The third piece of evidence was on June 6, 1928, one day after the *North China Daily News* published the article about Li Qingyun. The oldest and biggest news publisher in China, the *Shanghai Declaration News,* also published a news report. The following is the original text and photo of Li Qingyun.

Below in the news story where it says that Li traveled everywhere since he was ten years old, [28] this is different from what he told Yang Sen that he left home when he was thirteen years old.

---

[27]   *Wang Lao* (黃老) is a reference to the teachings of both the Yellow Emperor (黃帝, Huang Di) and Laozi (老子). *Having been burnt* is a reference to the tyrant emperor Huang Di of the Qin dynasty (秦朝, 221–206 BCE), who supposedly burnt and made illegal all books not conducive to his reign or legacy. However, this widespread burning is probably more of a myth than fact, as it has been used by many early scholars as an excuse to rewrite texts to their liking. Also, the Huang-Lao teachings were the predominant teachings of Daoism until the arrival of Zhang Daoling (張道陵, 34–156 CE), who revised Daoism into a religion and clergy—the Celestial Masters Sect (天師, Tianshi), and thus great effort was made to dispel the Huang-Lao teachings.

[28]   *The North China Daily News* first reported him as having been ten years old when he started traveling.

The Centenarian, the 250-Year-Old Man

He was born in Kangxi 17th year, had married
14 times, had 180 posterity and all had
manners of longevity.

According to the *North China Daily News*
report, one of the villages in Kaixian, Sichuan,
has an old man named Li Qingyun, 250 years
old, who does not dodder, has a strong body,
is full of energy, and looks like a few tens of
years old. Li was born in Kangxi 17th year.
When he was a few years old, he could write
and read. When he was ten years old, he
traveled everywhere. He traveled all over
Shangan, Xinjiang, Manzhou, Xizang, and
Annan, collected herbs for a living, time flew
by, and he was one hundred years old. Then
he went back and traveled among Hunan,
Hubei, Henan, and Jiangsu provinces, still
collecting herbs for a living. He often walks
over 50km a day and does not feel tired.
Li married fourteen times and has eleven
generations, he has 180 descendants. Li can
see and hear very well. His fingernails of left
hand were long and he kept his clipped
fingernails in a wooden box. The box was full
of fingernails. Li is very knowledgeable about
the history of Qing dynasty[29] and he could
answer any question about it. Li said, he had
some friends who lived longer than him, and
most of Li's disciples are elders. Some of the

---

29   Qing dynasty (清朝, 1644–1912).

oldest said their grandfathers knew Li, or had asked Li about methods of longevity. Li replied, "In meditation, sit like a tortoise, walk like a crane, and lay down like a dog." Li's teachings are popular. He received many gifts from his admirers.

Photo Inscription: The photo of Li Qingyun and the original news text published by *Shanghai Declaration News* on June 6th, Republic of China 17th year.

On June 6, 1928, after *Shanghai Declaration* published "The 250-Year-Old Centenarian, Li Qingyun," two days later, on June 8, it published an article in "Letters From Readers." The title was "The Evidence of the 250-Year-Old Man." In the text is mentioned "an officer," and it's very clear the officer is General Yang Sen.[30]

The Evidence of the 250-Year-Old Man

Editor's Note: The following article was published on June 8, Republic of China 17th year [1928]. The *Shanghai Declaration News* published "Letters From Readers," which gave proof to Li Qingyun being a true story.

> On June 6th, your newspaper quoted an
> article "The 250-Year-Old Man" from the
> *North China Daily News,* which was actually
> a true story. When I went back to Sichuan
> last April, I saw the photo of this old man
> in Wanxian. People said he was 249 years
> old at that time. I then went to Ning[31] to
> study in July. I was planning on posting this
> anecdote in the *Oriental Magazine* and *Science
> Magazine,* so that, experts and scientists would
> know and research on how a human being can
> live to 250 years old. However, since I didn't
> have the photo with me at that time as a
> proof, I didn't do it. I then mailed my brother
> who was in Sichuan and told him the news
> about the old man and asked him to send me
> a photo of the old man as soon as possible.
> But he was too busy with his full-time

---

30   This paragraph note and the following *Editor's Note* are by Wang Chengsheng. Neither Wang Chengsheng nor the newspaper list the writer of this "Letter From Readers."

31   *Ning* is abbreviation for Nanjing.

military job and couldn't do it. Now the article was published in a foreign newspaper and I have mixed feelings and feel kind of regretful. Some of the things I know are not mentioned in the article. Following is what I know.

Li Qingyun is from Guizhou, his posterity still live in Guizhou. He lived in Tiaodengchang, Kaixian, Sichuan, and was born in Kangxi 17th year. He is 250 years old now. But, he looks like a 70-something-year-old man. Last spring, an officer in Wanxian[32] heard of his age and story, then invited the old man to visit. He sent people to bring the old man back in a sedan chair, but the old man didn't want to sit on the sedan chair and preferred to walk. He could walk 30 to 35 km a day. His visit made a big splash in Wanxian.

Everybody in Wanxian knows about the 249-year-old man Li Qingyun. The officer took pictures of him and gave them out to relatives and friends. My brother got one of the photos, so we know about the old man. The old man said that when he was a little more than 10 years old, three herbalists came from Changbai Mountain, Jilin, who looked like 60-something-year-old men. They asked him to join them to travel around and collect herbs. He then joined them traveling to Tibet, north of India, Xinjiang, Sichuan, Gansu, and

---

32   Reference to Yang Sen.

Shaanxi. When he came back to Sichuan, he
realized it's been more than a hundred years
since he left Sichuan. After that, he went for
a long trip of collecting herbs again. Around
1914 or 1915, those old herbalists came and
visited him once. Those old men's physical
and mental health were better than him when
they visited him. They must be still alive now.
People asked him, how can he live for so long?
He said, he had eaten Lingzhi and it made his
life longer. Although it was a myth, maybe he
really had elixir herbs that would have great
benefit to human's health. Most of the people
did not believe his words. He said, "I don't
need to cheat, believe it or not, there are no
benefits or losses for me. I have never cheated
in my life." According to evidence, this old
man was at least over 180 years old.

My friend Xiong Zhiping,[33] originally
came from Kaixian, had visited the old man,
and asked another elder who lived around Li.
This elder said Li lived here before his father

---

33 Xiong Zhiping (熊治平, 1888–1981), later stylized as Xiong
Yanghe (熊養和) was a general in the Chinese Nationalist Army,
which is how he became friends with Yang Sen, and later became
a renowned Taijiquan teacher in Taiwan. Master Liang studied
with him for several years in Taiwan and wrote the preface to
Xiong's book, *Explanation on the Meaning of Tai Ji Quan* (太極拳
釋義, *Tai Ji Quan Shi Yi*) in 1963. According to Liang, Xiong had
visited with Li in Chenjiachang a few times before Li's visit to
Wanxian.

was born [and] Li's appearance did not change. His father died at seventy years old, and this elder is more than sixty years old. From this [elder's statements], Li is at least 180 years old. He [Li] saved his left-hand fingernails in a box , storing 10-inch-long fingernails, and the box was full of them. He could describe histories of early Qing dynasty in very great detail. In his spare time, he played cards. He is good at physiognomy and did not charge for it. He stored a lot of herbs and gave it to poor people. His herbs were often very effective. He was kind, so people loved to be alone with him.

Editor's Note: Mr. Xiong had written an article about Li Qingyun and published it in the weekly publication of University of Nanking. If readers want to know more details, please come visit my place at No. 25, Nanjing, Paul Street. I would wholeheartedly welcome this.

Familiar With Anecdotes Through Nine Emperors of the Qing

Because Yang Sen stayed with Li Qingyun for a long time, they had some long conversations, which provided Yang Sen with some further evidence.

First, what was the old man's knowledge and style of conversation? Li Qingyun entered into a private tutorial school when he was an adolescent, but left home at thirteen years of age. He went to school for just a few years, and as a teenager left home, and so he only knew some texts. For the years he grew up from a teenager to 250 years old he went into the mountains to collect herbs, and he taught students in Emei. From his living environment, the time in the Emei mountains was the only period when he had the chance and time to fully concentrate on studying classics and histories, and to read books intensively. His speaking was very logical and in colloquial language. Usually it took just a few words to clinch his point and make people think. And his ways of treating people and managing things were very appropriate and considerate. Yang Sen thinks this was because of his longevity and plenitude of life experiences. Maybe this is what Daoism means, "The method of Dao is the naturally-just-so."

Mr. Li Huan told General Yang that Li Qingyun's arts on Tu Na and Dao Yin were only at basic levels, and his "Dao of reverting back to Before Heaven and his skills of Tu Na are not proportional." So Yang Sen thinks his long life must be more than that of other common centenarians.

Second is his plentitude of life experiences and wide knowledge. Li Qingyun was born in Kangxi 17th year. He was a person born in the seventeenth century, but was still alive in the twenty-first century. He lived through the imperial reigns of Kangxi for forty-three years, Yongzheng for thirteen years, Qianlong for sixty years, Jiaqing for twenty-five years, Daoguang for thirty-two years, Xianfeng for ten years, Tongzhi for thirteen years, Guangxu for thirty-four years, Xuantong for three years, and the Republic of China for seventeen years. The total of these are 250 years, nine emperors of Qing Dynasty, and he experienced many events and things over these nine dynasties. When he talks with other people, whether it be about the middle period of Kangxi to the Republic of China's early years, all the historical facts and anecdotes he was able to answer quickly and fluently in detail. The strange part of this is because everyone knows the earliest newspaper in China was *The Declaration,* published in Tongzhi 11th year [1872].

Considering Li Qingyun's living environment, it was impossible to read newspapers frequently, so where did he get so much knowledge and anecdotal information? For example, Li Qingyun had said he was a soldier in the troops under Yue Zhongqi who was the provincial governor of Sichuan. There was great chaos in Jinchuan, and Yue Zhongqi being the governor of Sichuan pacified the chaos of Jinchuan. That happened in the 14th year of Qianlong [1749]. Li Qingyun was fifty-one at that time,[34] and he described everything about the troops of Yue Zhongqi. His description was very clear, like screen pop ups, very realistic, not like words he heard from somebody else. Some of his memories are valuable historical information.

Yang Sen asked him about an event when Li was reportedly living on Mt. Emei:[35] Had he ever heard about when Shi Dakai,[36] who was trapped at Purple Playing Ground [紫打地, Zi Da Di] and couldn't do anything but wait to be captured. When he was caught, was he transported by guards for execution in Chengdu [成都]?"

Li Qingyun answered, "That actually happened not so long ago." The words blurted out of his mouth, and he was not

---

34   Li Qingyun's age would have been seventy-two in 1749.

35   Mt. Emei (峨眉山), located in central Sichuan province.

36   Shi Dakai (石達開, 1831–1863).

lying because he explained, "Except Shi Dakai died when his military was defeated in Tongzhi 2nd year [1863]."[37]

It's sixty-four years later when Yang Sen asked him this question. In China, living to sixty-four years of age is itself longevity. However, for Li Qingyun, it was just a snap of the fingers.

In addition, Li Qingyun stored more than ten long fingernails. In Chenjiachang, thousands of people, regardless of age and sex, were all unanimously saying that their great-great-grandfathers, great-grandfathers, grandfathers, and fathers all had seen Li Qingyun and were familiar with him. Obviously, Li Qingyun living to 250 years old, it could not be faked.

As for Li Qingyun, he had mentioned the "Ways of Longevity," and Yang Sen recalled everything he could remember from the colloquial language Li Qingyun had used. He tried to relate this as though directly coming from Li Qingyun's own mouth. For example, they talked about seeking the way of becoming an immortal and achieving the Dao. Li Qingyun said,

It is not impossible to reach the way of immortals,
but first, it should start with learning how to purify
the mind and diminish harmful desires.

For those people who complained that the way
to immortality is hard to find, they should ask

---

37   This was a trick question that Li answered correctly. However, Wang Chengsheng must have reported this from what Li Huan had told him, as Yang Sen wrote that Li Qingyun told him that he "had heard information from woodcutters and mowers, but … I could not memorize it very clear.". Li Huan, however, discussed this incident with Li Qingyun, whom he said "was very familiar with these events and could talk about these stories nonstop like he experienced them himself."

themselves. Is my mind really pure and with little desire? If not, the more one attempts to force it, it will keep you farther away from the goal, then the mind will be sick until it is not able to be cured.

This means when people are obsessed by the goal of becoming an immortal, it becomes greed and ignorance, and these then grow in people's minds. Where does the the Way of Longevity dwell? Actually it is in our mind. So when we do one good thing, we are with the Dao, and in our mind we gain one point. When we do one bad thing, the Dao flies away. The Dao can not be forced. Meaning, the Way of Longevity resides in our minds, so advising people to do good things we can then persist in the Dao.

My master once admonished me, saying, "The grass and trees grow up from their roots, so without soil they would die. Fish and turtles all live in water, so without water they will die. Human beings live by their bodies, so without Qi we will die. Do you understand the abstruseness of these?"

At that time I replied, "The sages, the wise, immortals, and Buddhas all know the importance of Qi. Each of them equally know the treasure acquired in harmonizing the Qi, and that it is a process that brings about an auspiciousness. Therefore, Buddhism and Daoism both understand that nourishing the Qi is the first and most important lesson to learn." After listening to my answers, my master smiled and praised me. "You are right, very right."

Eat Three Qians of Gou Qi Daily

When I was 139 years old, before I met my master, my body was spry and easy. I could walk with vigorous strides and looked like I had learned kung fu pretty well. Some people suspected that I was either an immortal or a swordsman, and this made me feel a little awkward at the time. The main reason I could live to 139 years old and still be healthy is because after I was forty years old, I could control my mind and not be disturbed by outside issues. My mind was always calm. With a calm mind, my spirit would be peaceful. With a peaceful spirit, my body was strong and kept away all kinds of diseases. So, I am healthy and happy.

In the year when I was fifty years old, I went into mountains to collect herbs and met up with an elder. He didn't seem like a regular human being. He could run fast, fly and leap between big rocks. I tried to dash forward, but couldn't catch up with him. Then, after a period of time I met him again, I knelt down to ask for his secrets. The elder gave me some wild berries and said, "The only secret is that I eat this often. I took a look and it was Gou Qi[38] [枸杞]. After that, I ate three qians of Gou Qi a day. After a while, I felt my body become lighter and I could walk much faster. I didn't feel tired after a 50 km walk. My energy and foot strength were all better than ordinary people. I am not an immortal nor a swordsman, I just take three qians of Gou Qi a day only.

---

[38]   Gou Qi is commonly called "Wolfberry," and 1 qian = 3.78 grams.

[Daoist Poems on True Nature]

Li Qingyun liked to quote four True Word Verses by Lu Chunyang.[39]

No worry in mind for one day,
is like being an immortal for one day.

The Six Spirits[40] are healthy and naturally at peace,
the Qi fills my Elixir Field with a treasure.

Having the elixir, there is no need to look for the Dao
any longer.

If one keeps peace of mind, it is like looking at the self
in a mirror, and there is no need to sit in meditation
any more.

The Mountain Man, Pure Yang [白陽山人, Bai Yang Shan Ren] also composed a Four-Verse Chant:
If one has nothing to do, one can sit in meditation,
and so living for one day becomes two days.
If a person can live to be 70 years old,
that becomes 140 years old.[41]

---

39   Lu Chunyang (呂純陽) is Lu Dongbin (呂洞賓), one of the famous Eight Immortals, and attributed author of *The Supreme One's Platform on the Secret of the Golden Flower* (太乙金華宗, *Tai Yi Jin Hua Zong*). Lu Dongbin was also a great poet and swordsman.

40   *Six Spirits* (六神, Liu Shen), or Vital Organs, are the heart, lungs, liver, kidneys, spleen, and gallbladder.

41   From the *Secret of the Golden Flower* text.

Li Qingyun said the above examples are all about "keeping the mind calm to see the True Nature [真性, Zhen Xing]." We should set this as a standard, and follow this ideal without fail for our lifetime. He [also] talked about a paragraph in the *Grotto of the Immortal Spirit Scripture* [洞靈經, *Dong Ling Jing*]:

> To stretch and massage bones and muscle can keep one's body strong.
> To cut emotions and desires can make one's mind calm and quiet.
> To speak softly and cautiously can make a person content.
> If you can do all this, you are a sage.

Li Qingyun explained it:

> *Guiding the muscles and bones*—this is to exercise the muscles and bones so there can be physical health.
> *Cutting emotions and desires*—this is to control the Seven Emotions and Six Sense-Desires [42] so the spirit and Qi can be strong.
> *Speaking softly and cautiously*—do not speak unnecessary words to avoid troubles and so to be in a state of Chan.[43]

---

42 *Seven Emotions* (七情, Qi Qing): happiness, anger, anxiety, fear, sorrow, hate, and love/lust. *Six Sense-Desires* (六慾, Liu Yu): color, form, carriage, voice, softness, and features.

43 *Chan* (禪) and *Zen* are the same term.

[Five Ways for Protecting the Five Organs]

As for the "Five Organs" of the body, they all follow the Five Elements.[44] These mutually reinforce and neutralize each other. Li Qingyun thought that we must take care of them through five ways of protecting the Five Organs:

1. Remain indifferent when being favored or humiliated—and the Liver/Wood will be calm.
2. Be respectful when moving or sitting—and the Heart/Fire will stabilize.
3. Control eating—and the Spleen/Earth will have no outflows.
4. Regulate breathing and guard the speech—and the Lungs/Metal will maintain health.
5. Remain tranquil without desires—and the Kidneys/Water will be sufficient.

[Protecting the Orifices]

Protecting the "ears, mouth, and eyes," these three organs Li Qingyun believed are three key points of the "Way of Longevity." For this Li Qingyun explained:

The ears are orifices of Essence. If you concentrate on listening to something, the ears follow the sound and the Essence begins dissipating when concentrating on sound. The Essence then flows out and cannot remain intact.

The eyes are the orifices of Spirit. If the eyes are wandering about because of desires, then the Spirit

---

44 *The Five Organs, or Viscera* (五藏, Wu Zang) are heart, liver, spleen, lungs, and kidneys. *The Five Elements* (五行, Wu Xing) are the five elemental functions of Wood, Fire, Earth, Metal, and Water.

follows those desires and will get lost and not retain itself.

The mouth is the orifice of Qi. If the mouth talks too much, the Qi will follow the speech outward and not congeal within yourself.

[Food Taboos]

On food taboos, Li Qingyun explained:

No matter if it's Buddhism [釋家, Shijia], Daoism [道家, Daojia], or the Physicians [醫家, Yijia], they all advocate not to eat the Five Unclean Foods.

Buddhism's Five Unclean Foods are Chinese scallion, shallot, chive, garlic, and onion [but also taro].

Daoism's Five Unclean Foods are chive, garlic, rapeseed, Chinese scallion, and coriander.

Physician's Five Unclean Foods are onions, garlic, chive, smartweed, and mustard.

These are all smelly and spicy foods. Eating these will confuse the Spirit, hurt the Qi, and encourage false thoughts, and so shorten one's life. As for chicken, duck, fish, and other kinds of meats, these are not as harmful. The Five Unclean Foods are also known as just the Five Spices.

[Dos and Don'ts for Daily Life]

For daily life, Li Qingyun's ideas were:

In the winter, don't go hungry in the morning.
In summer, don't eat too much at night.

Don't wake up before the rooster is crowing, and don't get up after sunrise. Keep the mind pure, "the True Person embraces this," and keeps the Qi steady, then wickedness and filthiness will not grow in the body. If a person continually does this it is better than eating Ginseng and China Root.

During the daily life, what should we do and what should we not do? Li Qingyun's ideas were:

Things we should do: rub face frequently, blink eyes frequently, flick ears frequently, knock teeth frequently, keep the back warm, keep the chest protected, massage the abdomen frequently, knead the feet frequently, swallow the saliva frequently, and rub the waist frequently.

Things we should avoid: combing the hair in the early morning, seeking coolness in a shaded room, sitting on the wet ground for too long, wearing wet clothing in the cold, wearing long drying clothes, fanning ourself when sweating, sleeping with lights on, having sexual intercourse between 11:00 p.m. and 1:00 a.m., using cold water to wash the body, and using hot fire to burn the skin.

Eight out of ten are injured by: Staring for too long hurts the Essence, lying down for too long hurts the Qi, sitting for too long hurts the circulation of blood, standing for too long hurts the bones, walking for too long hurts the muscles. Anger injures the liver, anxiety injures the spleen, over thinking injures the heart, too much sorrow injures the lungs, eating too much injures the stomach, fearing too much injures the kidneys, laughing too much injures the waist, talking too much injures the secretions, spitting too much injures saliva, sweating too much injures the Yang energy, tearing [of the eyes] too much injures the blood, sexual intercourse too frequently injures the marrow.

Li Qingyun considered that "greed, anger, and arousing affections," along with "bitter sadness" [depression] and "being vexed by hatred" [negative compulsions], are what greatly affect our lifespan and our physical and mental health. Therefore, he had many warnings:

Greed, anger, and arousing affections are the most likely [emotions] to rob the human body and mind, and so keeping away from these are the Way of Longevity. When people embrace silence, the spirit will not be injured. Thinking less feels good, like candlelight shining in the mind. Don't get angry, and the Qi and Spirit will react smoothly. Be without worry and the mind will be calm and pure. Do not desire, and then there will be no effects of flattery and pride. Don't be stubborn, then everything will be flexible. Don't be greedy, then you can feel wealthy. Be conscientious, then why would you fear even monarchs? Lightly tasting will let you experience the sweetness of food. If the Qi is stable then the breathing pattern will naturally become thin and lingering. All mentioned above are for correcting the two aspects of "greed and anger."

Pouring the Liquor of Clarified Butter Over the Head to Increase Wisdom So Not to Arouse Affections [45]

In speaking about "arousing affections," his words enlightened people with perfect wisdom. Li Qingyun's ideas were:

When the mental or physical are blinded to specific things, the human body will attach itself to them and the Spirit will flee. When someone obsesses about some specific thing, it becomes like a daydream. The body becomes like a zombie and the Qi will dissipate, then the body will be incomplete and the person will die. Or, the Spirit will flee and cause death too.

Of grief, joyfulness, hatred, and anger, Li Qingyun shouted loudly, "These are the enemies of longevity!" He said,

Grief, joyfulness, hatred, and anger, any one of these can cause agonies to fill the whole body, and shorten a person's life. You see, when someone feels grief they cry with tears, just like smelling spices causes the nose to run. Hate can cause goiters. Anger can cause jaundice.

He also said,

No one can know when either praise or criticism will come. To be angry because of people's criticism or to be happy about praise are both emotional defects. The emotions will thus make you uneasy. Sensible persons

---

[45] Though it's not explained here, this title reveals a ritual spiritual practice of pouring clarified butter over one's head to eradicate sensual desire. The ritual was probably named in the title to indicate that Li Qingyun practiced it, but the editors thought it too mystical or controversial to explain the process, as the ritual would be dangerous without proper instruction.

will grin and bear criticism, and refuse praise politely.
Then the mind will be calm and clear like a mirror. So,
if people want to have longevity, they must guard
against happiness, anger, grief, and fear.

Li Qingyun also used the Physicians' statement as examples
to prove this, he said,
Physicians also had these kinds of statements: anger
hurts the liver, extreme happiness hurts the waist, too
much grieving hurts the lungs, and fear injures the
kidneys.

[The Six Qi and Sounds]

The 250-year-old man revealed that his "life's good health" is
because of the way of breathing. He provided explanations and
practicing methods:
Breathing should be delicate, refined, gentle, and
subtle. When exhaling, the air should go throughout
all the sensory organs. When inhaling, the air should
revert from all the sensory organs.

He explained that "The Six Qi"[46] are blowing, exhaling,
giggling, expelling, hushing, and resting breaths. He said this is
the Buddhist's way to get rid of visceral diseases. Li Qingyun
also read a chant for this,
Expelling the breath controls the heart, blowing
controls the kidneys, exhaling controls the spleen,

---

46   This can also be translated as, "The Six Breaths" (Chui 吹, Hu 呼,
      Xi 嘻, He 呵, Xu 噓, and Xi 呬). In Daoism these are called "The
      Six Healing Sounds" and the sounds and methods vary depend-
      ing on the system and school.

resting controls the lungs, hushing controls the liver, and giggling controls the Triple Warmer.[47]

These chants mean: Expelling breath [呵, He] can cure heart problems. Blowing [吹, Chui] can cure kidney problems. Exhaling [呼, Hu] can cure spleen problems. Resting breath [呬, Xi] can cure lungs problems. Hushing [嘘, Xu] can cure liver problems. San Jiao is in the stomach, so according to its different parts, the fluids will be different during the digestion operation. This includes digestion, absorption, and evacuation processes. So if the Triple Warmer has problems, giggling [嘻, Xi] is the cure.

He said that "Chui, Hu, Xi, He, Xu, and Xi" can treat and cure all kinds of visceral diseases. Even if there is no disease, using these six words can also "extinguish irrational thoughts and keep demons far away." The method for self-treatment, every day between 11:00 a.m. and 3:00 p.m., is to close the eyes, sit quietly, knock the teeth, swallow saliva, and then speak these six words softly.

Heart disease patients should cross their hands and put them on top of the head, then intone "He"[48] thirty-six times softly.

Kidney disease patients should hold their hands around the knees, then intone "Chui"[49] thirty-six times softly.

---

47 The *Triple Warmer* (三焦, San Jiao) is not a physical organ, rather an ethereal or Qi-infused organ, with upper, middle, and lower functions.

48 *He* [呵], Expelling Breath, is pronounced like "hoe."

49 *Chui* [吹], Blowing Breath, is pronounced like "chway."

Liver disease patients should cross their hand and put them on the back of head, close eyes and intone "Xu" [50] thirty-six times softly.

Lung disease patients should put their hands behind their back and intone "Xi" [51] thirty-six times softly.

Spleen problem patients should put their hands over the abdomen, bite the lips, and intone "Hu" [52] thirty-six times softly.

Stomach problem patients, the person should lay down, close the eyes, and intone "Xi" [53] thirty-six times softly.

Li Qingyun said these are the best ways to treat visceral diseases, and only people who have done it can understand thoroughly and know the effects. He was serious about the matter and said,

I have benefited a lot from *Chui, Hu, Xi, He, Xu,* and *Xi*. Before I was thirty years old I received these chants and did them every day for about 110 years. Even when I became a Daoist, I never stopped doing them.

---

50   *Xu* [噓], Hushing Breath, is pronounced like "shoe."

51   *Xi* [呬], Resting Breath, is pronounced like "shee."

52   *Hu* [呼], Exhaling Breath, is pronounced like "who."

53   *Xi* [嘻], Giggling Breath, is pronounced like "she-hee."

[The Sexual Taboo of Grafting]

Li Qingyun was opposed to the theories of Grafting With Dao Yin.[54] He said, "Grafting is a side door of Daoism. It is an unorthodox way." Saying further,

> For thousands of years within Daoism people tried practicing this to arrive at the Dao. This theory of "Grafting With Dao Yin" emphasizes too much staying on a tiny middle path, so it becomes partial and unusual. As for the Middle [Way] and Constant Dao, these just mean to purify mind and keep the mind stable and calm. I believe in the Great Heavenly Net,[55] as there is no one who can become an immortal practicing Grafting With Dao Yin. In the Way of Longevity, there are definitely none of these kinds

---

54 *Grafting With Dao Yin* (採補道引, Cai Bu Dao Yin) is a practice whereby men would sexually employ numerous young females along with incorporating Dao Yin breathing methods during sexual congress. This was derived from a practice called *Replenishing the Yang With the Yin*. Ghandi himself allegedly applied this practice by periodically sleeping between two young virgin females to absorb their pure Yin energy, but no sexual contact was engaged in, as this was purely a practice of absorption of Yin energy. Within the Grafting practice, however, sexual contact was frequently used and so it was more a practice of dissipation of Essence (Jing) than a practice of replenishing Essence. It should be noted that in Daoism, males lose their Essence through excessive dissipation, the loss of semen. Females, on the other hand, lose their Essence through excessive menstrual flow, the loss of blood.

55 *Great Heavenly Net* (大羅天, Da Luo Tian), also called Brahma's Net, is what surrounds our universe and no one can escape it or go beyond it unless fully enlightened, such as a Buddha.

of rules. If [people] get into this heresy, they will lose
their natural instincts, and will most certainly fall
into animal domains and suffer pain.

[The Four Methods of Daoism]
Li Qingyun then expounded on the basic methods of Daoism,
which are Clarity [清, Qing], Purity [淨, Jing], Appreciation [希,
Xi], and Being At-Ease [夷, Yi]. He also explained these as:

Clarity—so the mind is not too infected by human
society.

Purity—so the mind does not become too rash.

Appreciation—so the mind is not swayed by outer
appearances.

Being At-Ease—so the mind does not listen to the
surface of words.

Actually, these rules, as he said, are for "keeping the mind
pure and calm."

Live for a Hundred Years, But Only Today Is Today
Li Qingyun loved to recite one particular poem. When looking
into the details of this poem, it is pretty philosophical. The
original text of the chant is:

Life is everlasting. A person only lives in [his or her]
present life. A life may last for a hundred years, but
only today is today. If you believe in "only today
is today," you will still be in a good shape after all
kinds of suffering and tests. If you hesitate, live for
a hundred years and it is still like a dream. Life is
precious and it's difficult to see one's natural instincts
clearly. One should treasure the opportunity in every
moment. Do not miss it. This statement is so true.

It's all in our mind, and the mind is for achieving Dao through our lifetime. If someone missed out on the opportunity, they would be lost for the lifetime.

Another shorter poem reads:
Don't be afraid of having thoughts, be afraid of not being aware of having thoughts. Having wicked thoughts is sick, stopping them is the cure.

Li Qingyun explained this poem and said:
Thoughts refer to wicked thoughts. *Not being aware* means not being aware or discovering them too late. Having *wicked thoughts* is a mind disease, if one can sense it right away and stop the wicked thoughts, then it's just a blink to stop them. Once the wicked thoughts are stopped, then they will be cured.

He usually read three poems by the Heavenly Master Tranquility of the Void.[56] Li Qingyun said, "If familiar with these poems, you then can understand the purpose of Mind and Nature." It is said:

[The First Poem]
The Great Dao is not far away, it is in the human body. Visible things mean nothing, only Nature is real.

---

56 Heavenly Master Tranquility of the Void (虛靜天師, Xu Jing Tian Shi) is Li Qingyun's teacher. Based on his name, he must have belonged to the Celestial Masters Sect (天師派, Tian Shi Pai) founded by Zhang Daoling (張道陵, 34–156 CE) during the Eastern Han dynasty. *Heavenly Master* (Tian Shi) refers to his sect, and *Xu Jing* (Tranquility of the Void) was his Daoist name.

If a person finds their True Nature, the vital energy [Qi]
dwelling in the human body will return to the Elixir
Field, and life will be endless.

For the meaning of this poem, Yang Sen thought it was
similar to a story of Liu Gongquan,[57] a biography selected
from the old *History of the Tang*. Liu Gongquan knew how to
take care of his health. When he was eighty years old, he could
walk as fast as a young man. People asked for his methods for
keeping good health, he said, "I do not have secret methods, I
just don't let Qi out of my body through anger and extreme
pleasures, and I keep my Ocean of Qi[58] warm." Read it repeatedly and you can understand what it means.

[The second Poem]
If you seek a spiritual body, do not depart from
visualizing it in the mind; otherwise the visualizations
in the mind and the spiritual body will not be clear.
Dissipating the Spirit injures the bones and muscles.

If you want to understand the meaning of this, readers can
refer to the Sixth Patriarch.[59]

---

57 Liu Gongquan (柳公綽), 778–865 CE, Tang dynasty.

58 Ocean of Qi (氣海, Qi Hai).

59 Sixth Patriarch (惠能), Hui Neng, 638–713 CE. These verses are
    from the *Sixth Patriarch Altar Sutra* (六祖壇經, *Liu Zu Tan Jing*).
    This is the only Buddhist sutra written outside India. Hui Neng,
    a monastic, figures as one of the most important teachers of the
    Chan Buddhist tradition.

Bodhi is originally without a tree;
菩提本無樹
The bright mirror also has no stand.
明鏡亦非臺
Fundamentally there is not a single thing.
本來無一物
Where then could dust alight?
何處惹塵埃

[The Third Poem]
The Spirit leaves quickly and comes back quickly.
Because the Spirit returned to body, the Qi will come
back too. Practice it all the time, and the Essence, Qi,
and Spirit will merge and fill the Elixir Field.
Everything returns to its source.

No explanation is necessary for this third poem.

Lastly, the following is a praise Li Qingyun had taught
[while in Wanxian], *The Song of Entering the Dao* [60] by the True
Man Sun [孫眞人]. The words are:
Anger damages the Qi of the liver; excessive thinking
damages the Spirit. When the Spirit is tired, the mind
gets wearied easily. When the Qi is weak, it's easy
to become sick. Don't be too sad or too joyful, eat
balanced diets, never get drunk at night. The first
thing is not to get angry in the morning. Knock teeth
before sleeping [9:00 p.m. to 11:00 p.m.], stir and rinse
the tongue in the mouth before waking up in the

---

60 *The Song of Entering the Dao* (入道歌, Ru Dao Ge). The term
"song" carries the same meaning as "poem."

morning [3:00 a.m. to 5:00 a.m.], then diseases find it difficult to invade because the Qi fills up the body. If you want to avoid getting sick, restrain from the Five Dirties [foods], keep the mind calm and pleasant, and the Spirit and Qi will be preserved. The length of human life is not decided by fate, it is decided by ourselves. If you follow these rules, you can have longevity and health.

Although, this song is kind of rustic, it has very deep meaning. If you see through it, the truths are internally exquisite.

250-Year-Old Man, Li Qingyun

by Yang Sen

Nourishing-Life Seminar in Baizhuang

In Republic of China 16th year [1927], I was leading the National Revolutionary Army garrisoned in Wanxian, with the headquarters located at Western Hill Li Family Garden, Wan County, Baizhuang [白莊], and my private apartment which was next to the Baiyan [白巖] Academy. The scenery in this place is beautiful, ancient monuments everywhere. Ultimate White Rock Scenic Area was a place that poet Li Bai[1] of Tang dynasty stayed for study. He had written a famous sentence, "Come drink and play a chess game with me in West Rock." Flowing Cups Pool [流杯池] is at the foot of the hills. In the Song dynasty, the scholars and poets would get together and compose poetry here on the third of March, every year. On the bank of Flowing Cup Pool is a huge reclining stone. The stone was engraved by Jiangxi [江西], with the characters 黃魯直西 山.[2] The words are elegant, and the calligraphy is excellent.

There is also a writing on silkened bamboo by Huang Shangyi [黃尚毅] commenting on the *Mountain and Valley Orchid Poetic Essays* [山谷書幽蘭賦, *Shan Gu Shu You Lan Fu*].

---

1   Li Bai (李白, 701–762 CE). Also known as Li Po and Li Bo.

2   *Huang Lu Zhi Xi Shan,* roughly translates as, "Huang from Shandong went directly to the Western Hills."

At Green Goat Temple [青羊宮, Qing Yang Gong], nearby, Daoist priests liked to talk about the mystery of the Dao. Outside the temple, poetry and literature are etched into the stone walls by Yi Shunding from Hanshou,[3] Liu Zhenan from Feng Jie,[4] and by Tan Yida from Wan County.[5] These [inscriptions] are all beautiful, and plentiful enough to fill the eyes. I was either riding or walking on Western Hills every morning, enjoying the scenery and exercising consistently.

One morning in February, Chief of Staff Zhu Bicai [朱璧彩], Secretary General Yang Yukun [陽裕昆], Director of Military Law Yuan Huanxian [袁煥仙], Adjutant General Gui Yunjin, Clerk of Commercial Port Bureau Li Huan, and I had a seminar in my private apartment. The topic was about how to maintain good health and increase the human lifespan. Some people said Jian Keng [6] lived to be eight hundred years old, Lao

---

[3] Yi Shunding (易順鼎, 1858–1920) from Hanshou (漢壽)—inscribed "True Honor (實甫) Shifu." Yi Shunding was an official of the late Qing dynasty and part of a group of poets called the Seven Masters of Han Lu (寒盧七子).

[4] Liu Zhenan (劉貞安, 1871–1920) from Feng Jie (奉節)—inscribed "Among the Bamboo (問竹) Wen Zhu." Liu Zhenan was a Qing dynasty official and poet.

[5] Tan Yida (譚以大, 1872–1944) from Wan County (萬縣)—inscribed "The True Method (直方) Zhi Fang." Tan Yida was a poet from Wanxian.

[6] Jian Keng is another name for Peng Zu (彭祖), who reportedly lived for 800 years during the Yin dynasty (1900–1066 BCE).

Ran [7] was two hundred years old, Sun Simiao [8] lived to be over one hundred years old. In the first year of Republic of China, there was a 140-year-old man in Liangxiang county, Hebei. The former President Li Yuanhong [9] awarded him an inscribed board to praise him. On Green Land Mountain [青城山, Qing Cheng Shan] in the Emei Mountains, rumors said elders could live to be over one hundred years old because of practicing Daoist Qi refinements of the Spirit.

Westerners wrote books that say because of improvements in medicine, humans could live up to two hundred years old. In Turkey, elders who are over one hundred years old are everywhere because of eating yogurt. How long can humans live exactly? I asked this question in the seminar for participants to discuss. Everyone had their own opinions.

Adjutant General Gui Yunjin made a speech. He said, "I lived in Chenjiachang, Kaixian, where there is a 250-year-old man named Li Qingyun. He originally came from Qijiang county in Sichuan. I am not sure when he moved to Chenjiachang. I heard from local elders that their great great-grandfathers had seen him, but his tracks are not usually certain.

"This old man still lives in a hovel in Chenjiachang. He collects spring water and gathers wood sticks, and cooks for himself. Neighbors take turns supplying groceries, such as rice,

---

7   Lao Ran (老聃), a name for Laozi, is from *The Zhuangzi,* chapter 12, in the story of Confucius meeting with Laozi.

8   Sun Simiao (孫思邈, ?–682 BCE) was a famous traditional Chinese medical doctor.

9   Li Yuanhong (黎元洪, 1864–1928) was in office from June 7, 1916, to July 1, 1917.

vegetables, oil, salt, etc. His clothes and shoes are usually supplied by neighbors as well. He can walk to the top of Iron Phoenix Mountain from Chenjiachang in the morning and return in the evening the same day. The round trip is about a few tens of kilometers. During the lunar New Year holidays, I went home on vacation and visited him at his place and talked with him for a while. Isn't this conclusive proof of a 200-year-old immortal? If you would like to meet him face to face and talk to him about the secrets of longevity, I can invite him to Wanxian to stay for a few days."

The participants in the seminar all agreed with the suggestion and urged me to assign people from Commercial Port Bureau of Wanxian to go with Adjutant General Gui to greet Li.

Li Qingyun's height is about seven feet, and he is strong and healthy. Compared to General Feng Yuxiang,[10] Li Qingyun is still much taller. Because Li Qingyun is tall and big, we sent eight men for two shifts to carry him in a sedan chair.

When they arrived in Chenjiachang, lots of people came to see and people of all ages clapped their hands to welcome them. They were all happy for him and said Li was immortal.

[Editor's Note:] Yang Sen obtained the respect of Li
by the manner he greeted Li when arriving in Wan
County.

But Li Qingyun refused to sit on the sedan chair and walked all the way to Wanxian, and he walked quickly and didn't stop. When he arrived at the boundary of Wan County, the city residents cheered along the way. He arrived into the downtown area on Wenmiao Street and Daqiao Nanjin Street where the government offices are located. Everyone in the city

---

10   General Feng Yuxiang (馮玉祥) was six feet one.

came to welcome him. Pedestrians were everywhere and crowded on both sides of the road to deliver an "immortal style" grand welcome. Young people and children shouted loudly, "Look! the 250-year-old Li the immortal is coming." To show my respect, I was riding a horse and waited to welcome him in West Military Drill Ground, which is a place one must pass through to Wanda Road, and greeted him at the Commercial Port Bureau's special guest house. I asked General Services Section to prepare new clothes, fine food, and to take care of everything he would need for his daily life.

The Military Department, the subordinates of Commercial Port Bureau, and city residents who wanted to know the secrets of longevity came and visited him frequently. Lots of people came in and out, and the guest house couldn't hold up the traffic. Someone suggested that we should invite the old man to West Hill Park to meet the press in public and allow everyone to see the centenarian in person. I thought he was too old, so I didn't agree with it.

Li Qingyun's Background, Stories, and Footprints

Li Qingyun was settled in the guest house, and I went to visit him after he took some rest. He said he was born in Kangxi 17th year. Qijiang in Sichuan was his birthday place and he lived in Kai County for some time. He had married more than ten times and had many children. He had a lot of grandchildren and great-grandchildren, and could not count them all. Because he lived for so long, his wives died and then he would remarry again, and then that wife would die. Most of his grandchildren and great-grandchildren are all dead too. He lived alone for many years already. Now, he is used to being alone, so he does not feel lonely.

He also said, "When I was young I had been in military service under Yue Zhongqi's command. I had engaged in the battle at Golden River.[11] After that, I was tired of the military and then went to Snow Mountain [雪山, Xue Shan], which is on the border of Sichuan and Qinghai to collect herbs. I sold those herbs in Guan [灌] county and nearby areas. We slept in the wild and sometimes we only had a little food to eat for a few days in a row, then we would eat He Shou Wu, Huang Jing, or Baiji to fill our stomach. We then could work as usual and did not feel tired. Besides myself there were three other persons in our team to collect herbs. One was Zhou [周] who came from Eternal White Mountain [張白山, Zhang Bai Shan] in the Northeast, the other one was Zhang [張] from Dragon-Tiger Mountain [龍虎山, Long Hu Shan] in Jiangxi. Every time we entered the high mountains, we would often encounter wild animals, such as tigers, leopards, wolves, and bears.

"We never got hurt because we were very experienced in hunting and not afraid of anything. Sometimes we would encounter other dangers. Luckily, we were always able to turn misfortune into blessings. We often used the herbs we got to help people and treat diseases, and our herbs were very effective. We could get small rewards as our travel expenses. Although we only brought a little money for our long journeys, we got help from other people so we were never short of money and supplies."

I also asked, "Do you still remember some past events like when Luo Bingchang [駱秉章] captured Shi Dakai at Great Pass River [大渡河, Da Du He] and the bandits Lan Dashun [藍大順] and Li Yonghe [李永和]?"

---

11   The battle at Golden River (金川, Jin Chuan) took place in 1755.

94

He answered, "I was collecting herbs in remote mountains at that time. I had heard information from woodcutters and mowers, but it was not very detailed so I could not memorize it very clear."

Speaking on the Regimes and Methods on the Way of Nourishing-Life

Li Qingyun was about seven feet tall, and looked like a giant. He was bald and toothless. He had a ruddy face and loud voice. He appears to be an Earthly Spirit Immortal. If he did not have any secrets of regimen, how could he live for more than two hundred years? I asked him for his methods to dispel illness and prolong life. I wanted to let everyone know his secrets so we all could live longer.

He said, "Longevity comes from Mother Nature. During the days I collected herbs, I climbed mountains and waded creeks, breathed the wind and drank the dew, got the essence from the sun and moon, and received the Reiki [mushroom] from the natural earth. I drank mountain spring water when I was thirsty, and ate herbs when I was hungry. I slept in caves at night, climbed steep rocks in the morning. I was isolated from the outside world of human society. I visited many Daoist and Buddhist temples and had met extraordinary, intelligent persons who gave me directions.

"Some of them taught me Hanging Curtain, Guarding the Apertures, Tranquil Sitting, and the ways of Internal Alchemy[12] to refine cinnabar, mercury, etc., for compounding elixirs. Some of them taught me to adjust the breathing and practice

---

12   *Hanging Curtain* (垂簾, Chui Lian), *Guarding the Apertures* (守竅, Shou Qiao), *Tranquil Sitting* (靜坐, Jing Zuo), and *Internal Alchemy* (內丹, Nei Dan) are four types of Daoist meditation practices.

meditation to obtain wisdom, to be selfless so the mind would be like a bright mirror. Some of them taught me to cultivate body and mind to achieve the realm of perfection, and to understand thoroughly the meaning of life and its value.

"I think that Daoism, Buddhism, and Confucianism have different ways for cultivation. They approach from different angles, but they all lead to the same destination. In other words, this means to purify mind and let out the anxiety, put down all the fate, practicing Elixir Field breathing. If not, then longevity is impossible."

He also said, "Turtles, cranes, and deer know how to use their Elixir Fields and Embryonic Breathing [13] to extend their life. If human beings follow these rules, then humans can also get into the door of sublimeness."

Ming Gong [命公] said,

The senses of spiritual development of the body and mind are parallel. Follow the rules and do your best to practice. Then we will accord with our nature, and longevity comes.

---

[13] *Embryonic Breathing* (胎息, Tai Xi) is normally referred to as "reverse breathing." In "natural breathing," the abdomen is expanded when inhaling, contracted when exhaling. Embryonic Breathing is the opposite. The abdomen contracts during inhalation and expands during exhalation, which is why it's sometimes called "Reverse Breathing." The reason for using Embryonic Breathing is twofold: First, the inhalation provides a greater force and energy for pushing Qi up the back of the spine, and, with the exhalation, driving Qi down the front of the body. Second, it is called "Embryonic Breathing" because this is how we breathed when still within our mother's womb, and so this type of breathing recalls this state and so enhances the idea of creating a Spirit Embryo.

I was a fan of scientific sports. I was a layman and didn't quite believe traditional Chinese regimens; so I asked Yuan Huanxian who was very knowledgeable about meditation to record Li Qingyun's statement and make a copy in my diary. I think a person who wants to live longer should follow the rules of nature, such as to make good use of sunlight, air, water, and exercise, etc. These are very beneficial for a healthy body and mind. Chinese and foreign scientific studies and researches are all in agreement with this belief. Li Qingyun said he had experienced outdoor life for a long time, traveled over mountains and creeks, breathed fresh air, and had sunbathed often. So it seemed reasonable that he could live longer and healthier. These paragraphs were dictated by Mr. Yuan Huanxian from the health talks by Li Qingyun. Even though his statements appeared mysterious to some people, they are also highly esteemed by many others. I am not sure whether all of it is effective or not, so I made these documents public as a reference to be exported into the commentary. But as Laozi said, "The Dao models itself on the 'naturally-just-so.'" This is the gist of Daoism. It's the law everywhere, at all times.

Presenting Photos to Chairman Chiang Kai-shek

When I met with Li Qingyun in Wan County, we took an eight-inch photograph of his whole body. I still had the photo when I led the 20th regiment from Wan County to Quxian in northern Sichuan. At that time, I had official duties and sent Mr. Li Huan *(Editor's Note:* Ding Yu, he is now a representative of National Assembly of Republic of China in Taiwan) to Nanjing to have an audience with the chairman of the National Government. I asked Ding Yu to present Li Qingyun's photo to President Chiang [Kai-shek] and let our head of the country know that on the western border of China there was a 250-

year-old centenarian and for this reason bless a long life for the Republic of China and Chairman Chiang. The photo was presented on April 15,1928 [sic] [14] On April 16, I got a message from Li Huan, who told me Chairman Chiang viewed Li Qingyun's photo and asked many questions about his daily life and how could he live for so long? I explained every question in detail and Chairman Chiang indicated that if there was a chance, he wanted to invite Li Qingyun to visit the capital city to let Chinese and foreigners pay tribute to him and to show people that human life could be longer than two hundred years. Li was a reliable evidence and he looked forward to meeting him. Li Qingyun had been widely welcomed in Wanxian, but when he went back to Chenjiachang soon after, he passed away suddenly at age 250. I also felt sorry he lost the chance to have an audience with our head of the country.

Talking About Li Qingyun One More Time
I published the article "250-Year-Old Man, Li Qingyun in Sichuan" in *Zhong Wai Magazine*. Many friends were very interested about Li Qingyun's anecdotes and his secrets of longevity. They asked questions by written letters or inquired in person. They were very eager to know the answers, just like scientists like to get to the bottom of everything and explore mysteries of the universe. To be honest, immortals were also mortals. Mortals could become immortals. People who want to

---

[14]   This date is clearly an error as Yang Sen mentions this event in his "Preface to the *True Story of the 250-Year-Old Man, Li Qingyun*" and says it took place in 1930. Likewise, Li Huan, who was there, always says it was 1930.

live forever should refer to the two-sentence saying by Su Dongpo[15] from Sichuan:

Immortality cannot be learned.
We should instead learn how to live longer.

I think the first sentence "Immortality cannot be learned" is so true, because in the histories, the emperors of Qin and Han searched for immortality to extend life, but things turned out contrary to the way they wished.[16] This was a very good lesson. I had no comments on those unreal or unproven methods of longevity. I only believed scientifically proven exercises and that those are the only ways to keep good health and extend life. But everyone says, "Life is what I want, death is what I hate," and try to use various methods to reach the goal of extending life and to prevent or treat disease—including the Physicians' methods of medical treatment, health methods, and health care; Buddhist's Tranquil Sitting; [17] and Daoism's Dao Yin and Tu Na.[18] These are similar to the saying of Zhao Dongpo [照東坡], "We should learn how to live longer instead."

People explore mysteries of the universe, to do what they believe is good for them and pursue what they need. Any useful

---

15   Su Dongpo (蘇東坡, 1037–1101 CE) was a famous painter, poet, calligrapher, pharmacologist, and political leader of the Song dynasty.

16   The emperors of Qin (秦, Shihuang, 259–210 BCE) and Han (漢, Wudi, 156–87 BCE) attempted to attain immortality by employing false Daoist alchemists. Both suffered mercury poisoning and died.

17   *Tranquil Sitting* (釋家靜坐, Shi Jia Jing Zuo).

18   *Dao Yin* and *Tu Na* (道家導引吐納, Dao Jia Dao Yin Tu Na).

methods should be used—be it innate [Before Heaven] or acquired [After Heaven], physiological or psychological—to become immortal. I wish everyone could find out the suitable methods for longevity and to end well [to die well].

When thinking about these questions, I referred to a booklet I obtained named "250-Year-Old Man, Li Qingyun's Secrets of Longevity." It was dictated by Li Qingyun and compiled by Master Yang Hexuan.[19] This book was published by Shanghai Da Tong Bookstore. In the book, it mentions that Master of Nourishing Crane Pavilion was Li Qingyun's disciple. One of the sections of the booklet is a biography of Li Qingyun. It mentioned Li Qingyun was an herbalist from Qijiang in Sichuan. He traveled all over Shaanxi, Gansu, Xinjiang, Manzhou [Northeast China], Tibet, and inland areas of Hunan, Hubei, Anhui, Shandong, and Henan. These areas were more than Li Qingyun told me. He had married more than ten times, had many children, grandchildren, and great-grandchildren, which matched the hearsay by elders in Chenjiachang, Wan County, in Sichuan. It also said Li Qingyun met a Daoist priest in Kongtong who stated he was over five hundred years old and claimed he saw the civil army that was organized by Wen Tianxiang [20] to protect the emperor in De You [德佑] in the first year of the Song dynasty [1275 CE] and the soldiers had good discipline.

Li Qingyun asked the Kongtong priest for methods of longevity, and the priest told him the secrets and granted him a scroll of a Dao book. He then built huts on Mt. Emei, started

---

19 Master Yang Hexuan (養鶴軒主人, Yang He Xuan Zhu Ren, Master of Nourishing Crane Pavilion).

20 Wen Tianxiang (文天祥, 1236–1283 CE), Duke of Xinguo, was a scholar-general in the last years of the Southern Song Dynasty.

to teach Dao and Tortoise Breathing [21] to his students for more than one hundred years. Li Qingyun did not tell me about this priest. The book also mentioned that other than a drug shovel and a cloth bag, Li Qingyun had a small wooden box, in the box, there were many different lengths of fingernails. Those fingernails were trimmed on his routine life. This is the same box that Li Qingyun showed me when I met him. He let me see the box and there were many long fingernails inside. He kept more than ten long fingernails. The shapes looked like small curly pagodas. According to these many long fingernails, it seemed that Li Qingyun was indeed more than two hundred years old. He was not lying.

I remember I had assigned someone to Kai County, Chenjiachang in Sichuan, who looked for many elders whose age was between seventy and eighty and asked them questions about Li Qingyun. They all spoke in unison, "Sixty or seventy years ago, when we were little kids, we had seen Li Qingyun. He looked the same as now. This old man is so strange, he looked the same all these years and [we] could not see aging on him."

---

[21]   *Tortoise Breathing* in Daoism requires a very high skill of breath control. If falls into the category of Closing the Breath (閉氣, Bi Qi). Tortoise Breathing maintains the ability to close off the external breathing and function purely through circulating the breath (Qi) internally. The famous Song dynasty Daoist Ge Xuan reportedly could sit at the bottom of a pond for three hours due to his skills of Tortoise Breathing. In brief, adepts trained Tortoise Breathing by learning to first hold their breath for 120 heartbeats while generating breath from within their lower Elixir Field (Dan Tian), not from the abdomen. This is like treating the Elixir Field as if it were an inner balloon that expands and contracts.

The booklet said, "Li Qingyun went to Fujian [福建] and had seen Zheng Chenggong."[22] For this part, I believe that the writer did not have enough knowledge about history. The writer did not recognize that Zheng Yanping died in the first year of Kangxi [1662], but in the biography he stated Li Qingyun was born in Kangxi 17th year [1678], so this is contradictory.

In the booklet, Li Qingyun describes his "Way of Longevity" and Master Yang Hexuan recorded the dictation by Li Qingyun's teacher. I don't dare make comments about this because I am a layman of the Longevity and Immortality Secret Arts.[23] However, the principles of practicing the directional positions of the Eight Diagrams [八卦, Ba Gua] are similar to my statements about exercising the body and keeping the mind calm. It is like different routes leading to the same destination. Longevity and immortality are not just by luck.

Sichuan [四川] is blessed to have areas with Heavenly blessed caverns [immortal paradises], like on Mt. Emei [峨嵋] and Green Land [青城, Qing Cheng] Mountains. Many different Daoist sects practiced Nature Skills, or practiced Life Skills, and/or Nature and Life Dual-Cultivation,[24] and all these originated from here.

---

22   Zheng Chenggong (鄭成功) was a pirate who first took control of Taiwan. Zheng Yanping (鄭延平) is Chenggong's stylized name.

23   Longevity and Immortality Secret Arts (長生不老秘訣, Zhang Sheng Bu Lao Mi Jue).

24   *Nature Skills* (性功, Xing Gong). *Life Skills* (命功, Ming Gong). *Nature and Life Dual-Cultivation* (性命雙修, Xing Ming Shuang Xiu).

As far as I know, the most famous schools were the Liu Sect [劉門] of Shuang Jiang [雙江] and Luo Sect [羅門] of the same county. Liu Sect focused on mind practicing [Xing Gong], while Luo Sect focused on physical practicing [Ming Gong]. Master Peng [彭] from Yong Chuan [永川], Xixin Zi [洗心子] from Tong Liang [銅梁], and Duan Zhengkang [段正亢] who had lectured in Beiping [北平, presently Beijing], they preferred both physical and mind practicing in parallel [Nature-Life Dual Cultivation].

Previously, I had mentioned Yuan Huanxian who had helped me record quotations of Daoist practices by Li Qingyun. He served in my troops in Wan County as the director of martial law. I did not know he had the skills of Chinese alchemical processes [25] so I did not pay much attention to him. Later, he resigned from the position, then he went to preach to people in western and northern Sichuan. He had more and more followers and a great reputation. He went deep with various types of people.

At a later time when I was in the combat of suppressing the Communists in northern Sichuan, I went to Chengdu and attended a military conference. Someone told me that Wang Zuanxu [26] had kowtowed to Yuan Huanxian and learned methods of Dao. I asked Wang Zuanxu about this face to face, and he answered that it was true. Until now, I still suspect that the Dao which Yuan Huanxian was preaching was actually learned from Li Qingyun, but nobody knows. As for Wang Zuanxu's practice, he took one hundred pieces of Sichuan pep-

---

25   *Shao Dan Lian Gong* (燒丹鍊汞).

26   Wang Zuanxu (王纘緒) was a former commander-in-chief and governor of Sichuan province.

pers a day and never stopped for a few decades. Wang Zuanxu pretended to be mysterious and refused to tell people where he learned his methods. I also suspected that maybe it was Yuan Huanxian who taught Wang Zuanxu. If this was the case, then maybe Yuan Huanxian also learned it from Li Qingyun. I always doubt the effectiveness of these strange methods of longevity, so I don't quite believe them. But it is strange to say, Wang Zuanxu actually lived for a long time, and his physical condition was always healthy. In my memory, Li Qingyun was a very common person, rarely depressed. When I met him, he was already 250 years old. As one proverb says, "If a tree is not useful, then it will not be cut. Therefore it can live a long time." Maybe the reason that Li Qingyun could live for so long is because he was mediocre and rarely got depressed, was honest and behaved himself, didn't think and worry too much, and accepted circumstances with good will?

Unwittingly, this article has more than a thousand words. I would like to use a story of Han Wudi [漢武帝] as the ending. Wudi accepted the arrangement of providence and initiated fortunes for the country. His achievements were brilliant. He was one of the rare wise emperors in the history of China. However, after the second year of Yuan Feng [109 CE], he intently wanted to be an immortal. He looked for immortals and sought out all kinds of elixirs. The result is that swindlers came one after the other. There was a man from Qi [齊] who was named Shao Weng [少翁], who claimed he could summon immortals. Wudi then conferred him as a General of Wen Cheng [文成]. Wudi waited for him to summon an "immortal" for a long time, but it never came. Shao Weng's trick was exposed. Wudi then killed him.

After that, he was tricked by a Daoist priest, Luan Da [樂大], and conferred him as General of Wu Li [五利將] and Marquis of Le Tong [樂通候]. Wudi also granted him two thousand households and gave him one hundred thousand catties of gold. Later, the princess even married him. The result, again, was that the hoax was exposed. Wudi was very angry and ordered Luan Da to be cut in half. Wudi's own daughter then became a widow.

At the beginning of the Qing dynasty, a poet, Wu Meicun [吳梅村], wrote a poem after he read the *Emperor's Martial Record*, [27]

> Watching the sunrise to the east of Peaceful Mountain,
> asking the firmament in west of Heyuan;[28] great talent
> and vision were all gone in the later years, witchcrafts
> were mistaken as immortals!

If readers could ponder the deeper meaning of this poem, then read my article again, the "Way of Longevity." Maybe the reader could understand most of the meaning of the ways "to be immortal."

---

27   *Emperor's Martial Record* (武帝紀, *Wu Di Ji*).

28   Peaceful Mountain (泰山, Tai Shan). Heyuan (河源).

Anecdotes of the 250 Years Old Man

By Li Huan

Qinling Mountain [秦嶺山] range is winding like a dragon. The mountains extend into the east Sichuan, between Wan County and Kai County. It is also called Gaoliang [高梁山] Mountain range. From the ridge of Gaoliang Mountain range, on the left side it overlooks Yangzi River [楊子江, Yangtse Jiang], it squints at the town Kaixian [開縣] on the left-hand side. The ridge is called Iron Phoenix Mountain. Some said that a female and male phoenix [1] had visited and danced together in this region. The female phoenix took a rest on the mountain and that's how it got its name Iron Phoenix Mountain.

Mountains were high and reached to the clouds. It feels like winter during the summertime on top of the mountain and there was a Buddhist pagoda covered with iron tiles. A cycad stood next to the pagoda. The stems and leaves were lovely, looking like a Qiulong.[2] The trunk of the cycad tree is very big, taking dozens of people to wrap their arms around it. It is a sacred tree, a few thousands years old. At the foothill of the mountain is Chenjiachang, the juncture of Wan Kai highway. In the first year of Republic of China [1912], the highway was not excavated yet, and so traffic was very difficult to deal with. Living here with the towering mountains was like living in a paradise.

Li Qingyun stayed in Chenjiachang. He came from Qijiang county in Sichuan. According to local elders: their

---

1 Female phoenix (鳳, feng) and male phoenix (凰, huang).

2 Qiulong (虬龍), a small dragon with horns.

great-grandfathers had seen him. He didn't stay in one place for long, traveled around, coming and going alone. He looked leisurely, free, and unrestrained.

He had married many times, had many children but they had already died. Only grandchildren, great-grandchildren and younger generations are still alive. In the early years of Republic of China [starting in 1912], Li lived alone. He looked very at-ease and had no worries. His physical health was still good. He could gather firewood, carry spring water, and cook all by himself. He acted vigorous, collected herbs, and helped people by treating diseases for his livelihood. In Chenjiachang, many nice people gave groceries to him, so he was never short of food or money. He was very popular with his neighbors and some even called him the "Earthly immortal."

My friend Gui Yunjin came from Chenjiachang. When he went back to his hometown to visit his parents in the Republic of China 15th year [1926], he also visited Li Qingyun at his place. Li looked the same as he did years ago when Gui Yunjin's grandfather first saw him. I had a conversation with Mr. Yang Zihui [陽子惠, this is Yang Sen] about the 250-year-old man Li Qingyun. Mr. Yang admired him, so he ordered Gui to invite Li Qingyun to come to Wanxian to stay for a while and treated him very courteously. So I had the chance to talk with Mr. Li Qingyun several times at the left-hand side room of the Confucian temple there.

This old man was much taller than six feet, his body shape was tall and strong. He was bald with no hair, and just a few tiny mustache hairs. His face was ruddy, his voice was loud and clear. He wore a blue gown and mandarin jacket, straw sandals, and white cloth socks. His eyes were bright and full of expression. His eyes were so bright, like electric sparks. People were afraid of looking at his eyes directly. It seemed that you could tell his longevity when seeing his face. He was an extraordinary person of our modern time. The most strange thing was his fingernails. His fingernails were curly and about seven to eight inches long, shaped like pagodas. He showed the wooden box that was full of the fingernails he collected. I observed his dietary habits. He preferred rice cakes, fruits, and vegetables. He could eat three to four bowls of rice with little bits of meat, and he chewed and swallowed food slowly and calmly.

One morning in March, while serving Li, we roamed nearby suburb areas for sightseeing. I asked him about his birthday. He replied that he was born in Kangxi 17th year [1678] but he usually did not like to tell people.

Then I asked, "You have such a long life, do you have any secrets of longevity?" He answered, "The most important thing is to practice the Dao of Laozi, 'The Dao models itself on the naturally-just-so.'" He continued and said, "When I was young, I went to mountains to collect herbs between Sichuan and Qinghai every year. I did that for a living. Sometimes, when we stayed in the wild for days, we could not get enough food, then I ate herbs such as He Shou Wu. After eating the herbs, I didn't feel hungry and even didn't eat for a few days. But I could still work in the mountains and did not feel tired."

Then I asked, "When you went to remote mountains of Sichuan and Qinghai to collect herbs, were you alone or with other people?"

He answered, "Sometimes I went with my sons and grandchildren. But most of the time, I went with Mr. Zhang [張] who came from Dragon-Tiger Mountain in Jiangxi. But I have not seen him for a few decades, and I am not sure if he is still alive."

I also asked him about the historical events of how Ceng Guofan[3] pacified the Taiping [太平] Rebellion and how Luo Bingzhang captured Shi Dakai. He was very familiar with these events and could talk about these stories nonstop like he experienced them himself.

On the 15th of April, Republic of China 19th year [1930], I was in audience with Chairman Chiang of the Nationalist Government in Nanjing. Mr. Zi Hui [Yang Sen] commanded me to present a photo of Li Qingyun to Chairman Chiang and explain Li's daily life in detail. Chairman Chiang was very interested and wanted to invite him to Nanjing so he could meet the centenarian in person. But after Li Qingyun went back to Kai County from Wan County, Li's life expectancy arrived, and so he died in nature. I felt regret that he could not go to Nanjing to have an audience with the head of the country.

---

3   Ceng Guofan (曾國藩, 1811–1872 CE).

A Big Hit in the U.S.
When Zhong Wai Published the
Article of "The 250-Year-Old Man"

By Zhang Qichang,[1] sent from New York

Recently, I chatted with my American friends, there were two very hot topics. One is about an old man and the other is about young kids; one is from the past and the other is in the present. Of course, the one about the "Young kids" and "Present" is the Chinese Little League baseball team which won the championship of the Little League World Series, and of their discipline and good behavior when they were in the United States.

The United States is commonly known as, "Hell for elders, a battlefield for middle aged men, and a paradise for children." Children's activities generally received more attention. Not to mention that the championship of the Little League Baseball World Series is the best of the eight best teams that advanced from 7,300 leagues and 60,000 teams around the world. They have to go through serious intense competitions before they can obtain this highest honor. The United States is recognized as the baseball kingdom internationally. Little League baseball is a major international competition and draws attention from all over the world. Even U.S. President Richard Nixon had

---

1   Zhang Qichang was a famous Chinese painter and calligrapher living in New York. He was a friend and contemporary of Picasso and Master Liang. He wrote this article in 1969 for *Zhong Wai Magazine* and was included here in Yang Sen's book.

watched the games in person and cheered happily for the children and gave autographs for them.

The American's favorites, these teenage stars like the United States' eastern team, northern team, western team, they were all defeated by the Chinese junior baseball team. At that time, all U.S. mass medias and the American people were all surprised and stunned. They used terms like, "miracle," "couldn't be imagined," "incredible," and "haven't ever seen this before" to describe the Chinese Little League baseball team. Moreover, it initiated a kind of fever about baseball, and people were acting crazy about baseball again. The American impression of the children in the Chinese Little League baseball team was "they're all native Taiwanese."

Before they became famous, they did not even have real baseballs and bats. They used bamboo poles and rocks to practice with. Everyone was surprised that the world's No. 1 team was from a small village with a population of a little less than five hundred people. They also said, "The Republic of China is not a country that is famous for its baseball teams, and this was their first time to play in the Little League Baseball World Series. They amazed the world with their very first attempt and won the championship." So, they then asked forcefully: "If they are not genius and it's not a miracle … then, what is it?"

The Little League Baseball World Series was held in the city of Williamsport. A well-known local newspaper published a comment recently. Although the comment has just a few paragraphs, it is actually the most efficient way to promote our country and gain visibility internationally. This is what other countries would pay any price for and yet couldn't get it. One of the paragraphs in this commentary was,

We believe that before the Chinese Little League
baseball team came to the city of Williamsport, there

were a lot of people who did not know where Taiwan, the Republic of China, is, and how far away is it from Williamsport? But after people watched these Chinese children's performance, they started to realize that the Republic of China is actually so close to them, and as close as just on top of their heads.

"As close as just on top of their heads," of course, is not based on a geographical concept. The purpose of this article was to correct a common phenomenon of Americans ignoring the Republic of China [2] via the fact that the Chinese Little League baseball team had just won the world championship. The newspapers pointed out directly, the Chinese could better the American!

As for the "old" and "past" that was mentioned in the first paragraph of this article, this is related to the *Zhong Wai Magazine* that you are reading now. The origin of this hot topic article was actually a coincidence. When volumes 5 and 6 of *Zhong Wai Magazine* arrived at my apartment in New York, I was eager to read the magazine as usual. When I was just starting to read Mr. Wang Chengsheng's masterpiece on page 30 of the magazine, "How Could You Live to 250 Years Old?" somebody rang my doorbell. I put down the magazine and opened the

---

2   A statement about when Chiang Kai-shek and his wife requested military and financial aid to defeat Chairman Mao in China, a request that was ignored even when Madame Chiang came to America in hopes of addressing the U.S. Congress on their plight. Master Liang, who was the second highest ranking officer for British Customs, felt that if the United States had come to the support of Chiang Kai-shek, Mao could not have overtaken Beijing in 1949 and contemporary China would be very different.

door. It was my neighbor Mr. Jones who came over to borrow a repair tool. I invited him in and seated him in the living room while I searched for the tool he needed. On page 30 of *Zhong Wai Magazine,* there was in English a news title regarding the 250-Year-Old Man Li Qingyun published by *North China Daily News* on the 5th of June, 1928. I believe that because the news was written in English, it caught Mr. Jones' eye. He picked up the magazine and read the English paragraphs at a stretch. Suddenly he was excited and shouted.

While I was in the storage area looking for the tool, I heard Mr. Jones shout. I wondered what happened and rushed out. The sixty-four-year-old Mr. Jones suddenly looked thirty or forty years younger and behaved like a young adult. He pulled me to the couch and forced me to explain the rest of the article which was written in Chinese to him, a total of six big pages. At that same time, he was rubbing his hands and looked eager. He was also muttering to himself: "It's a miracle, a miracle! Can't believe it! Incredible! There was a person who really lived to be 250 years old!"

It was difficult for me to interpret the magazine to him. (By the way, I want to say thanks to Mr. Wang Chengsheng and the *Zhong Wai Magazine.* Every article in the *Zhong Wai Magazine* makes the AD year as the reference for the years that were prior to Republic of China. This not only indicates that the magazine has a good style, but also that the articles it publishes have good historical and referencing value. This also made it easier for me; otherwise, I couldn't have even interpreted the first two paragraphs on the thirty-third page in a short time).

When I was interpreting page 30, the white-haired Mrs. Jones came to my house to check out why it was taking her husband so long to borrow the tool. Mr. Jones shouted to Mrs.

Jones right away and told her about his "astonishing discovery." Mrs. Jones then learned there was a person who lived to be 250 years old. She was surprised and amazed. She was so excited and couldn't help dancing for joy. The excitement is nothing less comparing to the day she saw Neil Armstrong landing on the moon (broadcast on TV, of course). Thanks to Mr. Jones' consideration, he repeated to his wife word for word of what I just interpreted to him, and added some of his own descriptions.

He stopped at exactly where I stopped. It seemed that Mr. Jones was paying close attention to my interpretation of the article to him. He even pointed at the sentence of "至於李青雲所談及的延年益壽之術" and asked me to continue to interpret for him.

The problem is that, the following paragraphs were too difficult for me to translate, such as "寵辱不驚 — 肝火自寧，動靜以誠 — 心火自定."[3] I was sweating while I tried very hard to interpret these [verses] to them. Unfortunately, these sections were the key areas that Mr. and Mrs. Jones wanted to know the most, the "Methods of Longevity." For them, the value of the article and the excitement on what they have found was like Columbus discovering the new Americas.

---

3   These four verses roughly translate as:

寵辱不驚, *Favor and disgrace are not to be feared.*

肝火自寧, *Repose yourself if there is fire in the liver.*

The idea here is that when meeting with blame or praise, do not get angry as this will injure the liver, and you will need to repose yourself so as not inflame the liver.

動靜以誠, *In the bustle of activity and talking, be truthful.*

心火自定, *Bring order to the self if there is fire in the heart.*

These lines say that within the noise and confusion of daily stresses, you need to settle the heart/mind and bring order to your thoughts. Otherwise, the frustrations will injure the heart.

But the more I interpreted, the more I felt that I could not express the real meaning of those sentences. I was scratching my head and thinking very hard on how to translate into English, phrases like "貪嗔癡愛, 葱韮薤蒜蕖."[4] I felt dizzy and I didn't know how many of my sweating hairs were scratched off. When the time was getting closer to the sunset, Mrs. Jones finally saw my embarrassment of being in the hot seat and urged her husband that they should go home now and wait until I read the whole article. Then they would be all ears coming back tomorrow afternoon for the secrets that could make them live to be 250 years old as well.

Mr. and Mrs. Jones thanked me over and over again, and we made an appointment for 3:00 p.m. the following day. When they walked out of my door, they looked full of energy and walked swiftly. It seemed like they have already learned the secrets of longevity and guaranteed that they could live one hundred or two hundred more years. They used to look very unanimated, like an old couple who relied on just Social Security benefits at the end of their years. Now they are like two different people and full of energy. I had to admit that I was very tired that day and also worried about the test for tomorrow afternoon. However, I also felt pleased that I could bring a little bit of hope and joy to them.

---

4   These two verses roughly translate as:
     貪嗔癡愛, *Greed and anger are foolish emotions.*
     葱韮薤蒜蕖, *Scallions, leeks, shallots, garlic, and lotus.*
     The reason Zhang Qichang had trouble translating these verses
     was that the ideograms used were more classical than colloquial
     Chinese. Likewise, interpreting just a sentence without knowing
     the context of the entire text always proves difficult in Chinese.

My apartment is next to Mr. Jones' apartment. Mr. and Mrs. Jones are retired and both stay at home most of the time. They have nothing to do and are very lonely. I follow Chinese tradition and try to keep a good relationship with my neighbors and to show my hospitality and make guests feel at home when they visit my humble apartment. I believe this was what makes Mr. and Mrs. Jones closer to my family than other neighbors. Mr. Jones is a very honest and frank person, but also a bit stubborn and simple. Sometimes, he tends to be affected by his preconceptions. I remember soon after we moved to this apartment, Mr. Jones and I were just getting to know each other. At the time, he read some news from mainland China [5] that was reported by a few foreign reporters who took bribes from the Chinese Communist Party. We talked about Taiwan and he said something that made me wonder should I laugh or cry, "Taiwan is not better than the mainland China."

Because he is pretty old, I thought I should not be mad at him, so I smiled and asked, "Why is that?"

He answered justifiably, "Foot binding had disappeared for a long time in mainland China, but there are still women with bound feet in Taiwan. This is a brutal custom."

I said, "That's true," but I asked him right back, "Did you know when foot binding started to become popular?"

He knew and said: "It started during the Southern Tang dynasty [937–975 CE]. China was in the feudal system and this was a savage and inhumane custom which was developed under a patriarchal society."

"So," I asked, "Have you ever heard of when China prohibited foot binding?"

He shook his head.

---

5   People's Repuplic of China (PROC).

"When the Republic of China was founded in January, 1912, Dr. Sun Yat-Sen [6] was elected as the first provisional president, he immediately ordered the prohibition of foot binding across the country.

Mr. Jones gladly agreed and said, "I think it's correct that it was prohibited at that time, because Dr. Sun Yat-Sen was a reformer."

Then I asked him, "From 1912 to now, how many years have passed?"

Mr. Jones calculated and answered, "Ah, it's been fifty-eight years already!"

"Chinese women usually started binding their feet when they were three or four years old," I calculated for him carefully. "The government of the Republic of China prohibited the foot binding since the first year of Republic of China [1912]. This means, if there were still women with foot binding in China, they should be at least sixty years old."

He pondered it over, nodded and said, "That's right!"

"Here is our conclusion, Mr. Jones," I told him seriously, "If there are no women with bound feet in mainland China, that means women over sixty years old were all killed by the Chinese communist party with vicious ways of persecution, such as hunger, labor, abuse, and torture. Because in the Chinese communist party's eyes, women over sixty years old have no productivity, they only consume resources. The existence of these women to them is a waste. So, Chinese communist party had to get rid of them. On the other hand, in the Republic of China [Taiwan], not only "elders are able to enjoy their later years and children can grow up smoothly with care," but also every elder can still do

---

6   Sun Yat-Sen (孫中山, 1866–1925) was a Chinese revolutionary and premier of the Kuomintang.

things that they love as per their interests and physical conditions. They can live life the way they want.

In Taiwan, there is a 103-year-old woman who is having fun with her grandchildren, enjoying family times and later life. In Taiwan, the elders are respected and valued by the society and people. So, of course, there are still foot-bonded women in Taiwan."

After hearing this, Mr. Jones now realized the fact. After this conversation, he had changed his preconception and attitude about Republic of China, Taiwan. At the same time, we became very close neighbors.

Mr. Jones and I had an appointment the next afternoon. It was a Sunday, at 2:00 p.m. sharp, Mr. and Mrs. Jones arrived right on time. When they walked through the door and told me that they have "a few" friends who are very interested about Li Qingyun's story, who were even more interested than himself, and they would like to hear it also. Mr. Jones wanted to ask for my consent and see if their friends could come to my house to listen to the "speech" also. At that time, I was thinking that today I have to expend the energy to speak to them anyway. It doesn't matter to have a few more old gentlemen and old ladies, so I agreed with them without hesitation.

Unexpectedly, at 3:00 p.m., there were so many people who arrived, my house was suddenly like a busy market. That never happened before. Some of them are neighbors we had never greeted or met with before, some of them are Mr. and Mrs. Jones' friends and relatives, and relatives of friends. There were more than thirty people who came in, and my living room was packed with visitors. We didn't have enough chairs and cups for the guests, and even the air conditioner was not strong enough. You can imagine how embarrassed my wife and I were. Fortunately, these visitors were so kind and told us again and again that they just wanted to see the photo of Li Qingyun and listen to the story about the 250-year-old man, and the most important thing is that, they wanted to know the "Way of Longevity" that Li Qingyun taught Yang Sen. But they also said they felt kind of presumptuous being uninvited guests. So we felt embarrassed that if we were not good hosts, it would make them feel even worse, so we just followed everyone's suggestion, let the visitors sit wherever they liked in my living room. Then I started my "speech."

I spent a lot time the night before and in the morning of that day to review Wang Chengsheng's masterpiece many times. For those rarely used words, I had checked a dictionary and made notes. This made it much easier for me to explain to them. In the mean time, I felt that Li Qingyun's statements were honest and correct, reliable, and with evidence. It was not the heterodoxy that would lead people into derangement nor superstition, or bizarre composition. Introducing these principles to foreigners may have better results than with Chinese people because they had never heard nor seen ideas before. At least these teachings are harmless and beneficial for them. If they could keep practice unremittingly, they might be able to live to be 250 years old.

I spent two hours explaining this masterpiece by Wang Chengsheng. The guests felt very satisfied after hearing it. Some of them recorded the whole session, some people made notes. They looked very serious, so I believed that Li Qingyun may have successors in the United States.

I had the chance to get to know more American friends through these two interpretation events of Li Qingyun. The story spread out by word of mouth and more and more Americans are interested in people and things of Republic of China. Originally, it's been almost twenty-five years since World War

II ended. People have enjoyed peaceful and prosperous years for almost a quarter of a century.

Scientific discoveries are booming and progress moves faster. When the author wrote this article, human beings had landed on the moon twice. Life is so beautiful and the future ahead is so bright and magnificent. Who does not want to live longer? Who does not want to become the second Li Qingyun? My American friends were crazy about the story of Li Qingyun. They are just like a swarm of bees rushing to be followers. Actually, everybody feels the same way. It's nothing to wonder about.

The story of Li Qingyun had such an impact in my small living circle. Of course, it's nothing compared to when the Chinese Little League baseball team swept the Little League Baseball World Series in the U.S., and the outcomes of these events were obviously different. But these two events reminded me that it was because our wise and great President Chiang who implemented a nine-year compulsory education [for children]. This allowed a lot of children to be free from taking too many supplementary lessons and obtained an educational and balanced development morally, intellectually, and physically. In less than two years, we are already seeing the Chinese Little League baseball team become famous abroad and dominate the World Series. At the same time, it's also because President Chiang promoted the Chinese Cultural Renaissance Movement, so there are many excellent publications arising at the right moment. *Zhong Wai Magazine* is one of these and is very popular abroad. It published this article that even helped promote our country, an unexpected success of civil diplomacy. Old and young, past and present, all of writings have shown that President Chiang's farsightedness and all the decisions he has made have vast and profound effects.

12/12/1969, in New York

Do You Believe That Human Beings Can Live for 250 Years?

By Yan Lingfeng

One

There is an old saying, "A person seldom lives to be seventy years old." However, the living environment and medical and pharmaceutical sciences have advanced tremendously in modern times. People living to be seventy years old is no longer difficult at all. No wonder the ex-vice curator of National Palace Museum, Mr. Zhang Shangyan [長尚嚴] carved a seal for himself on his seventieth birthday. The words on the seal read, "What's rare in the old days is not rare in the modern days." Although these words might imply some other meanings, people being older than seventy years of age is not rare any more. This doesn't mean that there were no long-lived ones in the past, just that people then only had a few ways to prolong their life, such as exercise by working in the fields, worrying less, and eating simple food.

Two

Zhong Wai Magazine has had articles mentioning the 250-year-old Sichuan man, Li Qingyun. In many issues, such as issues 1 and 3 of volume 1, issues 4 and 5 of volume 6, and issue 1 of volume 7, however, it's not easy to convince people that this is a true story. But it seems to be arbitrary to call it impossible. For instance, it was only in the fairy tales that humans could land on the moon. In the story of Chang-E [1] she ate a magic pill and could float into the sky. She ended up landing on the moon and lived there. Or the story of Emperor Ming of the Tang [2] who visited the palace on the moon in his dream. Now, human beings have landed on the moon. So it could mean these [old stories] are true, or maybe not.

An old book described that Ancestor Peng had lived for eight hundred years, but I believe it's more likely that it was his family that lasted for eight hundred years rather than his own age. One of the chapters in Sima Qian's [3] *Records of the Grand Historian* [史記, *Shi Ji*] says that "Laozi lived for more than 160 years. Some people said more than two hundred years. His longevity was due to his practice of Daoism."

If it is true that Laozi had lived for more than two hundred years in the ancient Chinese times, then the 250-year-old Li Qingyun was very likely a true story. However, the book used the words "some people said" people lived for more than 200 years, which is still a story without direct evidence. The chapter on "Yang Zhu" [4] says that, "One hundred is the limit of human's life. It's barely one out of a thousand who can live beyond one hundred years." The *Spring and Autumn Annals* [春秋, *Chun Qiu*] also says, "A human's life could last for more than one hundred

---

1   Chang-E (嫦娥) is the Chinese Goddess of the Moon and, in present times, the name given to the Chinese space program.

2   Emperor Ming of the Tang (唐明皇, Tang Ming Huang), or more popularly titled, Tang Xuanzong Huang (唐玄宗皇).

3   Sima Qian (司馬遷, 135–86 BCE) of the Han dynasty.

4   Yang Zhu (陽朱, 440–360 BCE) is mentioned in the *Book of Liezi* (列子篇, *Lie Zi Bian*). Yang Zhu was a Chinese philosopher during the Warring States period.

years, but the average years lived is sixty at most." One hundred-year-old people were very rare in the old times. For those who had less desires and worry and practiced Daoism, living for more than one hundred years was not impossible.

Three

Following are two sets of statistical data of long-lived people around the world and the life expectancy of some countries:

Centenarians Around the World

According to records from various sources, below are a list of famous centenarians:

—Canadian: Marie Rosalie Lizot, 109 years old (1738–1847)
—British: Ryin, female, 123 years old (1811–1934).
  Her real English name could not be found.
—British: Elizabeth Hanbury, female, 108 years old
  (1793–1901).
—British: Ann Pouder, female, 110 years old (1807–1917).
  The text is wrong. The true dates are 1807–1907.
—British: Miriam Sparks Banister, female, 111 years old
  (1817–1928).
—British (Irish): Katherine Plunket, female, 111 years old
  (1820–1932).
—Russian: Dabinbo, female, 111 years old (1824–1936),
  she was the daughter of Russian Princess Baskov. Her
  real English name could not be found.
—Danish: Christian Jacobsen Drakenberg, 146 years old
  (1626–1772).
—Spanish: Zidansh, female, 125 years old (1781–1906), died
  in Madrid due to Pneumonia. Her real English name could
  not be found.

—Turk: Zaro Agha, 157 years old (1626–1772), some say
he lived to 162 years.

—German: Kolin, 270 years old (no reliable source).

—French: Maria, female, 158 years old. (Birth and Death dates
are not determined. People say her major food for the second
half of her life is goat milk and cheese, 162 years.)

—Australian: Amanji, 122 years old (delivered her youngest
son when she was 121 years old). Her real English name
could not be found.

—Japanese: Takeuchi Sokufu, 300 years old. (Served as a
government officer for 244 years. Lack of reliable proofs.)

—Japanese: Emperor Jimmu, 127 years old (was the first
Emperor of Japan, lack of modern evidence).

—Japanese: Mrs. Leyuku, 124 years old (1826–1950).
She was a farmer and died of stomach diseases.

—Japanese: Fujimoto, 116 years old (1835–1951).

—American: Louisa Kirwan Capron Thiers, 111 years old
(1814–1926).

—Chinese: Dongfang Shuo, 3800 years old (more of a fiction).

—Chinese: Heizhao, 290 years old (he was a monk, lack of
reliable evidence).

—Chinese: Jiang Ziya, 136 years old (lack of reliable evidence)
Mentioned in an article in *Hong Kong Observatory Daily
Newspaper* on 11/06/1969.

Life Expectancy of Some Countries

Country	Male	Female
Australia	66.1	70.6
Austria	54.6	58.9
Belgium	62	67.3
British	66.4	71.2
Canada	65.2	69.1

Denmark	67.8	70.1
Finland	54.6	61.1
France	61.9	67.4
German	57.7	63.4
Hungary	54.9	58.2
Israel	67.3	70.1
Japan	61.9	62.7
Netherlands	69.4	71.5
New Zealand	65.5	68.5
Norway	67.8	71.7
Poland	55.6	62.9
Sweden	67.1	69.7
Switzerland	62.9	67
United States	65.9	71.5

These are the countries that have higher life expectancy in our present time. Among all these countries, females have a higher life expectancy than males. (Quoted from *Hong Kong Observatory Daily Newspaper* on 11/06/1969.)

Four

Besides the data listed previously, following is the information collected by the author regarding long-lived people.

1. In the newspaper, 5/10/1966
    Xu Jixun [許濟遜] from Hong Kong, 104 years old. Xu's Clan Association held a birthday party for him. He could still eat regular food. He ate two pieces of chicken and appeared to really enjoy his birthday party a lot.

2. In the newspaper, 5/10/1969
   In Taiwan, Kaohsiung, Ye Biao [葉標], 104 years old, living together with five generations of his.

3. In the newspaper, 8/5/1963
   Selikanov in Russia, 107 years old, could climb mountains taller than 2000 meters.

4. In the newspaper, 4/13/1963
   In Macau, Li Runqing [李潤清], 110 years old, had five generations in one family. Died a natural death.

5. In the newspaper, 2/21/1963
   An Argentine farmer, Jeasantolina, he hasn't suffered from serious diseases. His daughter was 90 years old on the date.

6. In the newspaper, 2/13/1963
   Lai Ruiwen [賴瑞文], a Taiwanese farmer who lived in the mountains of Miaoli, 115 years old. He didn't smoke, never drank, and so remained healthy.

7. In the newspaper, 11/22/1960
   In Hualian [花蓮], Taiwan, a native female Taiwanese, Xu Jian [許簡], 119 years old. The government gave her a wooden cabin as a gift.

8. In the newspaper, 9/5/1963
   In Jamaica, a female farmer, Dali, died on 9/3, 121 years old.

9. In the newspaper, 12/26/1960
   In North Carolina, U.S., a farmer, Davis, 122 years old, died on 12/25. He was born on the Christmas day and died on the Christmas day.

10. In the newspaper, 9/18/1964
    In Turkey, a 99-year-old woman, Huating, just delivered twins on 9/17. Her husband is 127 years old.

11. In the newspaper, 2/2/1963
    A Colombian black woman died in Cauca on 1/30, lived for 131 years.

12. In the newspaper, 2/13/1962
    In Haifa, Israel, an old man, Abalaham, died a few days ago [in Feb. 1962] at age 134. When he was 93 years old, he married for the fourth time, and he started to form his third set of teeth.

13. In the newspaper, 12/20/1962
    In Latin America, an old man, Kuiwas, is 137 years old. His secrets to longevity: work every day and get sufficient sleep every day.

14. In the newspaper, 1/14/1964
    Ayuku, a Nigerian, died on 1/12 at age 140. He had seven wives and a posterity of about one hundred.

15. In the newspaper, 9/5/1965
    An Argentine Indian farmer Floru died on 9/3, at age 144.

16. In the newspaper, 8/14/1959
    An Azerbaijani man named Muhammad Awazov died at age 151. He had about two hundred descendants.

17. In the newspaper, 4/7/1963
    Muslimov is a Russian Caucasian. He is 158 years old. He never gets sick and he works constantly. He can still eat lamb and vegetables, drink homemade beer and goat milk.

18. In the newspaper, 1/13/1963
    A Syrian named Waton died on 1/12 at age 163. His ID indicates that he was born in 1800.

19. In the newspaper, 12/1958
    Kutachi from Tehran claims that he is 185 years old. The government sent two doctors to investigate and verified it is true. He is still healthy and only his vision and hearing are a bit decrepit.
    Note: This man reportedly died in 1961 at age 188.

20. In the newspaper, 9/1/1963
    An Iranian lives in Bekahdan, his name is Sayade Abutaron Musawei, and he is 191 years old. He is still very healthy and full of energy. He has a few hundred descendants.

21. In the newspaper, 12/21/1964
    The north Sumatera farmer, Hadimohamres, died on the 20th. He liked hot meals. His 120-year-old wife and nine sons are still alive with more than three hundred grandsons and unnumbered great grandsons.

22. In the newspaper, 10/23/1958

There is an old man, Ali, who lives in the Jilusa village on the 22,000 feet height mountain. Couldn't find a mountain in Iran measuring 22,000 feet high. Mt. Damavand is the tallest, which is 18,406 feet. He is 195 years old and has an ID issued by the Arkuli county. Couldn't find this county in Iran. He married when he was twenty-five years old in 1790. He has five children and four are still alive. His daughter, Canun, who was born in 1848, is 110 years old now. If this man is still alive, he would be 206 years old (in 1970).

The photo of the 195-year-old Iranian, Ali. Reported on 10/23/1958 in the *Hong Kong English Tiger News.* If the man is still alive, he would be 206 years old.

Five

According to the data listed previously, there is a man who lived to be 195 years old, or 206 years old if he is still alive now. Compared to Sichuan's 250-year-old, Li Qingyun, that's only fifty-five years apart. From this, it seems possible that Li Qingyun had such a longevity. However, based on the findings of the physiological studies, after fifty years old, a human being's physical health decays gradually and constantly. This is like the running of a marathon. After running four or five miles, it gets harder and harder with every next step. It's also like a parabola in physics. After passing the vertex, the object is dropping off at an accelerated speed. Not to mention such a long period of time like fifty years. Also, I have some doubts on what is described in Mr. Yang Zihui's articles. My doubts are listed below for readers to review and take under advisement:

1) Li Qingyun's age is lacking strong historical documents for evidence.

2) 1928 in Wanxian, if the Yi Fang Photo Studio took many pictures of him, and the photos were so popular, they even made a good profit out of those. Then why aren't any of those photos available, [and] he [Yang Sen] had to use the picture published in the *North China Daily News?*

3) At that time, Mr. Li already had grandsons of the eleventh generation, and a total of 180 descendants. Then why couldn't he just give the name of one of his descendants?

> Even Han Dynasty's Sima Qian was able to record this, Laozi had a son named Zong. Zong was a General of Wei. He was invested and served in Duangan. Zong's son was Zhu, Zhu's son was Gong. Gong's great great-grandson was Jia. Jia was an officer and served in the government of Emperor Wen of Han. Jia's son was Xie. Xie was the teacher of the prince, Commander Jiao.

Information and communication technology nowadays is highly developed, so why couldn't he even name one of his descendants?

4) He was from Guizhou, and his descendants were supposed to be living around Qijiang and Guizhou. But how come nobody in Guizhou had ever mentioned this? Maybe they are not aware of this?

5) He was just a soldier in Yue Zhongqi's army, and didn't have much education. He spent most of his lifetime traveling around, and didn't have time and chance for study and research. However, his wording of explaining *The Grotto of the Immortal Spirit Scripture* [洞靈經, *Dong Ling Jing*] and also his rules and secrets of regimen is very delicate and in depth. I believe only a person who is an expert in both Daoism and Buddhism and who also well understands Chinese medicines could deliver a speech like that. This is another doubt that the author would hope to have a firm answer.

Six

From all the information we had, we can believe that Laozi indeed lived for 160 years. Sima Yi commented about Zhuge Liang [5] and said, "He has tons of things to do and worry about, and only has a little time for meals and eats very little, how could he live for long?" The author thinks this is only half right.

All the centenarians do not live extravagantly with meat and wine, promoting big cities and industrial or business

---

5   Sima Yi (司馬懿, 179–251 CE); Zhuge Liang (諸葛亮, 181–234 CE).

centers—such as New York, Paris, Tokyo, Berlin, and London. Instead, they live in remote simple-living areas. These people are, so-called, the ones who live in the valley and nature caves. They don't need fine food and luxurious clothes. The patients who suffer from stroke, heart diseases, and various cancers are mostly from the big cities, living a good life, and enjoying fine food. As for "tons of things to do and worry about," it's not only work related matters. Affairs like opening ceremonies, tossing the ball to start a game, birthday parties, funerals, wedding parties, celebrating parties, rushing to airports, back and forth to harbors, and even making public speeches are all included. The key issue is these are all "mentally unhealthy."

The *Book of History* says,[6]

If you have peace and kindness in your mind about
helping people, the mind will then be calm and there
will be nothing to worry about. Then, the good things
will come day after day. If you have hypocrisy and
cupidity in mind, and hurting people in the dark. The
mind will not be calm, and you find your position is
getting increasingly more difficult day after day.

Ambition and scheming are the worst two among all! Ambitious people, even if in a good way, are determined to succeed. However, their desires usually expand with their success, and with no good end. They will want everything in their reach or not. Nothing will satisfy them.

Following is a quote from *The Book of Liezi* in the chapter on "Yang Zhu," and is very well said,

---

6   *Book of History* (尚書, Shang Shu), *The Canons of Yao and Shun*,
     is a record of high officials in ancient Chinese dynasties.

A ten-year life can end in death just as a one hundred year life can end in death. Kind people and sages will all become deceased, bad people and ordinary persons will also become deceased. After good emperors like Yao and Shun passed away, their bodies decayed and just their skeleton was left. After bad emperors like Jie and Zhou were deceased, their bodies decayed and only a skeleton was left. When looking at the skeletons, can anyone tell the difference and know which one is which?

Qin dynasty Emperor Shihuang [秦始皇] and Han dynasty Emperor Wu [漢武帝] both had great accomplishment in expanding and managing their empires. Even so, they begged supernatural beings and alchemists for secrets and medicine for immortality. But, as we all know, the result was in vain. Therefore, for the people who are seeking longevity, the only way is to purify and calm one's mind and to limit desires, live a simple life, and be satisfied. People like emperors Shihuang and Wu who sought for immortality are like what Zhuangzi said,
Pursuing all subjects, but never coming back
successful, is like silencing an echo by one's shouting,
or running a race with one's own shadow. Alas!

Lunar New Year's Eve 1970, Taipei

135

Replies to the Queries Regarding the 250-Year-Old Man

by Li Huan

Not long ago, Mr. Wang Peiyao [Chengsheng] visited me and showed me an article that was written by Mr. Yan Lingfeng *"Do You Believe That Human Beings Can Live for 250 Years?"* The article describes things in a very detailed way and cited evidence extensively. From this we can tell that Mr. Yan Lingfeng was very interested in the topic of "investigating long life." He must have spent a great deal of effort in the research. I admire his brilliant exposition and penetrating analysis. He can be called an expert of Daoism.

After an intense discussion, Mr. Peiyao thought I had personal contact with Li Qingyun, so he asked me sincerely to write my feedback in response to Mr. Yan's questions in the article. I am glad that I can help to clear things up, and it's no big deal. But before ending this, I have five statements:

1. In the issues of October and November, 1970,[1] the article "How Do You Live to be 250 Years Old?" by Mr. Peiyao, created strong public interest around the world and was read by many people. Before he wrote the article, Mr. Peiyao visited and interviewed Mr. Yang Sen and myself many times. He made records, notes, and commentaries. After serious inspection and deliberation, he then completed this valuable article. I don't dare to claim the credit for replying to these queries on Mr. Peiyao's article

---

[1] *Zhong Wai Magazine,* volume 6, issues 4 and 5.

without his authority, because this may cause readers to misunderstand that I was the author of this great article. The purpose of this is to write an article to answer questions for Mr. Peiyao. First, Mr. Peiyao asked me many times to do this and so I could not refuse.

Secondly, I was one of the persons who provided information for that article. Also, in the 16th year of Republic of China [1927], I was a clerk of Commerce Bureau of Wanxian. I received an order from Hui Gong [2] to serve Mr. Li Qingyun and to stay with him for a few months. I had many conversations with him during the time. Besides, in the 19th year of Republic of China [1930], on April 15th at 10:00 a.m. in Nanjing, I presented this centenarian's photo to President Chiang. He was Chairman of the National Government then. President Chiang was very busy every day with government affairs, but he spared some time and inquired about Li Qingyun's daily life and conditions, and asked me to tell General Yang Zihui [Yang Sen] to try to escort Li Qingyun to Nanjing, [so as] to allow Chinese and foreigners to pay tribute to this Earthly Immortal. I still remember that Mr. Zhang Zhen (later served as the chief commander of R.O.C. Military Police) was the secretary of recording. These past events are like they just happened yesterday. Mr. Peiyao thought, since I was not only one of the persons who was involved in interviewing the centenarian Li Qingyun, but also the one who provided the report to our supreme leader, this is a major event with an historical value, so I have the responsibility to address these suspicious queries.

---

2   Hui Gong (惠 公) is the stylized name of Yang Sen.

2. About the basic attitude of writing this article, I believe that we, Yang Huigong [Yang Sen], Mr. Peiyao, and myself, essentially have the same standpoints. Those are:

   Is Li Qingyun a real person? The answer is that Li Qingyun was not Mr. Bogus, nor the son of nonexistent, nor the grandpa of imagination. He was a real person and his stories are true. Many people had seen him. Yang Huigong [Yang Sen] and I had irrefutable evidence, because these were our experiences and we had contact with him in person. As to did he really live for 250 years? We could only list facts about Li Qingyun and several local circumstantial evidence. Including statements of local elders from Chenjiachang, Kaixian in Sichuan, where Li Qingyun lived for a while in his "later years," and the news reported by our two largest English newspapers: *Shanghai Declaration* and *North China Daily News;* the facts and the detail of the days that General Yang and I stayed with Li Qingyun; and various topics we talked about together. We only reported the truth and the facts that we knew, nothing more.

3. According to my memory which hasn't decayed yet, I can approve Mr. Peiyao's article. What he described in the article were very clear and proper. He did not embellish it with ideas of his own. It also complied with the principle of "show me the evidence." He never made conclusions for the reader and, not to mention, he isn't arbitrary.

4. The purpose of this article is to take the matter on its merits. For this topic that everyone is interested in, we can discuss openly. I firmly believe that Mr. Yan, Mr. Peiyao, and myself, we did not have preconceptions.

5. The following replies have included Mr. Peiyao's opinions and mine, so I am just the one who wrote down our discussions.

Mr. Yan Lingfeng made a comment on the story of "Sichuan 250-Year-Old Man, Li Qingyun," saying "It's not easy to convince people that this is a true story. But it seems to be arbitrary to call it 'impossible.'" He listed a total of five doubts he had. I would like to reply to these one by one:

1) "Li Qingyun's age is lacking strong historical documents for evidence."

When describing people, we should provide the historical information to prove that the person is real and the story is real, not a baseless fabrication. For example, the lineage of Confucius' family was very clear. They have a very organized family tree through the ages. But other famous lineages, it seems only a few are comparable. Mr. Yan is a famous scholar and an authority in this field, so please allow me to use the founder of philosophical Daoism, Laozi, as an example. In the "Biography of Laozi" in the *Records of the Grand Historian,* it is said,

> His surname was Li, and his given name was Er. His courtesy name was Boyang. He was from Kuxian, Chuguo.[3] Some said Laozi was also a citizen of Chu. Laozi lived more than 160 years old, or some said he was more than two hundred years old. They said Laozi

---

3   Li Er (李耳), Boyang (伯陽). Kuxian (苦縣), Chuguo (楚國), the state of Chu.

looked like an old man, but some said otherwise. No one could prove which is correct.

It also said,

Laozi had a son named Zong; Zong was a General of Wei.

This short [quote] showed three different historical records of Laozi. Even until now, we are still not sure what is correct and nobody is discussing this. However, Laozi was an originator of Daoism, he wrote in five thousand characters,[4] lived between one hundred to two hundred years old, but who in the world could deny his existence rashly?

In fact, there are many examples of ancient people who lived to be a few hundred years old, yet, with only rough descriptions in history, and no record of lineages at all. A Sichuan man named Li Ba Bai, for example, lived to be eight hundred years old and lived through three dynasties of Xia [夏], Shang [商], and Zhou [周]. But historians did not even know his name.

Sun Simiao [孫思邈, 540 or 581 to 682 CE] was summoned by Sui Wendi [隋文帝, 581–604 CE], to be the Nation's Doctor at Zijian [子監, Imperial College]. He lived until the first year of Yongchun [永淳] of the Tang dynasty, which made him more than 100 years old and it was not well recorded in history. Li Qingyun was a neoteric, not an ancient, so it's not fair to compare him with Laozi, Li Ba Bai, and Sun Simiao. However, that fact that Li Qingyun lived to 250 years old could be proved by many people, such as my good friend, Gui Yunjin, who was

---

4   Reference to *The Scripture on the Way and Virtue* (道德經, *Dao De Jing*).

also my colleague and a former Adjutant General of the 20th regiment. He had studied military science in the U.S. Gui Yun-jin's great grandfather, and even many people in Chenjiachang, Kaixian, and Wanxian, all of them had seen Li Qingyun per-sonally, talked to and had contact with him and have testified to this. Li Qingyun's spiritual and good character was different than other people. He had [at that time] white hair like crane feathers and a ruddy face like a child. Looking at him you would know he had lived for a long time. From what he de-scribed, he went through the vicissitudes of life. This makes me think of the tale of the *Peach Blossom Spring* [桃花源, *Tao Hua Yuan*], in which people went into a hard-to-find valley trying to avoid wars during the Qin dynasty and never came out. After many, many years, until the Jin dynasty, they did not know what dynasty controlled the outside world, and didn't even know there was a Han, Wei, and Jin dynasties.[5] Li had married many times and none of his wives could grow old together with him. This could be a proof that he was very old. As for the status and where were his grandchildren, great grandchildren, and younger generations. It seems to me that it's too demand-ing if we asked a 250-year-old man who had been secluded for a long time to explain this one by one.

Besides, we are not sure whether newspaper records could be considered as "historical documents." Because Mr. Yan listed twenty-two long-lived people in his article, and they were all according to "newspapers," these did not have annotations of any sort of "historical documents." So we do think newspaper records should at least be able to be considered as a good basis or reference. Mr. Yan's so-called "In the newspaper" were just

---

5   Qin (秦, 221–206 BCE), Han (漢, 206 BCE to 220 CE),
     Wei (魏, 386–535 CE), and Jin (晉, 1115–1234 CE).

three words. He did not list countries, places, and from which newspaper. But Mr. Peiyao's article attached the original text of the news and the photo by *Shen Pao* [Shanghai News] and *North China Daily News,* which were two newspapers that had good reputations and authority. This information should be much more reliable than just "In the newspaper."

2) "1928 in Wanxian, if the Yi Fang Photo Studio took many pictures of him, and the photos were so popular, they even made a good profit out of those. Then why aren't any of those photos available, [and] he [Yang Sen] had to use the picture published in the *North China Daily News?*"

For this question I would like to divide it into two parts to answer.

The first: The reason why we used the photo that was published by *North China Daily News* is that because we wanted to provide a "historical proof" or something close to it. I believe that anyone who had been a newspaper editor would feel the same way and use this direct and effective approach. Besides, the photo published by *North China Daily News* was actually one of the photographs from Yi Fang Photo Studio.

The second: We had to leave so many things behind on Mainland China. Take General Yang Zihui as an example. When he was in the final retreat from Mainland China, he followed an order to do a very difficult task. In that very dangerous time, he was the Commander-in-Chief of the garrisons at Zhongqing [重慶]. He served the highest leader side-by-side trying to protect our land. Later, on the night before Chengdu was occupied by the enemy, he received an order and took a plane flying through Haikou [海口] and arrived in Taipei. Not only did he not bring the photos of Li Qingyun, he didn't even have time to take his money with him. After General Yang arrived in Taipei, he had an audience with the highest leader and they dined together. His next meal was in a restaurant, when he wanted to pay the bill, he found out that he had no cash with him. And at the end, it was paid by his daughter who arrived earlier [in Taiwan] and was studying at National Taiwan University. From this, we can understand [his] situation roughly at that time.

3) "At that time, Mr. Li already had grandsons of the eleventh generation, and a total of 180 descendants. Then why couldn't he just give the name of one of his descendants?
 "Even Han Dynasty's Sima Qian was able to record this,
  'Laozi had a son named Zhong. Zhong is a
  General of Wei. He was invested and served
  in Duangan ...'

"Information and communication technology nowadays is highly developed, so why couldn't someone name even one of his descendants?"

Mr. Yan Lingfeng compared Mr. Pei Yao to be parallel with Sima Qian. This made Mr. Pei Yao feel jittery. It is true that the information and communication technology is well developed, but whether well developed or not, [this has] nothing to do with the names of Li Qingyun's descendants. The point is, what Sima Qian recorded was the history and biography of Laozi. Writing a biography would need a list of names of the protagonist's descendants. We wrote the stories about Li Qingyun based on what we knew, and we didn't think it was necessary to record his family tree and list the names of his descendants. Even then, I remember, I had no interest in his descendants' names, so I did not even ask nor did any research about it.

144

4) "He was from Guizhou, and his descendants were supposed to have lived around Qijiang and Guizhou. But how come nobody in Guizhou had ever mentioned this? Maybe they are not aware of this?"

We need to declare that we did not say Li Qingyun came from Guizhou, so I don't know where Mr. Yan got this information. Because Li Qingyun always said he came from Qijiang in Sichuan, and Mr. Peiyao didn't make a mistake in his article. In issue 4, volume 4 of *Zhong Wai Magazine,* you can find in column 7 in the third paragraph on page 4, that the Adjutant General Gui Yunjin had said, "... he came from Qijiang, we don't know how many years he had lived in Chenjiachang ..."

Also, in column 20 of the second paragraph on page 6, "according to his statements, his ancestors were in Guizhou, then moved to a remote mountain in west Qijiang, Sichuan, which is at the border of Guizhou." "Ancestors" and "moved" were very clear explanations. Li Qingyun grew up in Sichuan, so people in Guizhou not knowing about him is normal. Moreover, we would like to ask Mr. Yan, "Did Mr. Yan ever ask people in Guizhou, talk to them or hear anything from them?" Otherwise, how could Mr. Yan "arbitrarily" claim that people in Guizhou "never mentioned Li Qingyun" or "they did not know about him?"

The final question that Mr. Yang Lingfeng asked is particularly interesting, because he said,

5) "He [Li Qingyun] was just a soldier in Yue Zhongqi's army, and didn't have much education. He spent most of his lifetime traveling around, and didn't have time and chance for study and research. However, his wording of explaining *The Grotto of*

the Immortal Spirit Scripture [洞靈經, *Dong Ling Jing]* and also his rules and secrets of regimen is very delicate and in depth. I believe only a person who is an expert in both Daoism and Buddhism and who also well understands Chinese medicines could deliver a speech like that. This is another doubt that the author would hope to have a firm answer."

The following is our response:

First, in the *Shuowen* [6] it says,

> *Teaching* [教, Jiao] is where a teacher teaches and
> students are then able to learn knowledge and
> to follow the instructions.

It also says,

> *Guiding* [育, Yu], this is raising children and teaching
> them to do good things.

In the West, they also divided education into two categories: school education and society education. Westerners believe that the purpose of education is to help create independent individuals for the society and to create a corporate society for individuals. Their method is to immerse students in the stimulating environments, motivate them to develop themselves, moving forward and create a better new life. In fact, everyone had been educated. Soldiers live a battle life, they were educated for skills and knowledge needed for combat. The education they received is not necessarily less than students. Whether in modern or in ancient times, in China or

---

6   *Shuo Wen* (說文), *Explaining the Characters,* is a famous Chinese dictionary compiled in 100 CE. The two compound characters 教育 mean "education."

elsewhere, there were many soldiers who became generals or went on to even higher positions. We should not have the wrong perception that soldiers were not educated.

Second, well-educated people may not have read the *Grotto of the Immortal Spirit Scripture,* and not only well-educated people can understand the *Grotto of the Immortal Spirit Scripture.* (Of course, the "well-educated people" here is in the narrow sense of the meaning and what Mr. Yan means is people who had been to school).

Third, it seems to me that Mr. Yan should not say that Li Qingyun did not have the opportunity to study the *Grotto of the Immortal Spirit Scripture,* and "Daoist Principles of Long-Life," because in Mr. Peiyao's article "How Could You Live to 250 Years Old?" there was a long paragraph describing when Li Qingyun was 139 years old he met a Daoist master who taught him some mnemonic chants and techniques of longevity. He built huts on Mt. Emei and lived there. He then started teaching the "Ways of Longevity." On Mt. Emei, he practiced the secrets and techniques learned from his Daoist master. Meanwhile, he taught his followers, and he lived on Mt. Emei "for about one hundred years, and gained more and more followers, usually around one hundred people."

Li Qingyun had one hundred years to research with his one hundred or more students. They learned and gained the benefits from each other. How [then] can we say that Li Qingyun "traveled everywhere and did not have chances for studying and doing research?"

Fourth, Mr. Yan's so-called [reference to Li Qingyun using] "elegant wording and in-depth speech." To tell the truth, I had made fun of Mr. Peiyao for this a few days ago. I said, "Mr. Peiyao, your article was outstanding!"

147

He replied humbly and said, "Thank you! It's not very presentable." Then he asked me, "Why did you say that?"

I laughed, "You recorded the techniques of longevity that Li Qingyun talked about. Yang Huigong [Yang Sen] said very clearly to use colloquial language to make it feel like a real conversation. But through your pen, Li Qingyun's demotic words became what Mr. Yan described as 'elegant wording and in-depth speech.' Doesn't this mean you had written a good article?"

At that time, Mr. Peiyao smiled and said, "I wish that when Mr. Yan wrote his article, he could have made it simple and easy like a good article, then we could have enjoyed it together; if we have different opinions, we could discuss these with each other and laugh it off."

The rest of the contentions in Mr. Yan Lingfeng's remarkable article are not within the scope of this article. Allow me not to comment.

The Secrets of
Li Qingyun's Immortality

Preface to The Secrets of Li Qingyun's Immortality

by Yang Sen

When the 250-year-old man Li Qingyun was 129 years old,[1] he went into Gansu to collect herbs and met an old Daoist priest. Li Qingyun had abundant experiences with interpreting people, so he knew this old priest was not an ordinary person. He asked this old priest of his methods of longevity, initially, but the old priest refused to tell him. Finally, unable to bear Li Qingyun's begging, he taught him some methods of longevity and chants for practicing the Dao. After that, Li accepted three to five disciples then went to Mt. Emei to build cottages and stayed there, where he then started teaching methods of longevity.

The previous paragraph is the story of Li Qingyun seeking longevity. Its already in this book in Wang Chengsheng's masterpiece "How Could You Live to 250 Years Old?" Mr. Wang Chengsheng recorded Li Qingyun spending roughly one hundred years on Mt. Emei practicing and teaching Dao. In those years, he had increasing numbers of disciples, usually around one hundred. Most of them were elders who had white hair

---

[1] Yang Sen says that Li Qingyun was 129 years old when he met his Daoist teacher, which is different than other reports in the book. The note on this said, "This must be a typographical error because on page 91 it is stated he was 139 years old. Actually 139 is the error and 129 is the correct age." Who inserted the note is uncertain, but it seems likely that it was from Yang Sen. If Li Qingyun was 129 when he met his teacher and then taught for one hundred years on Mt. Emei, this would time out with the publication of *The Secrets of Li Qingyun's Immortality* in 1908.

like crane feathers [and] ruddy faces like children. Just a few people's ages were under one hundred years old. According to Mr. Wang Chengsheng's description, we know that Li Qingyun's methods of longevity and chants of practicing Dao, which he received from an old priest, are just an entry level of practicing Dao.

He went to Mt. Emei to practice Dao to teach students, who benefited and brought out the best in each other. Usually there were around one hundred elders who stayed together to practice Dao and did so nonstop from day to night and learning from each other. For Daoist theory of practicing, it could be said it's thoroughly tempered and could prove the methods of Daoist longevity can stand the test. Li Qingyun and his disciples had researched and practiced the methods of longevity around one hundred years; certainly it was a major event for Daoism.

Due to the result of this unprecedented event, not only Li Qingyun and his disciples enjoyed the great years because of the mind and body practicing, the other and most important result was that Li Qingyun and his capable disciple, who is the Master Yang Hexuan, worked together and wrote a surprising book, *The Secrets of a 250-Year-Old Man Li Qingyun's Immortality.* Maybe most of the contents were compiled by Master Yang Hexuan. This surprising book has five sections and those are "The Way of Longevity," "The Basis of Longevity," "The Way of Achieving the Dao," "Natural Temperament," and "Superior Quotations of Qingyun." Three of these sections included here—"The Way of Longevity," "The Basis of Longevity," and "Superior Quotations of Li Qingyun"—comprise the valuable record of Li Qingyun and his student [Master Yang Hexuan] who spent one hundred years of doing research and learning from each other, earnestly practicing. It can be said this is a joint research report by a teacher and disciple. "The Way of Achieving the Dao" and "Natural Temperament" are words of wisdom from One Hundred Schools of Thought,[2] and were compiled by Li Qingyun and his students together. Certainly, [these teachings] went through experiments and investigation by Li Qingyun and his disciples.

The whole book was written in classical Chinese, but later the editors punctuated the article. If the readers can read the sentences carefully, the difficult lessons can become easy to understand. It is not too hard for readers to understand thoroughly and get the essences from the book. Use it as a reference to study methods of longevity. Then, use this article as a preface to introduce the antecedent of this surprising book and the purposes of the issue [for attaining longevity].

---

2   *The One Hundred Schools of Thought* (諸子百家, Zhu Zi Bai Jia) flourished from the sixth century BCE to 221 BCE. This school literally embraced all Chinese philosophical teachings. The most traditional source for the history and functions of this school were described in *The Records of the Grand Historian* (史記, Shiji) by Sima Qian. The school was originally based on the teachings of Confucianism, Daoism, Legalism, Mohism, School of Yin and Yang, and the Logicians. During its history other schools were embraced as well, such as the School of Diplomacy, Yangism (Yang Zhu), Agriculturism, Military School, and so on. Much of the work compiled by the One Hundred Schools of Thought was said to be lost during the period of the *Burning of the Books and Burying of Scholars* (焚書坑儒, Feng Shu Keng Ru). See note 27, p. 60 for more information about this event.

Part One
The Great Dao of Long Life

[長生大道章, Chang Sheng Da Dao Zhang]

The Secrets of Long Life

The art of the Dao of Longevity consists of ten methods:

Sitting Meditation	打坐,	Da Zuo
Settling the Mind	降心,	Jiang Xin
Refining of Your Nature	練性,	Lian Xing
Transcending the Realms	超界,	Chao Jie
Sincerity and Reverence	敬信,	Jing Xin
Cutting-off Affinities	斷緣,	Duan Yuan
Control the Mind	收心,	Shou Xin
Simplify Daily Activities	簡事,	Jian Shi
Maintain Proper Views	眞觀,	Zhen Guan
Fixed Peacefulness	泰定,	Tai Ding

To speak about lengthening a person's life, you must first have an adequate understanding of these ten principles so that the subtleties can be grasped. After this, the means for longevity can be spoken of, which are the methods for driving away disease to prolong life, the secrets of reverting old age, and the method for restoring youthfulness. All of these methods are interconnected.

155

Sitting Meditation: To simply put the body into a dignified posture with the eyes shut is not the true way of meditation. Nevertheless, meditation in this manner should still be performed twice daily, during two of the six two-hour periods [between 11 p.m. and 1 a.m., and 11 a.m. and 1 p.m.]. Whether walking, standing, sitting, or lying down, the mind must be as still as a mountain, unmovable and unswayable. The Six Roots[1] must be prevented from escaping and the Seven Passions[2] must not enter within so as not to disturb the mind. It is said:

> If wealthy and noble, act according to your position
> and be without arrogance. If poor and of low standing,
> act according to your station and do not engage in
> flattery.

There should be no experience in life that is not met with calmness, and there should be no situation in which you are not at ease. When you can be like this, there is no need to sit absorbed in a state of Chan [Zen] nor to enter samadhi [三昧, San Mei], because at this point you are already a living Buddha or immortal.

Settling the Mind: This means that the mind becomes so deep and unmoving, so obscure and abstruse, that not even the Ten Thousand Things[3] appear. The mind is so mysterious and profound that the internal is not distinguishable from the external,

---

[1]   *Six Roots* (六根, Liu Gen) sight, sound, smell, taste, touch, and perception.

[2]   *Seven Passions* are the Seven Emotions (七情, Qi Qing) of joy, anger, sorrow, fear, love, hatred, and lust.

[3]   Term for all phenomena.

nor can the minutest desire or thought be produced. This is true samadhi, not necessarily the settling of just the mind.

The mind, however, moves about quickly, hither and thither, with many thoughts and desires. From above and below things are sought, even in absolute silence you hear and see things. With these innumerable illusions appearing before you, the result is that the mind deteriorates and your virtue is injured. You cannot but want to settle your mind!

Refining of Your Nature: When adjusting the tuning mounts on a lute, you must be careful not to turn them too rapidly, otherwise the string can be snapped. If you go too slowly the proper note cannot be found. The string must be wound tightly, yet gradually, if the right pitch is to be obtained.

This is similar to casting metal to make a sword. Steel is easily broken and iron is easily warped, but iron and steel combined can produce a strong and sharp sword. This kind of alchemical excellence must be duplicated when refining your true nature [to become a Buddha or immortal]. So it is then best to always be compassionate and to transfer all your virtue and merit. This is the way of refining your nature!

Transcending the Realms: There are three realms in the world of existence: desire realm, form realm, and formless realm. When becoming entirely unmindful of selfish desires, one transcends the realm of desire. Being unmindful of sensual pleasures, one transcends the realm of form. In realizing the state of voidness, one transcends the realm of formlessness. Transcending these three realms results in the eradication of suffering, and one will be far apart from the evil influences of mara.

Sincerity and Reverence: This is the very foundation of the Dao. It is said that it is best to just master one thing and not go off on to many other things. Sincerity means to be absolutely without doubt. This is called bringing forth the genuine and not the false aspects of one's true nature. Those who are able to maintain reverent sincerity are sages, immortals, and Buddhas.

Confucius said, "Reverent sincerity is brought forth from benevolence for the people and from cultivating friendships with good people." Even sages set this principle to work.

Cutting-off Affinities: This means to cut off defiling causes and conditions of affinities. If defilements are not cut off, the mind will become extremely dull and all forms of wisdom will be obscured.

The layperson's mind is incapable of disassociating itself from thoughts of either purity or defilement, or gain or loss. To eradicate these, one must bring about thoughts of skillful means,[4] yet even these must eventually be eradicated.

In all our various activities and undertakings we seek to profit and to keep with the times and trends. Therefore, from this type of behavior we become confused and disturbed. However, the causes and conditions of these defilements, in a short time, can be turned into tranquility and so the spirit can be retained internally. But most people wait until nearly reaching

---

4   *Skillful means* is a term meaning to apply the teachings that instruct and aid the cultivator towards eliminating the attachment of duality, such as adhering to precepts and conducts that prevent attachments. But even these are no longer needed once a person has "crossed over to the other shore" (Buddhism) or "Returned to the Dao" (Daoism).

the end of their years before shunning these defilements and affinities. The ancients said,

> Renounce all concerns for the physical pleasures of the body and it will no longer suffer. Non-action [wu wei] will make the mind naturally tranquil. Do not disclose your virtue or skills. Uncover your true nature and don't hinder others from doing the same.

Altogether, desires either for purity or defilement, gain or loss, should not bring about attachment within one's thinking. Likewise, the matters of birth and death, old age, and sickness should not be entangled within your mind. In summation, to commit defiled acts causes injury to one's true nature. The ancients cultivated the methods of longevity according to these principles.

Control the Mind: This will result in the immediate advancement of a further step towards immortality, making you master over your body and mind. Your entire spirit will become more yielding and you will be purified, bringing about wisdom. But if your mind is moved by desires, you'll only bring forth obscurity and ignorance.

Human desire is all confused, much like a dreamland—taking reality as fact and illusion as reality. Those who are attached to these illusions only stain themselves and do not acquire the merits of purification and reform. Therefore, to conceal desire internally is to hide the sun of profound wisdom. When embarking on the Dao, you must heal yourself by ridding the mind of defiled desires. You must be capable of daily reform and renewal, escaping from the circumstances of the red-dust world. Be as pure and empty as a cavern and do not attach yourself to any one thing. Unite your mind with Dao, which is called returning to the source. Once having returned to the source, you will never depart from it. This is called being absorbed in tranquility.

Once having returned to the source and being absorbed in tranquility, it will follow that the mind will become peaceful and function naturally. Within, there will be emptiness and the mind will be nowhere attached externally. This is wu wei [non-action]. Neither defilement nor purity, slander nor praise will bring about disturbance. Neither wisdom nor ignorance, benefit nor loss, nothing will be sought after. Be among those who observe propriety and be ordinary and reverent in your conduct. Allow both misfortune and fortune to come and go naturally. This is the foremost way for attaining true wisdom.

The mind is no different from the eyes. When fine particles of debris enter them, irritation results. The mind, likewise, when entangled by even small trivial matters, becomes disturbed, agitated, and unsettled. The affliction is often very subtle and difficult to detect.

It is best to adhere to these basic principles to regulate your conduct. Remain unmoved when observing and experiencing the natural order of life and the changes of phenomena. Simply experience life and make peace with it. This is self-realization and tranquility.

It is as though you were unaware of night and daytime. Whether walking, standing, sitting, or lying down, the proper deportment must be maintained in all affairs—the mind then can be tranquil. The mind must be as if in samadhi, where, moment to moment, tranquility is maintained. Without this, affliction will result. Even with small attainments of samadhi, you can find peace. Gradually, the mind will become evermore controllable, evermore clear and removed from defilements. This is the true way of controlling the thoughts.

Simplify Daily Activities: It is said it is incorrect to seek that which is beyond one's ordinary daily activities. To do so is like placing delicacies within simple nourishing food, making all your garments from silk alone, or adding gold and jade to an already abundant treasure. These are but extras to your lot and are only meant for mere enjoyment. They do nothing more than confuse the mind and spirit, so it is best to avoid such thoughts. The chief purpose of simplifying your daily activities is to avoid confusing the mind and spirit, nothing more.

Maintain Proper Views: Each time we sleep and each time we eat there is an increase and decrease. So it is that with each word and action, fortune and misfortune will follow. Being able to foresee the causes of such results, errors can be nipped in the bud and thus eradicated from your life.

If you are unable to dispense with the idea of your existence, if you cannot put this down, you must then humbly seek out the instruction of a competent teacher. Also, pay no attention to the obstacles created by the mind, nor think that perplexities are developed through some mental defect. The eradication of these afflictions has nothing to do with anything other than simply ending carnal passions. Know that excessive lust for form and beauty are brought forth only through thoughts. Hence, if these thoughts are not produced, then the matters concerning form and beauty will be extinguished. Form is nothing but emptiness, and thoughts are only deceptions. The mind should be fixed solidly as ice, otherwise how could life's affairs be dropped? We must use our intuition to foresee these deceptions in advance. Then we will not suffer so needlessly. It is said, to observe the truth of something, the wise person uses intuitive perception.

Fixed Peacefulness: This is to go beyond the worldly dust and arrive at the final stage. When cultivating the fundamental principles of Dao, we can reach the origins of nature successfully through tranquility. By nourishing this tranquility all affairs can be concluded.

The body should be like dried wood, and the mind like cold ashes.

To be without thoughts is samadhi, wherein the mind is in absolute and fixed concentration. An ancient hymn called this "being absorbed in tranquility."

The mind has the capacity for undertaking the necessary work for cultivating the Dao, and practicing the Dao brings forth a state of ultimate tranquility and the realization of wisdom. The wisdom is inherent, born within the original nature, yet existing nowhere. The ancients called this "divine light" because the mind is muddled and dim, but the tranquil mind is illuminated. Wisdom is light, but knowledge is considered a hindrance to samadhi. Bringing forth this wisdom is not difficult. Those who conceive it as difficult cultivate in vain.

Since ancient times, many have achieved this state of being unmindful of the body. Few, however, achieve being unmindful of the self. Wisdom obtained from being unmindful of the body is not very useful, because true wisdom comes from being unmindful of the self. Zhuangzi said,

> Nourish wisdom with tranquility, but do not seek
> to just use the wisdom—tranquility will then be
> nourished by that wisdom. Therefore, wisdom
> and tranquility nourish each other.

The self can then be regulated and brought into harmony with its realization of true nature. Tranquility and wisdom produce samadhi and prajna [般若, Bo Re]. This harmonizing and regulating is the work of cultivating virtue [德, De]. With tranquility, one will find peace. Otherwise, the wisdom attained will have no value. The Dao is complete when virtue is perfected.

Knowing these ten paths and thoroughly investigating the mysteries of them will result in longevity. Then the eternal realms of the immortals become evermore accessible.

Chapter on Nourishing Life

Li Qingyun said, "I am 250 years old, still move agilely, and many people think about whether I am an Earthly Immortal? The length of a person's life is dominated by the Qi [氣, vital-life energy]. Vitality has various thicknesses. Those people who are good at regimens, even though their vitality [Qi] is originally thin, because they are good at maintaining health, they can still prolong life. People who are not good at health, although their vitality is thick, but they use it improperly, they will shorten their life. Just like candles having different lengths, when placing the long candle in the wind and rain, the burning time is much shorter, or even immediately extinguished. When placing the short candle in the covered cage, the extinguishing time will be extended. The reasons of regimen are similar to this. However, in ancient times, living to one hundred years old was not surprising. Long life and activity is still unabated, but modern people are different. When less than fifty years old, they look old and clumsy. Is it because of the time differences and the vitality of different thickness? Of course not, it is because of different health methods.

"The ancient people who knew good health, would follow the changes in the law of Yin [陰] and Yang [陽], and follow the correct health methods for exercise and dietary restraints. They kept a regular daily life, not working too hard. Therefore, they could maintain good physical and mental health, then live up to the time limit of the natural human life, which is more than one hundred years old. Nowadays, people are not in accordance with the laws of nature, drinking wine as a beverage and having sexual intercourse after getting drunk. Indulging in lust and wine, the kidney essence will be depleted and the genuine Qi will dissipate. People do not know to keep their own vital energy strong and rest the spirit. Only having eyes on happiness, they break the rules of health, so a fifty year old is already aged like a hundred year old. Therefore, mountain people live longer than city residents, because mountain people have normal daily routines, no fame in mind, and no machinery to disturb the spirit. Keep the mind innocent, like people of the ancient tribes. Do not pursue fame and fortune, then one can live longer. If people living in cities do not restrain their diet and keep their daily activities regular, the root causes of illness and delusion will be produced within their hearts, and [the mind] will be distracted by the externals of seeking for fame and fortune. Furthermore, sensual affairs will disturb people's spirit. The ideas of wealth, honor, and disgrace haunt people's minds, then the mind and spirit will feel uneasy, and be confused without end. All these are enough to shorten a person's life. Lu Qing Xian Gong[5] said,

> 'Enough rice and firewood is a carefree life; do not
> evade taxes, do not let your emotions become unstable,
> and don't be stimulated easily. Do not borrow money
> from others, do not step into a pawn shop. You just
> need simple food, and then you can have longevity.'

"This skill of regimen is a very good approach of longevity. Following these principles will lead to longevity and you will not need to go looking for panaceas or smelt elixirs. Laozi said,

> 'Do not toil the body to exhaustion, do not bring
> about mental unrest and stupor, do not let anxiety
> bother the mind. Think less to raise Shen, lust less
> to raise Jing, and talk less to raise Qi.'

---

5   Lu Qing Xian Gong (陸清獻公) is Lu Gansu (陸甘肅, 1630–1692 CE), famous Qing dynasty scholar.

"The true meaning is often ignored by people who are not good at regimen. The ancient theory of regimen was nothing more than being compassionate, frugal, gentle, and calm. If people are compassionate, not being destructive or hurting others, and if their Qi is directed at kindness, they produce harmony between Heaven and humanity. Laozi considered frugality to be a treasure. Frugality not only refers to money matters, but being frugal in diet is good for the spleen and stomach. Being frugal in lust can collect the spirit. Being frugal in speech can raise the Qi. Frugality in making friends [means to] select friends who have good morality and to take them as a model. To be frugal with wine and women will purify the mind and diminish lustful desires. To be frugal in thought will eliminate worry. The more you save from having frugal disciplines, the more you will benefit. To be kind is the way leading to the auspicious. When the ruler and the ministers get along well, the nation will prosper. When the father and son get along well, the family will be happy and at peace. When brothers can get along well, they will support each other. When couples get along well, the boudoir will be quiet and harmonious. When friends get along well, they will help each other. So, the *Book of Changes* [易經, *Yi Jing*] says, 'Harmony leads to the auspicious; disharmony leads to disaster.' To be calm means not working too strenuously, then the mind will not be impulsive.

"Su Laoquan said, 'Even if Mt. Taishan collapses in front of my face, I would not change my countenance; even if an elk danced by my side, I would not look at it.'[6] This is the highest realm of calm. *The Scripture on the Way and Virtue* [道德經, *Dao*

---

6   Su Laoquan (蘇老泉, 1037–1101 CE), Song dynasty poet, pharmacologist, writer, painter, and political leader. This quote is saying to stay calm even when meeting with unexpected events.

De Jing] has five thousand words, its gist is nothing more than this. People who wish to maintain good health must keep compassion, frugality, kindness, and calmness as their foundation.

"For sleeping and eating, my thoughts have no discrepancy with the *Scripture on the Way and Virtue*. Do not eat too much; eating too much will hurt the stomach. Do not sleep too long; sleeping too long will waste the vitality.

"I never ate too much food nor slept too long. This is probably why I have lived to be over two hundred years old. Moreover, any seemingly unimportant thing that people are most likely to ignore could hurt their health. If happiness, anger, grief, and joy are excessive, they will be injurious. Talking, laughing, eating, and resting can also be injurious if done excessively or at the wrong time. Being careless of cold and hot weather, walking too fast, and indulging in debauchery, all are harmful. Accumulating injurious habits to their limit can cause death.

"Ancient people did not walk too fast, nor overuse the eyes and ears, did not sit for too long, nor lie on the bed for too long to avoid fatigue. Wear extra clothes before feeling too cold, take clothes off before feeling too hot. Do not eat if not hungry, do not drink if not thirsty. Do not let happiness, anger, grief, and joy haunt your mind. Do not let wealth and fame disturb the heart. People used to say: hunger, cold, pain, and itch, only I can sense these, parents cannot know these for me. Aging, illness, and death, only I can bear these. My wife cannot replace my suffering. The principle of self respect is that if you do not care about yourself then who can be blamed? These vigilance phrases could be the standard for regimen, only experts who know the key tricks know how."

Chapter on Regulating the Mind

Someone asked Li Qingyun, "The feeling of happiness, anger, grief, and joy, the desire of wealth and fame, are all from the heart. The way of regimen is to forget everything and begin regulating the mind. However, what is the way of regulating the mind?"

Li Qingyun smiled and replied, "What you ask is a big question and it has deep meaning. There is no way to regulate the mind other than getting rid of the wishful thinking. Buddhism says, 'People have an illusionary mind and an enlightened mind.' The mind of illusion is the distraction of thoughts arising and extinguishing, a trancelike state [stupor] with no return. The mind will not be at peace and the spirit not stable. If one is aware of the mind of illusion, and can cut the thoughts immediately, the mind can be made clear as an autumn lake and calm like an old well. Do not let distracting ideas arise in the mind, but also do not diminish the ideas of the mind, as they lead to the mind of enlightenment.

"If people obtain enlightenment, without any treatment their minds can also be cured. But most of the time, people stay in confusion and because they are confused, they cannot eliminate the childish mind or realize and see their nature, so they cannot live over one hundred years old. People who die young, their lives are just like the short lives of mayflies. What a pity! The mind of illusion is in wishful thinking.

"There are three types of wishful thinking [those centering on the past, present, and future]. Thoughts on the wealth and status of the past, sensual joys winding about in the mind, and recollecting past events—these are the types of wishful thinking of the past.

"Focusing on the present, feeling envy, distinguishing likes and dislikes, and hesitating in making decisions—these are the types of wishful thinking of the present.

"Expecting future wealth and status, wanting accomplished descendants, and seeking more acquisitions—these are the types of wishful thinking of the future.

"These three types of wishful thinking cause the mind to be unstable, fickle, moody, and confused. These [states] are difficult to eliminate, even though the mind wants peace, and the spirit wants calm, but how can they be stable? So, one must keep away from worries, cut off lust, forget honor and disgrace, end hatred, cease wishful thinking, eradicate the mind of illusion. From the bottom of the heart, the mind of enlightenment will then gush out. The mind will be as clear as the sunny sky, as clean as a glass lamp that sits in front of the Buddha, and as bright and immaculate as the moonlight. Then [the mind] will achieve the goal.

"The human mind is meant to be stable, but many people only worry about imaginary troubles, and this leads to wishful thoughts; having wishful thoughts is the disease of the mind. The propriety then goes to where the money is. The inception of contention is where fame and fortune reside. People who seek for these will develop ingratiating habits. The mind of likes and dislikes is the beginning of either anticipating gratitude or revenge. When competition is initiated, injury and suffering come about, then when having troubles, people run away. When seeking advantages, people will flatter to please others, because they only worry about personal gains and losses; emotions of sadness and joy come from external influences, but fame and wealth are internal, and then wishful thinking arises. The sick mind comes from wishful thinking.

"The way of regulating the mind is to discard all distracting thoughts of fame, and matters of gain and loss should not be so prominent as to interfere with the spirit. The matters of illness and death should not be so prominent as to whirl about in the mind. Let vast and clear vitality fill the mind, and the limpidness and clearness appear externally. This is what Confucius meant when he said, 'If we want to cultivate our own virtue, it must be correct in our mind first.' The Buddhist [釋 氏, Shi Shi] also says, 'Do not have the mind-intention of just self. Do not do unfavorable things to others. Treat everything on Earth equally well.' This is what Daoists call, 'Clarity and Tranquility.'

"For a person who is practicing, initially they might not be able to get their heart calm and keep away from wishful thoughts. When the heart is not calm, wishful thoughts will grow. However, the key is to be conscious of the issue. People who are not conscious, they have shallow minds. Actually, very few people can avoid not worrying too much and shortening their lives.

"A sage [聖 人, Sheng Ren] said, 'Who can be entirely free from error. If you make mistakes, just do not fear to correct them.' Having wishful thinking is like making a mistake. When you are conscious of it, just correct it. Person who are conscious of their wishful thinking, and then correct it, cause the wishful thinking to be as if it never existed in their mind.

"The Buddhists say, 'Don't be afraid of desirous thoughts coming about, only be afraid of being unaware of them too late. To be aware, then the mind will be calm. Even if one is not looking for longevity, one will live longer naturally.'

"Worldly people [世 人, Shi Ren] say, 'The methods of prolonging life and preventing disease are no more than eating light food, restraining lust, talking less, getting rid of anger, keeping in shape, and training the Qi.' Most people just treat the surface symptoms, not the true cure. Illnesses are in the mind, using just treatments cannot have [the right] effect. We must rely on consciousness. My descendants who want to regulate their mind, they should start from clearing and emptying the mind, then the progress will come."

Chapter on Purifying and Illumining

This so-called "purifying and illumining the mind" is just to remove the excess distractions from the mind and keep to pure and simple thoughts. The sages of the Three Religions said, "Use these two words as the foundational way for treating others and conducting oneself in society." This has been repeatedly discussed, especially concerning Daoism's central doctrine, having a pure and bright mind, loyalty, and filial piety. So, people who have no distracting thoughts and have total concentration, their minds are actually pure and clear already. "Form is just emptiness, they are not produced and not destroyed."[7] People who are loyal and have filial piety, their Qi is correct and their spirit is clear. Qiaoyangzi[8] said,

> Through the ages, there are many methods of practice,
> but why does Daoism specifically emphasize the pure
> and illumined mind, along with loyalty and filial piety
> as its doctrine?

A master [先生, Xian Sheng] said, "There is no other meaning to purifying and illumining the mind." They mean to be

---

7   From the *Profound Perfection of Wisdom Heart Sutra* of Buddhism, "Form is just emptiness, emptiness is just form … they are not produced nor destroyed."

8   Qiaoyangzi (樵陽子) is the author of *Secrets on the Profound Golden Elixir* (金丹妙訣, *Jin Dan Miao Jue*).

conscience of the functions of trust, loyalty and filial piety, and these are just to prop up the proper conducts of morality. [9]

Worldly people used to hear these words, but ignored past stories about them, so mostly they are not practiced correctly. The loyal person will feel respect for all things. To the person who has filial piety, there's no difference between relatives or strangers.

What is "clearness" [清, Qing]? It's not to be contaminated with bad habits. What is "purity" [淨, Jing]? It's not to be exposed to bad environments. Not to be contaminated and exposed, a person will be able to realize loyalty and filial piety. The Master also said, "A loyalist is loyal to their ruler." The mind is the ruler of everything in the universe. Having the idea of hiding the truth from the mind, this is to be unfaithful. When serving parents, some think it means to spare no effort, but this is not filial piety. Filial piety must come from the mind, then it can be recognized by the parents, and then the special providence is also recognized. This is called "filial piety touching Heaven." Human nature was originally bright and connected to Heaven, but because of being infected with bad habits, indulgences, misinterpreting the principles of conduct, it cannot even be termed humanity. Not even worthy of being called, the Three Powers, [10] or together with Heaven and Earth?

---

9   The term *Gang Chang* (綱常) is used here, meaning the *Constant Guiding Principles, which,* in turn, refers to the *Three Bonds* (三綱, San Gang) between prince and minister, father and son, and husband and wife. These relationships function because of "trust," "loyalty," and "filial piety," and also because of the Five Constant Virtues (五常, Wu Chang) of "Benevolence," "Righteousness," "Propriety," "Wisdom," and "Sincerity."

10   Three Powers (三才, San Cai): Heaven, Humanity, and Earth.

What is called "anger" [忿, Fen] not only means rage, fury, indignation, and hate, but it is related with jealously and narrow mindedness, being superficial and ungenerous, caring too much about everything and being mean spirited. These all belong to anger. If we can repent past mistakes and be open minded, then anger will not occupy the mind.

What is called "sense desire" [慾, Yu] not only means having greedy, evil, and lustful thoughts, it is also related to indulgence and nostalgia, between the lag of things [failures we experience in life]. If greedy for something, sentimentality gets attached and will not give up, these all belong to sense-desire. If we can block the source of the sense desire and stay alert, then the water of desire will not flow downstream. Nevertheless, there has to be an understanding of the principles. To understand the principles is to never forget the Heavenly Mind. With the Heavenly Mind, there is the principle. The spirituality of a pure and bright mind has a very equal and impartial knowledge which can access the worldly and posterity without shortcomings.

The most important matter is this: don't be against the mind and don't be wasting your life, this is true loyalty and filial piety. Serving parents is the priority, to be fair and faithful, and being a top-grade person in the world. Think things over every day. You should be able to look up into the sky without feelings of guilt, be able to lower your head without feelings of guilt towards other people, and be introspective of your own heart without feelings of guilt. When faced with difficult conditions, use your sensible mind to deal with them. This is just like dismembering an ox as skillfully as a butcher. Process everything very properly, each step should follow a special providence, doing our best, keeping the ideas of loyalty and filial piety in the mind.

If people do not reward good people, then Heaven will know it. To understand this teaching, do not act as if unkempt and be persistently silent. In ancient times, humanity was not seeking to go beyond the secular or to destroy the feudal ethical code. A saying goes, "If wanting to become an immortal, a person has to practice being mortal first." Many times I have seen a person claiming to be a priest, but they still used schemes to trick people. If the treacherous and absurd mind is not removed, then the evil thoughts will still exist. Even if they can speak a great deal about things like Yellow Ivory, White Snow, Black Mercury, and Red Lead,[11] these in the end are still just vain words. So, of the tens of thousands of people practicing Dao, just one or two can find success. Why do I say this is so? Because their minds were never organized. All things are empty, only honesty is the fundamental.

From ancient times, people who practiced the Dao towards immortality were all just paying attention to practices. However, why then does the great teachings of Purity and Illumination not emphasize those practices? My answer was, I heard True Master Immortal Du[12] say,

> The Clarity and Purity teaching is a school of
> thought to cultivate people's upright hearts and
> moral characters. It is not just a secular doctrine for
> practicing vital energy [Qi]. Cultivating one's upright
> heart and moral character is to teach earthly mortals
> to organize their mind and morality naturally, as
> people tend to ignore the work of restraining their
> own desires. Instead, people look for other quick ways

---

11   These four old terms are used in Daoist internal alchemy and are metaphors for Heaven (Yellow Ivory, 黃牙, Huang Ya), Earth (White Snow, 白雪, Yin Xue), Fire (Red Lead, 紅鉛, Hong Qian), and Water (Black Mercury, 黑汞, Hei Gong).

12   True Master Immortal Du (都仙眞君, Du Xian Zhen Jun).

to success, such as necromancy [communicating with spirits] or compounding elixirs. They did not know to first look internally and regulate their minds. Otherwise, it is like learning how to fly when not even knowing how to walk.

Someone then posed the question,

In the Clarity and Purity teachings, it is said, "Heaven established the Central Yellow and Eight Poles and the Reverting to the Origin of the Illimitable." [13] May I know more about how these Eight Poles [14] occupy Heaven?

Master Du said,

It is termed, "Revert to the Origin" so you may go back and Return to the Source. [15] The Illimitable is the Dao, and the Central Yellow and Eight Poles are the principles, so it was the Dao that created these principles. To understand the principles and not forget the origin is the main idea of the Clarity and Purity teachings.

---

13   *Central Yellow and Eight Poles* (中黃八極, Zhong Huang Ba Ji) and the *Reverting to the Origin of the Illimitable* (返元無上, Fan Yuan Wu Shang). These are terms used in internal alchemy practices.

14   *Eight Poles* is also a reference to the Eight Diagrams (or trigram images) from the *Book of Changes* (易經, *Yi Jing*).

15   *Return to the Source* (還源, Huan Yuan).

True Master Immortal Du told me before,

> Within the Nine Halls of the Central Heaven is the view of the Supreme One's Central Yellow, and it is called the Heavenly Mind. It also called the Earthly Ancestor, because it is the source of all the things in the world, and the basic rule for all things.[16]

When dispersed about in the human body, the Heavenly Mind is called "Barring Off the Elixir" [丹扃, Dan Jiong]. In the human mind, there is the Supreme Ultimate [太極, Tai Ji], which cannot avoid all the good and bad responses, and the causes and effects of them. Just like a shadow follows the body, this is also the original relationship between reality and the higher realms [a Buddhist ideology]. So people who are learning Dao, they must thoroughly understand the meaning of Life [命, Ming] and control the rule of it. Then Life's role can be fully expressed and the value of Life can be achieved, so that the self will be in harmony with the universe.

Sensible people understand their own mind very clearly, and do not conceal their own behavior, they do not make mistakes against reason, and do not do anything, even slightly, that is against reason. They just want to keep the mind clear, so they

---

16   *Nine Halls of the Central Heaven* (九堂中天, Jiu Tang Zhong Tian), *Supreme One's Central Yellow* (中黄太一, Zhong Huang Tai Yi), *Heavenly Mind* (天心, Tian Xin), *Earthly Ancestor* (祖土, Zu Tu). The *Nine Halls* are the nine Qi centers in the brain that surround the Upper Dan Tian, called here the *Supreme One's Central Yellow,* as well as *Heavenly Mind* and the *Earthly Ancestor.*

can find the whereabouts of their Nature [性, Xing].[17] Once we know our Nature, the source of Life can be recreated.

We should begin practicing so we can return to our original status. It is time to clean up bad habits and the sediments of Yin [陰姿, Yin Zi]. Then one can go up to the supreme realm of purity and nothingness. The realm of destruction cannot reach the Supreme Dao with either floods, fires, or hurricanes. After this, it can be said that one is beyond the numerous changes of Yin and Yang, and outside of the life and death.

Someone asked about prayer, "Why do some people have no interaction with Heaven?"

The sage said, "The rainy day and the sunny day is connected between Heaven and Earth's vitality [Qi]." If a person prays very sincerely, how could they not get a response from Heaven? If a person's daily conduct and cultivation does not comply with the will of Heaven, then when they pray for a response, isn't it just too difficult [for Heaven] to respond? When putting forth your best effort towards such things, the principles of Heaven appear naturally.

Someone asked, "Have you seen True Master Immortal Du's sword that can cut a Rain Dragon [蛟, Jiao]?"

---

17   The term *Xing Ming* (性命) has a broad meaning. In brief, *Ming* (Life) is a term expressing the idea of cultivating, and *Xing* (Nature) is what the person experiences from cultivating (Life). Almost all Daoist texts on cultivation make use of this term. It is even used in Confucianism. Since Ming can mean "destiny" and Xing, "temperament," the term lends itself to the idea of "realizing one's destiny." Xing also means "innate" (or in Daoist terms, Before Heaven) and Ming, "acquired" (After Heaven). So, the meaning of the term is cyclical. We cultivate Life (Ming) to realize our Nature (Xing), and once Nature is realized then we can know our destiny (Life).

The sage said, "It is a Daoist sword and the Qi of the sword has righteousness, wisdom, and bravery. It is silent before it's out of the sheath, and is called the Dao of the supernatural. After the sword is unsheathed, it becomes a weapon of reality. Stars fall onto the Earth and become stones, like thunder striking and leaving its mark. But these are the sediments of Yin Qi [陰氣]."

Now, the sword which was kept in the Cauldron Monastery at Mysterious Pool Mountain [觀廬陵玄潭, Guan Lu Ling Xuan Tan], it is not iron or stone, it is the sediment of real knowledge and wisdom. The reason people's minds are moved is because all living things change. In the beginning, people are connected with all things. People should reflect on themselves and stop at the source. This is called *Returning*. The reason for all things is that there is no moving without returning. Thunder and storms are ever changing, but eventually they will calm down and go back to their origin.

The Illimitable [無極, Wu Ji] is what the Exalted One[18] called, the Valley Spirit [谷神, Gu Shen], it means the nature of things. The Supreme Ultimate [太極, Tai Ji] is the Mysterious Female [玄牝, Xuan Pin]. It means the application of things. The valley should be empty to get a good response, even of the gods with endless variations, so that the matters of the spirit are put in the place of emptiness. If this is done, then change is the rule of the Way of the Creative [乾, Qian], it causes all things to acquire their own life, and this is why the Mysterious Female is the root of the world.

The natural gives life for people as the flesh of the human body, it is a visible virtual element, only nothing is eternal. Surely a spirit is the root of beginning and it begins from the Supreme

---

18   *Exalted One* (太上, Tai Shang), title of the deified Laozi.

Origin.[19] So what the eyes can see is the shape and appearance of things. The eyes can see things but we cannot see how we can see things. What ears can hear is the sound. The ears can hear sounds, but we cannot hear how we can hear sounds. Human's ears, eyes, and hands are all visible, however, these are controlled by an invisible [consciousness]. This is like the void and formlessness, using the body of all things as its form. Only emptiness can contain everything and be complete, and can be the fundamental of the Dao. Only reality can show the subtle function of emptiness, and then achieve the Dao.

When I started to learn the Clarity and Illumination of the Great Dao, I had not yet read many Daoist classical books, only read a few Confucian classics. Those books praised the noble character and focused on moral character. Every time I read it, it reminded me to remain vigilant and prudent. Saying words that are contradictory to reason [Dao], and retractable words that are also contradictory to reason. Doing things that are contradictory to reason, will also retract the results that are contradictory to the reason.

These kind of words touch the inside of the heart, I do not dare to be against them at any moment. Every time chickens or dogs are lost from a home, the people cannot wait to get them back. In our life, there are some things that had been lost already and which are more valuable than chickens and dogs, but we never go looking for them. In the night hours, the Qi is not sufficient to hold onto it, it is almost the same as animals, then people will feel the shame naturally. I felt appreciation in that moment, it was like boiling water or a thorn of fire in my body and mind, so I was thinking, if I practiced slowly, even if

---

19   *Supreme Origin* (太始, Tai Shi) is the Before Heaven (innate) Original Spirit.

I did not understand the Dao very well, then I would be a sinner from a sage's point of view. It left me feeling uneasy even when eating and sleeping. Later, I was very fortunate and had some progress. I felt heaven and my mind had arrived in heaven. I felt a little happy about that, when I sit back and think about it. It was because of the force of feeling of shame that made this possible.

I have three old sayings for learners to keep in mind:
Put higher standards on ambition and integrity.
Do not learn dirty and contemptible things.
Do not seek the short-term visible result. Try to
be tolerant, don't be narrow minded, and don't
be discontented.

Integrity has to be straight, not selfish, and do not
follow evil thoughts to seek things.

A sage said, "In this world, some careless people who are learning the Dao, often say that they did nothing wrong." How could this be true? If we sit back, think, and compare it carefully, the achievements of the ancient people, how many steps did they strive? If people cannot be humble, then how could they expect to have progress in seeking the Dao.

Someone again asked, "Is there any way to be clear of evil thoughts?"

A sage said, "This should be work on the tiny sign of thoughts." What is the tiny sign? For example, when a bad plant starts to germinate, we should remove it immediately with the root. If you wait until it has grown up, it becomes difficult to remove.

The *Book of Changes* [易 經, *Yi Jing*] says, "Stepping on hoar-frost, people should think of the freezing day coming." It means the Yin Qi turned strong. So it also said, "A nobleman can notice the events of subtle change beforehand, and seize the opportunity to act."

The principles of this Dao: it is to learn the way to be a good person, to manage the mind, and to be loyal and have filial piety. Everyone should follow the rules and be responsible for their own self. To learn this Dao, for career or seclusion, it will help to be successful wherever you go, so the staff will be loyal to the monarch, people will obey their parents, worship their ancestors, and be nice to their posterities. We wear summer clothing in summer and wear leather cloth in winter, we drink when thirsty, eat when hungry. There is no difference with the normal people. The only extra is to use some regulation effort for the heart. It is unlike the secular so-called "practicing," with strange dressing, cutting off contact with relatives and friends, sinking directly into the realm of emptiness. Therefore, in practicing Dao you should not be too extreme about only caring for yourself, as this confuses human relations, and hurts the doctrine.

Chapter on Breathing

The vital energy [Qi] of Heaven and Earth cycles in one year. The Qi of the human body cycles in one day.

[Yang and Yin Qi Cycles]

The Yang Qi [陽氣] in the human body, starts at midnight, the hour of Zi,[20] and the Qi begins to flow from the left foot upward, through the left thigh, from the waist into the left armpit, to the left shoulder and left side of the brain, then across to the right side of the brain, down to the right shoulder, through the right arm and armpit, down to the waist, and into the right foot. When this cycle is complete, it is back to midnight [hour of Zi] again.

The Yin Qi [陰氣] in the human body, starts at noon, the hour of Wu,[21] and the Qi begins to flow from the right palm up through the right arm, up to the right shoulder and then across to the left shoulder, moving through the left arm and armpit, and then to the waist and down into the left foot. From outside the kidneys [and down through the testicular area] it moves into the right foot. From the right armpit it moves down to the waist. When this cycle is complete, it is back to noon [hour of Wu] again. (Editor's Note: intersecting at noon and midnight.)

The operation of Yang Qi and Yin Qi is nonstop day and night, and a day is a cycle. With the Qi of Heaven and Earth, a year is a breathing cycle. For the Qi of the human body, a single inhale and exhale is a breathing cycle, as an exhale and an

---

20   *Hour of Zi* (子時, Zi Shi) runs from 11:00 p.m. to 1:00 a.m.

21   *Hour of Wu* (午時, Wu Shi) spans 11:00 a.m. to 1:00 p.m.

inhale forms one breath. The long endurance of Heaven and Earth, and the lifespan of humans all rely on this breathing. Also, the power of good fortune, the changing of destiny, and having extraordinary talent, all rely on this breathing. So this breathing, it is the power of Yin and Yang, birth and death, having the authority to make all things live or die.

[Embryonic Breathing]

Thus, Daoism starts from learning Embryonic Breathing [22] as a basis of Entering the Dao, and those who want longevity need to learn how to breathe with these tactics to prolong life. Umbilical Breathing is learning about how to raise the Qi [up along the spine] and learning to stay calm [when doing so], there should be no emotions of joy or anger.

The mind is to be kept clear of all distractions, keeping the will free of any disturbances. Sit still and face the easterly direction. Use a thick sitting pad to make the body feel comfortable and so not to tire quickly. Wear loose clothes so the Qi will not be hurried. Shut the Six Doors[23] so the Spirit [神, Shen] will not disperse. Keep sitting over a long time, the Spirit will be clear and the Qi will become stable. Then the mind will be clean and all the thoughts will be silenced.

Allow the Spirit to move through the Qixue,[24] but do not have any thoughts of making this movement happen, as there is no need to think about it, particularly because the Spirit and breath will become interdependent. Do not allow the Qi to

---

22   *Embryonic Breathing* (胎息, Tai Xi) is sometimes called *Umbilical* or *Reverse* breathing.

23   *Six Doors* (六門, Liu Men), means the Six Senses.

24   Qixue (氣穴), acupuncture points.

escape the body. When inhaling the air, the mind will follow it and arrive in the Qixue of the Qi Hai.[25] When exhaling, the mind will follow it and arrive in the Ling Tai.[26] The breath is to be continuous and indistinct. Do not use the eyes to look, even if the eyes are opened, the mind should see nothing. Do not use Spirit to perceive things, and the mind should perceive nothing. Sit until the mind is clear, and forget about outside objects and even oneself. The Spirit and the True Qi[27] will gather in the Yellow Court.[28] After that, nothing can get out and nothing can get in. It is like a baby inside the mother's womb. The Spirit interacts with the breathing [息, xi], so there will be no need to adjust the breathing, it will be balanced by itself. But [the Spirit] cannot be interfered with so the Qi in the Yellow Court will heat naturally.

[Embryonic Breathing Exercises of Qian, ☰, and Kun, ☷]
[Qian[29] ☰ Qigong]

After that, contract the neck and raise the shoulders, squat like a monkey, and breathe through the heels for twelve breath

---

25   Qi Hai (氣海, Ocean of Qi), below the navel.

26   Ling Tai (靈台, Spiritual Terrace), between the eyes.

27   True Qi (眞氣, Zhen Qi).

28   Yellow Court (黃庭, Huang Ting), lower abdomen.

29   These two terms, *Qian* and *Kun,* are the first two hexagrams of the *Book of Changes* (易經, *Yi Jing).* Qian represents the "creative," and Kun, "the nourishment of all phenomena." Qian is all Yang, ☰, and Kun is all Yin, ☷. It is from these two hexagrams that the remaining sixty-two hexagrams of the *Book of Changes* are derived.

cycles. Put a little bit of force on the lower abdomen, close the anus [30] tightly, and use the mind to direct the hot Qi to the Tail Gateway.[31] Then breathe twelve cycles through the heels again to direct the Qi into the twin gates of the Doubled Spine.[32] Then breathe twelve cycles through the heels for one more time. The Doubled Spine will feel a little bit itchy and warm.

Then direct the Qi through the Jade Pillow.[33] This acupoint has a very solid vestibule and is the smallest orifice among all the others. Keep the eyes looking up into the Muddy Pellet,[34] so the head and nostrils are also directed upwards. Open and close the eyes nine times. Accumulate the Qi to fill up the Muddy Pellet.

[Kun ☷ Qigong]

After the Muddy Pellet is penetrated, keep the head down and then breathe twenty-four cycles through the heels.

Close the eyes and gaze down, while directing the Qi from the Muddy Pellet to the Illuminated Hall,[35] then down to the Base of the Mountain,[36] and press the Qi to move into the

---

30   Anus (穀道, Gu Dao), literally means the "Grain Path."

31   Tail Gateway (尾閭, Wei Lu) is the tailbone area, same location as the kundalini gland.

32   Doubled Spine (夾脊, Jia Ji), also called Double-Gate, Double Pass, or Spine Handle, the middle of the spine.

33   Jade Pillow (玉枕, Yu Zhen), the occiput.

34   Muddy Pellet (泥丸, Ni Wan), top of the head. Also called, Cavity of One Hundred Returnings (百會穴, Bai Hui Xue).

35   Illuminated Hall (明堂, Ming Tang), midpoint between the eyes.

36   Base of the Mountain (山根, Shan Gen), the nose.

Receiving Serum.[37] Make sure to position the tip of the tongue so it touches the upper jaw, and direct the Qi to cross the Magpie Bridge.[38] Then holding the breath,[39] swallow the Qi down through the Double Pagoda.[40] Moving it down through the Crimson Palace.[41] Then use the mind to direct the Qi down so it returns to the Yellow Court. Moving the Qi up the back and moving it down the front of the body forms a complete cycle and is called a "Lesser Heavenly Circuit of Qi."

Do this process six times to perform the method of Qian [乾], resulting in a total of 216 breath cycles, this is Ascending Yang.[42] Next, perform the method of Kun [坤], resulting in a total of 144 breath cycles. This is Descending Yin.[43] Yang ascends and Yin descends, the total equals a full circle of days in a year, or 360 degrees. Practice this the same time every day, after midnight [midnight to 1:00 a.m.] and before noon [11:00 a.m. to noon]. When the Yang Qi inside the body is aroused, the body will sense the time of midnight.

When the Yang Qi is aroused, there will be no need to limit the practice between midnight and noon punctually, just go ahead and practice the heel breathing cycles and direct the

---

37   Receiving Serum (承漿, Cheng Jiang), under the tongue.

38   Magpie Bridge (鵲橋, Que Qiao), roof of the mouth.

39   *Holding the breath* (閉氣, Bi Qi).

40   Double Pagoda (重樓, Chong Lou), esophagus.

41   Crimson Palace (絳宮, Jiang Gong), solar plexus.

42   Ascending Yang in 216 breath cycles (6 times 12+12+12).

43   Descending Yin in 144 breath cycles (6 times 24).

Qi through the Tail Gateway. Follow the previous procedures and complete a cycle. By doing this everyday, gradually, the Yang Qi will be stimulated more frequently. Every time the Yang Qi is stimulated, perform a Lesser Heavenly Circuit of Qi, not limiting the time between midnight and noon, not limiting the number of times either. From the Bubbling Well[44] of the left foot, move the Qi up to the Tail Gateway to run a Heavenly Circuit. Also, from the Bubbling Well of the right foot, run a Heavenly Circuit. With the two feet together, running once, and then letting the Qi sit still in the Yellow Court, this is called a Greater Heavenly Circuit of Qi. Doing this once per day is good enough. In a word, the Yang Qi is stimulated to operate the Qi inside the body, not too fast and not too slowly. If the Yang Qi doesn't move, then hold the Qi. Do not force it nor neglect it. These are the real secrets of Embryonic Breathing. But when doing Breathing Through the Heels, it is not appropriate to inhale any cold air into the abdomen,

If trying to restrain the breath, the breath will be stopped. Then the Qi is obstructed and the blood will be stagnated. As a result, the person will get sick.

[Regulating the Breath]

Regarding the technique of Regulating the Breath [調息, Tiao Xi], it also known as the method of mind moderating. It is to train the Qi and purify the Qi. The goal is to make the Spirit and the Qi interdependent with each other so as for Closing-Off the Barriers [閉關, Bi Guan]. A sage said, "The blood and Qi in the human body are connected."

Nourishing the immune and circulatory systems of the body should be done spontaneously every day. Some think they can

---

44   Bubbling Well (湧泉, Yong Quan), center of the balls of the feet.

learn how to direct the Qi apart from these two systems, but this is like putting an extra head on top of a head. Furthermore, a new life [infant] is only born in harmony with these systems, I never heard of a new life born apart from them.

People have to know how to retain Qi in the Yellow Court. It is the key method of Embryonic Breathing. Directing the Yang Qi in the body is the function of the Ren and Du Meridians. These two are the secrets of peace and tranquility.

There are six key points of breathing:

1. Hold the head upright.
2. Avoid squinting the eyes.
3. Keep the chest wide open.
4. Exercise the lower abdomen continuously.
5. Straighten the bones of the lower back and spine.
6. Situate the hands and feet in a natural position.

Only after understanding these six key points can one then think about starting to learn breathing; otherwise, it will be like a blind person riding a horse along a cliff. It will be hard not to take a wrong step and fall off. If someone already knew of these methods, but did not get the right directions from a real teacher, it is also in vain.

So for people who are learning the Dao, it is necessary to find a real teacher, then people can begin to practice Dao. As to learning the methods for prolonging life, how is it different from learning the Dao?

So I say, "It is easy to get the real secrets, but it is not easy to understand them. Although there are real teachers, it is not easy to find them. If people can find a real teacher and get the real secrets, it will not be hard to become an immortal."

Responses to Lianxiazi's Questions [45]

Lianxiazi asked the Old Man, Qingyun, "I had heard from my master that people nowadays drink wine as though drinking water, they regard the reckless things as normal, and have sex after getting drunk. Their Qi and Essences [精氣, Jing Qi] are exhausted because of their lust, and their True Qi [真氣, Zhen Qi] is dissipated because of this waste. They do not know how to reserve an exuberance of the Essence. They do not know how to manage their Spirit, often giving themselves to the sensual pleasures and only seeking temporary pleasures, these are signs of shortening life."

He also said, "The Seven Emotions [七情, Qi Qing] and Six Sense-Desires [六慾, Liu Yu] are thieves of longevity. I can basically understand the wise thoughts of my master. But he is over 250 years old, has married fourteen times, had more than 180 posterities. Too many for him even to recognize or even call their names if seeing them face to face.

"My master said, 'Restrain desires and limit passions.' I do not understand how to explain this? I would like to know your opinion. Is this the Daoist's so-called, 'Cultivation of Qi through having sex with multiple women to attain long-life?'"

Qingyun, the old man smiled and said, "What you have said is incorrect. You have doubts in your mind so now you ask me these questions. You are intelligent, but your mind has still

---

45 This section is about sex, *Refining the Rosy Clouds.* So, respecting Chinese sensibilities on the subject, the text includes this so-called person, Lianxiazi (煉霞子), as the interlocutor and disciple of Li Qingyun. *Lianxia* means *Rosy Clouds,* an old Chinese term for the activities of sexual intercourse. Thus, the device of using Master of the Rosy Clouds (煉霞子, Lian Xia Zi) as the questioner.

not broken away from vulgar thoughts. When I was 139 years old, I met my teacher in the Kongtong Mountains and he taught me about the Dao. Before I was 139 years old, I never practiced Dao, and I had already married nine times and had a few tens of posterities. Even if I wanted to acquire the secrets of Grafting [採補, Cai Bu] to prolong my life, where would I have received [these teachings and young females] from?

"This is all so obvious, I should not need to explain this. You should have already understood this. However, since you still have doubts in your mind, I will explain the details to you, so you won't go in the wrong direction and impair your efforts of practicing the Dao.

"The Seven Emotions are happiness, anger, anxiety, fear, love, hate, and desire. The Six Dusts[46] are color, sound, smell, taste, touch, and thought. For people who are learning longevity, the best is to stay away from these [Emotions and Dusts]. However, inside the human body there is a complete Illimitable [無極, Wu Ji] hiding. When the Illimitable is present, we will see it as the Supreme Ultimate [太極, Tai Ji]. When there is the Supreme Ultimate, Yin [陰] and Yang [陽] will come.

"When Yin and Yang are in harmony, then life will last forever. It's decided by the Heaven and Earth, and Yin and Yang. As for the Supreme Ultimate, before its formation it was called the Illimitable, and this is the Qi of both chaos and of vitality. As the Illimitable gathers the energy, but when not yet distributing it, plants will not grow and birds and animals will not come forth. These have to wait until the Illimitable turns into the Supreme Ultimate so the Yin and Yang can become harmonious. Then Heaven and Earth join propitiously, and the

---

46   *Six Dusts* (六欲, Liu Yu, or 六塵, Liu Chen).

myriad things[47] in the universe will be born and created. So people say, 'Once Yin and Yang are in harmony then all things will grow.' This is Daoism's point of view.

"The age of Heaven and Earth is very long. How could people say that the intercourse of Yin and Yang [sexual intercourse], which creates all living things in the universe, could shorten their own lives? When it is because of the harmony of Yin and Yang, and the vital energy [Qi] generates life, giving birth to everything. Human life is identical [in process]. The human who is endowed with masculine Qi becomes a male. The one who is endowed with feminine Qi becomes a female. Each is determined by Yin and Yang. Male is Yang and female is Yin. It is also the sign of Qian [乾] and Kun [坤]. When Yin and Yang mingle together, they give birth to posterities. It is harmonious and it is proper, just like the propitiousness of Heaven and Earth, which manifests all things and beings. Who could say this is wrong?

"Xiang Chuanzhi [象川之] said,
'The male is Yang; however, inside the Yang there must be Yin. The cyclic number for Yin is eight, so 1 x 8 [the 8-year-old male], the Essence [semen] of Yang wants to leak out and so is externally [sexually] attracted; 2 x 8 [16-year-old male] the Essence [semen] becomes overflowing with Yang and so he is able to reproduce. The female is Yin; however, inside the Yin there must be Yang. The cyclic number for Yang is 7, so 1 x 7 [the 7-year-old female] the blood of Yin wants to leak out and so is externally [sexually] attracted; 2 x 7 [14-year-old female] the blood overflows with Yin and so she is

---

47   *Myriad things* (萬 物, Wan Wu), the Ten Thousand Things, all phenomena.

able to be impregnated. The Yang Essence and the Yin blood are the quintessence of the Five Flavors [48] regarding diet.'

"He also said,

'Essence can produce Qi. The Qi can then produce Spirit. Both nutrition and the immunity of the body will reach its maximum when these are achieved. So people care about regimen, and will do their utmost to treasure the Essence. Once the Essence is full, then the Qi will be vigorous. Once the Qi is vigorous, the Spirit will flourish. Once the Spirit is flourishing, then the body will be healthy. As long as the body is healthy, it won't get sick. Inside the body, the Five Organs [heart, liver, spleen, lung, and kidneys] will be blooming, the skin will be moist and silky. The face will be glowing. Ears and eyes will hear and look sharply. Even when people get old, they will still be vigorous and strong. From these, we can see that sages admonished people about treasuring the Essence, but never admonished people for not using the Essence.'

"The *Treatise on Nourishing Nature* [養性篇, *Yang Xing Pian*] also said, 'The Essence of a human is precious, and yet it is also little.' In the human body, there is usually 1.6 liters,[49] and this is before the male starts dissipating Essence [semen] starting around age sixteen. A male who treasures and accumulates it, could maintain up to three liters. The man who does not

---

48   The Five Flavors are sweet, sour, bitter, pungent, and salty.

49   One liter = 10 deciliter. One deciliter = 3.38 fluid ounces.

reserve it and overuses it, the total Essence could be less than one liter. So, overusing the Essence will then damage it; reserving too much Essence will then cause it to overflow. Excess is just as bad as deficiency. Either of these ways are not good. So when the Essence is too full, it will overflow. If a man does not restrain lust, then the Essence will eventually be used up. Having intercourse one time, the Essence will lose one-half deciliter. If one-half deciliter of Essence was taken from the fullness of Essence, then it will not cause damage and can even help in the balancing of the Spirit. If taken from one whose Essence is overused, he has to raise and cause it to recover, otherwise it will be damaged permanently. Thus, *The Yellow Emperor's Inner Classic* [黃帝內經, *Huang Di Nei Jing*] said,

'The Essence is generated from grains. For those whose Essence is not enough, they should be eating nutritious food [especially grains] to make up for it. However, the flavorful and sumptuous meals cannot raise the Essence. Only simple and natural foods can generate Essence.'

"The above is [mentioned] also to teach people to use good complementary nutrition to increase Essence. It does not teach people not to use the Essence at all. One of the main reasons a man marries is to have children. If one acts in a diametrically opposite way, it is inauspicious. However, during the Winter Solstice, a man should prohibit lust. During the Summer Solstice he should restrain lust.[50]

"In the winter and summer seasons, people should save their Essence. The sage said, 'There are three ways to be unfilial, the worst is not to produce offspring.' Let alone within the Great Heavenly Net [大羅天, Da Luo Tian], there is no single immortal who has not been filial. For people who care about the regimens for long life, they should also treat this filial obedience as their priority. I have never seen anyone who is not filial and still receive care from Heaven for achieving longevity.[51] Although I married fourteen times and have more than a hundred posterities, [this] did not shorten my life because I had intercourse at the right time, and I restrained and controlled lust. I was good at using the Essence before it became full and overflowed. When the Essence was decreased, I then ate natural food light in flavor to make up for it. Letting

---

50   During the period of the Winter Solstice, men should forego having sexual intercourse. During the period of the Summer Solstice, they should regulate, but not prohibit, it. The idea is that men should follow nature by engaging in sexual activity during the spring and summer seasons, and not in the autumn or winter season, just as seen in nature.

51   This is purely Confucian ideology. Meaning, Confucians propagate the notion of biological immortality, not spiritual immortality. Buddhists and Daoists hold different views on this subject as well. Chinese Buddhists are unconcerned about sex and reproduction, seeing them as hindrances to attaining enlightenment, and so they adhere to celibacy. Daoists view sex as a natural function that can be used for restorative and transformational purposes. However, Li Qingyun's statement that all immortals produced children, at least historically, is not altogether true.

the old [Essence] release and the new [Essence] be produced. This is just like controlling flowing water within a trench. Keep the water flowing smoothly, neither letting it become too full, nor letting it dry up. Adjusting the Yin and Yang so that the Qi is harmonized. Therefore, it will not harm life.

"If talking about the method of Dao Yin via Grafting, then it is nefarious and against the Law of Heaven. This only exists in the animal domain. You only see that I am old and still in good health, and have many posterities, but you do not fully understand the subtle secrets of Yin and Yang. Therefore, you have doubts in mind. Today, after I explained them to you, you should be able to understand thoroughly now."

Lianxiazi then said, "The whereabouts of the subtle secrets is that only people with wisdom can find and get it. I understand it now." Then he expressed his gratitude and left.

Part Two
Discourses on the
Beginning Foundations of Long Life

[長命初基說, Chang Ming Chu Ji Shuo]

People admire immortals, admire that they live a life forever, free, and unfettered by the world of mortals. The reason they can be immortal is because they can comprehend the subtle principles of the Great Dao [大道, Da Dao]. It is hard for mortals to comprehend the subtle principles of the Dao. Those who can comprehend it will become immortal. However, there are a few things that everyone can do, and everyone should learn to do. These little things, people usually ignore and do not care about. In the eyes of these people, these things are kids' toys. And they only spend time envying the immortals who can live forever. It is truly a pity!

These, then, are some lessons that everyone can learn, and are the Dao outside of the Dao. They are the basis of longevity. What does this mean? In a nutshell, it is the improvement of health. The methods to improve the health should focus on Jing, Qi, and Shen, which have been described in detail previously. Methods to maintain health should be to keep on exercising, but there are so many ways to exercise. The people around Shandong and Henan areas, they exercise hard and their bodies are strong. However, long-lived people among them are still short of one hundred years old. Is this nature? Definitely not! It's that their method of exercise is not correct. The way they exercise emphasizes the use of hard and bold vitality by methods of ravaging force to make the body stronger. This way is like when a person is tired and the eyes want to close and rest, but someone uses ginger and hot pepper to rub on the eyes to force the person not to sleep. This kind of exercise is over intense. It is not a good method. I also see people who are cultivating in the mountains, but their bodies look as thin as a lath and their faces are brown and not shiny. They pursued longevity by melting lead [and mercury] to create an alchemical pill of immortality. Eventually, their whole body will be sick. Both the body and the spirit will be damaged. Then, their body will rot along with the grass and the plants in the mountains. So they would tell people, "Immortality is just a lie. There is no such thing in the world." Their bodies are not healthy, yet, they only concentrate on useless or even harmful works. Isn't it difficult to look at persons seeking longevity using these efforts? There is not one single unhealthy immortal. There is not one whose body is not strong and healthy. There are so many methods that appear to be able to improve health, but those methods that can mingle the hard and soft, and can harmonize the Yin and Yang are very rare.

Today, I will introduce the methods that I learned from my master to all of you. If these methods can be widely spread out to the world, and people can study and practice with diligence, even if we may not be able to become a Heavenly Immortal, it is very possible that we can be an Earthly Immortal. As for my method to improve the health, it accords with Yin and Yang, harmonizes the hardness and softness. These methods are not extreme and are good methods to make the body healthy and strong. According to my master, this method was not an ancestral method of Daoism. It was passed down from Buddhism.[1]

Even though doctrines of the Three Religions [Confucianism, Buddhism, and Daoism] are different, the goal is the same. So for anything that benefits people, we shouldn't care which sect it belongs to, or where it comes from. Therefore, Daoists have also learned from this. But later generations even regarded this as the deepest rules of Dao Yin, which is a misunderstanding. Nobody knows the name of this method from ancient times, but people nowadays are calling it Seated Eight Brocades Qigong. I do not know what the actual origination of this method is. However, similar methods are spreading between people, but these are not fully rational. And those methods have quite a number of different ways and knacks. I think it was because that those methods have passed through so many hands or places that some started to distort it.

My "Basis of Longevity" methods can be divided into several categories, [and] I will explain them in detail. I hope everyone

---

[1]   This is an interesting statement because later Li says his teacher handed down these methods to him, calling them *The Methods of the Eight Diagram Elemental Skills,* an obvious Daoist terminology. There is also the problem that Bodhidharma's *Muscle-Tendon Changing Classic* (易 筋 經, *Yi Jin Jing),* the basis of Buddhist qigong, was not introduced into China until the fifth century CE. In Daoism, Dao Yin (導 引) exercises (the basis of the Eight Brocades exercises) long predate Bodhidharma's arrival in China. Li himself was obviously not sure about his teacher's statement when he says, "I do not know what the actual origination of this method is." I think it's best, as Master Liang suggested, to take Li's teacher's statement about Eight Brocades being handed down through Buddhism as possibly meaning he learned the exercises from a Buddhist teacher.

will not judge the usefulness of these methods by how soon the efficacy appears. But to practice with diligence and spread it out widely, the beneficence is boundless and longevity is assured.

The Method of Tranquil Sitting
[靜坐之法, Jing Zuo Zhi Fa]

Meditation is the first important rule for the fundamentals of longevity. This stabilizes the Jing, concentrates the Shen, and controls the Qi. We had talked about its theories many times before, now we will only talk about the methods.

First, find a secluded spot to sit in, and construct a quiet room. The decoration in the room should be simple and clean. It should not have too much complicated furniture. The only necessary thing is to set up a Cloud Bed [雲床, monks' meditation bench], maybe a table with an incense burner, and a few chairs. No more than these. The heart will be more easily cleared when surrounded by only a few simple objects.

The Putuan [2] on the Cloud Bed could be just a general sitting cushion. It should be soft and thick. Initially, when just starting to learn and practice, if the cushion is too hard, the feet may too easily experience pain, and this disturbs the Spirit. As time passes and a person gets used to it, then it can be positioned more evenly on the ground.

During the meditation, the clothes should be loose and comfortable, so the chest and the abdomen can expand. When in the Lotus sitting position [跌坐, Fu Zuo], place the left foot on top of the right thigh, then the right foot is crossed and placed on top the left thigh.

If in the beginning you cannot make the Full Lotus sitting posture, then you can start with the Half Lotus sitting position [半跌坐, Ban Fu Zuo]. The Half Lotus sitting position is to place the left foot on top of the right thigh and the right foot is un-

---

2   *Putuan* (蒲團), sitting cushion for meditation. Japanese Zafu.

derneath the left thigh. When feeling tired, the left and the right [legs] can be exchanged.

During the meditation, the head should be upright, the eyes should be half closed, the chest should be expanded, the spine should be straightened up, the two hands should be stacked or holding each other and the hands placed in front of the abdomen.

The best time of the day for practicing the Lotus sitting posture is between midnight [11:00 p.m. to 1:00 a.m.] and noon [11:00 a.m. to 1:00 p.m.]. The first practices should not be too long, as the limbs will not yet be strong enough. If practicing too long, it may cause injury instead. You can use a stick of incense as a timer. Insert it in an incense burner. Initially, take the time of burning one half stick of incense as one session, then gradually increase the time. When one can sit for two hours, then [you] don't need to worry about sitting too long causing injury. During meditation, the first thing to avoid is noise, the second thing to avoid is the mind wandering around. The third is to avoid practicing in a humid place. The fourth is to avoid letting the room get too stuffy and hot. The fifth is to avoid not being persistent. These are five problems we should avoid. If one commits these problems, the mind and the Spirit will not be in control, and we should be paying more attention.[3]

---

3   For more information on this method of meditation, see *Clarity and Tranquility: A Guide for Daoist Meditation* by Stuart Alve Olson (Valley Spirit Arts, late 2014).

The Method of Circulating the Breath

[調息之法, Zhou Xi Zhi Fa]

The method of Embryonic Breathing is the most important part of the regimen. Previously, we did an article talking about this. Breathing dominates human life, and as long as the breath lasts, life continues. If the breath is smooth, then the bones of the whole body will be harmonious. When the breath is extinct then the person will die. When the breath is imbalanced, then people will get sick. This is why the breathing is so important within the method of longevity. For Heaven and Earth, one breath cycle is one year. For humans, one exhale and one inhale forms one breath cycle. Talking about the breathing, we should start from adjusting the exhale and inhale.

So in a quiet environment, it is the best time to pay attention to the method of breathing. During the exhale and inhale, the mind should follow it. The Spirit and breath are interdependent, but each has its own subtle effects.

[Embryonic Breathing Method (repeated)]

One should contract the neck and raise the shoulders, squat like a monkey, and breathe with the heels for twelve breath cycles. This will help create a little pressure on the lower abdomen. When doing so close the anus tightly, and use the mind to lead the warm Qi to the Tail Gateway [尾閭, Wei Lu]. Then breathe twelve cycles with the heels again, leading the Qi to the Double Gate [夾脊, Jia Ji] on the spine.

Next, breathe twelve cycles with the heels one more time, leading the Qi to the Jade Pillow [玉枕, Yu Zhen]. Then breathe twenty-four cycles with the heels, leading the Qi from the Muddy Pellet [泥丸, Ni Wan] through the Bright Hall [明堂, Ming Tang, middle of the brain], then down to Base of the Moun-

203

tain [山根, Shan Gen, above the nose on the forehead], and then move the Qi to the Holding Serum [承漿, Cheng Jiang, third eye]. Make the tongue touch the upper jaw, and lead the Qi to cross the Magpie Bridge [鵲橋, Que Qiao, upper palate], then holding the breath and swallow the Qi down to the Twelve-Storied Pavilion [重樓, Chong Lou, esophagus], passing through the Crimson Palace [絳宮, Jiang Gong, solar plexus].

Next, use the mind to lead the Qi down and return to the Yellow Court [黃庭, Huang Ting, lower abdomen], going up the back and going down the front. This is one rotation. Once the Qi can be completely controlled by the mind, then there is no need to adjust the breathing. The breath will be harmonious as though it's on autopilot.

When practicing breathing, the eyes should look at the nose, and the nose to look at the mind.[4] The mind will follow the Qi and circulate throughout the whole body. This can eliminate the distresses from the outside world and cut down on worries. Then you will achieve a stable state of mind and a peaceful spirit. Continued practice for a long period of time will prolong a person's life. If the mind is not clear, it is because of attempts to force oneself to suppress desires. But this way, even if one thought is suppressed, there will be ten thousand more distracting thoughts arising right afterwards. Then it's not only that the Qi will be scattered, the spirit will be confused. But it is also that the benefits of the practice will all disappear, and even worse, one may become mentally disordered or the

---

4   This statement is saying that by focusing the eyes on the tip of the nose, the spirit is thus focused directly on the Third Eye, as a direct line connects the tip of the nose with the eyes, Third Eye, and center of the brain.

Jing will fail. Such kinds of serious diseases can eventually become incurable.

Buddhism says, "Mind is Buddha," and that is what it means [Buddha means "pure mind"]. In the past, there was a pedant who got the skill of lead and mercury [the elixir] from an alchemist. He claimed that he could Abstain From Grains [辟穀, Pi Gu]. Later he went into Bowing Assembly Mountain [會稽山, Guiji Shan] to practice. After three to four years, someone found him in the mountain. Although he was still alive, he looked dull-witted. Finally, he was carried back home from the mountain and never recovered for the rest of his life. This is an obvious example of when the mind is not cleared, yet trying to force oneself to practice, then the result is that the Qi is scattered and the Spirit is confused. Thus, those who look for longevity, the first thing is to adjust the breathing; otherwise, not only may they not reach longevity, but also experience negative affects on their life.

The Method for Calming Spirit

[安神之法, An Shen Zhi Fa]

People who want tranquility and to calm their Spirit should first clear their mind. People who want to clear their mind should first dispel their desires. As Laozi said, "The human Spirit tends to be calm and clear, but it is the mind that disturbs it. The human mind tends to be quiet and clear, but it is desires that draw it away."

The place in which Spirit resides is called the Spiritual Hall [神室, Shen Tang].[5] The place where the mind dwells is called the Spiritual Terrace [靈臺, Ling Tai]. These are like people living in their house. Those who live in the city, their mind is susceptible to interference; those who live in the mountains, their minds are easier to calm. The Spirit and the mind reside in our body. If my Wisdom Root[6] is good enough, no matter where I am, my mind will be clear and peaceful, just like living in the mountains. If my Wisdom Root is blunt, then no matter where I am, my mind will be disturbed, just like living in the city. So people with good Wisdom tend to understand the Dao more easily. People without a good Wisdom Root tend to have difficulty understanding the Dao. On the journey in looking for the Dao, we must not let thoughts of fearing the difficulty haunt our mind, the result will then be in giving up on ourselves. If we are determined, even if we live in the city, we will feel like we are practicing in the mountains. A clean pool can produce the lotus, but in Buddha's eyes, a place as dirty as the latrine, a thing as dirty as feces, the lotus still has a chance to grow.

---

5   Spiritual Hall (神室, Shen Tang), middle of the brain.

6   *Wisdom Root* (慧根, Hui Gen), intuition or insight.

In daily life, people should always hold onto the Spirit Hall. Do not let it out easily. There are methods to keep the Spirit in the hall. Initially, people may have difficulties calming the mind, but then during the hours we are not busy, we can relax and sit. Count [the breath] silently from one, two, three, four, to ten, then to one hundred, then to one thousand, even to ten thousand, to a billion. By doing this, the mind is concentrated on counting, then the spirit will follow the mind, and all distracting thoughts can be wiped out. And all outside devils will flee from then on. Therefore, as the time passes the mind will be clear and the spirit will be calm. We can gradually increase the degree of difficulty [for thoughts to enter], by counting until there is no number in the mind, then the nature of mind will be clean and enter into the Dao. We should practice this whenever and wherever possible. It is not that this can only be practiced during the certain time of the day. At the time when the breath is not harmonious, the spirit at the same time is likewise not stable. Then the mind is disturbed, and then there is no way to get rid of the distress of the outside world. This is the key to which everyone needs to pay the most attention.

The Methods of the Elemental Skills

[行功之法, Xing Gong Zhi Fa]

I call these methods Elemental Skills.[7] My teacher handed
down these exercises to me as *The Methods of the Eight Diagram
Elemental Skills.*[8]

---

7   *Elemental Skills* (行功, Xing Gong). Xing could be translated here
    as "active," but it seems more likely that the ideogram is used to
    reference the Five Elements (五行, Wu Xing), thus connecting
    these methods with the theories of the Eight Diagrams and the
    Five Elements. To the Chinese, unless these two systems are
    correlated with any given system or method, it is simply not
    worthy or accurate.

8   *The Methods of the Eight Diagram Elemental Skills* (八卦行功法,
    Ba Gua Xing Gong Fa) are more commonly referred to as the
    Eight Brocades Exercises (八段錦, Ba Duan Jin). See *Qigong
    Teachings of a Taoist Immortal: The Eight Essential Exercises of
    Master Li Ching-yun* by Stuart Alve Olson. In the varying texts
    on Eight Brocades in Daoist literature, especially in the older
    Daoist manuals, there exists two "Windlass" methods: the *Single
    Windlass* and *Double Windlass* (which comprise the Fifth and Sixth
    Brocades, respectively). In this text, Li Qingyun is presenting the
    version more commonly found in Buddhist works, which doesn't
    distinguish between the Single and Double Windlasses. Also, in
    the Buddhist tradition, the exercises are presented in verse form
    and not numbered chronologically (or described as Brocades)
    as they are in Daoist manuals. The drawings come from a Daoist
    book published in 1591 (遵生八箋, Zun Sheng Ba Jian).

These exercises can be performed by anyone as they are very simple. They are regarded as Dao Yin methods. The secrets of these exercises are versed:

Seated, close the eyes and darken the heart.
Grasp the hands firmly and meditate on the spirit.
Knock the teeth thirty-six times.
The two hands embrace the Kunlun.
Left and right beat the Heavenly Drum,
Sounding it twenty-four times.
Gently shake the Heavenly Pillar.
The Red Dragon stirs up the saliva;
Rouse and rinse the saliva thirty-six times.
Evenly fill the mouth with Divine Water;
Each mouthful is divided into three parts and swallowed.
When the dragon moves, the tiger flees.
Close the breath and rub the hands until hot;
On the back, massage the kidneys.
Entirely exhaust one breath;
Imagine the heat aflame at the Navel Wheel.
Left and right turn the Windlass.
Stretch out both feet loosely;
Afterwards both hands support the Void.
Repeatedly bend the head over and seize the feet.
Wait for the water to be produced;
Rinse and swallow, dividing it into three parts;
Altogether swallow the Diving Water nine times.
Swallow it down with the sound of gu gu;
Then the hundred pulses will be naturally harmonized.
Complete the motion of the River Cart.
Direct the fire to circulate and heat the entire body.

The purpose for these exercises is to prevent harmful influences from approaching, to provide clearness during sleep and within the dreams, to prevent cold and heat from entering, and to keep pestilence from encroaching.

These exercises should be practiced after the hour of Zi [子] begins and before the hour of Wu [午] ends. This will create harmony between Qian [乾, *The Creative*/Heaven] and Kun [坤, *The Receptive*/Earth], which are connected together by a cyclic arrangement. There is excellent reasoning for both restoring and returning.

A Verse Song in Praise
> Massaging with warm hands and making use of the
> saliva produces a beautiful facial appearance.
> Pushing up the palms and shaking the head results
> in the ears not becoming deafened.
> Cultivating to high level, the two hands can remove
> all obstacles.
> It is wrong in principle, if when pounding the body,
> that it causes aching or pain.
> Massaging the soles of the feet until hot will make
> for lively walking.
> Pulling the Windlass is to be free of the work of
> changing the sinews and tendons.
> Gazing fiercely like a tiger and arching the back
> regulates the wind.
> With proper breathing the Five Viscera can all be void
> of any harmful afflictions.

From these above verses we can observe *The Methods of the Eight Diagram Elemental Skills,* which really are the very best and most wondrous methods for invigorating the body. Yet, most people, because of their life situation, even if they acquire these verses and songs, are unable to understand their profound meaning. Because of this they live in contradiction of what is natural. It would be wise for them to begin by putting forth every effort into these exercises, so that they will no longer suffer and toil their life away. Some will want to cultivate only during their leisure time, but this type of training is insufficient. Alas! How unfortunate the result, as these types of persons only bring about their early and hurried death.

Formerly, when my master first considered me able enough to teach these skills, I originally had found the principles of the skills beyond my comprehension. So subtle and abstruse, limitless and yet of one nature, but different in form. However, I did understand that these skills could aid society and benefit the minds of all people. After a time I found the desire to teach.

Once I asked my teacher why he had not previously dared to transmit these teachings to others, especially to other various Daoist sects. His response was,

Because those within [other] sects obtain teachings
and then change them according to their likening and
to suit the tenets of their sect. They in turn go on to
transmit it to others; then these persons change it
again to their likening and proceed to transmit it—
too much of the original teaching is then discarded
and lost. Therefore, I am giving you the responsibility
of imparting this teaching correctly. You must transmit
it as broadly as possible, for if only one person were
able to practice these skills, then only one person
would obtain a good old age. If only one thousand and
eight persons practice these skills, then only that many

persons would acquire health in old age. However, by widely transmitting this profound Dao of living beyond one hundred years, then all the people of China could obtain a good old age. Finally, the ancient state of the great Han could also obtain a good old age as a nation.

Therefore, the following commentary on the original text of the Eight Diagram Elemental Skills is given so that these teachings can be widely transmitted to the various Daoist sects. For herein lay the secrets, explained line by line, which reveal the subtle knowledge contained within these skills. This will hopefully aid everyone in practicing these Eight Diagram Elemental Skills in their proper sequence, and impart correct understanding of the procedures so all may experience and practice the refinement of these [methods].

Seated, close the eyes to darken the heart.

[閉目冥心坐, Kai Mu Ming Xin Zuo]

To *close the eyes* in effect will nourish the spirit, and *darkening the heart* is to control the false thinking.

After you are seated, the procedure is to securely close the eyes to internally contemplate the mind. All the confused thoughts will begin to vanish and return into the darkness—the mind can then thoroughly and intuitively illuminate all things.

When sitting in the cross-legged position, do so on a thick cushion. The head must be held upright and the spine kept erect and straight. Your entire being can then enter the Four Voids[9] self-reliant and independent in all things. The Tail

---

9   *Four Voids* (四空, Si Kong), the Four Dhyanas in Buddhism.

Gateway [尾閭, Wei Lu] must also be kept upright, not leaning to one side or another. This is very important.

Grasp the hands firmly and meditate on the spirit.

[握固靜思神, Wo Gu Jing Si Shen]

To *grasp the hands firmly* means to clench both hands into fists. The clenching of both hands into fists, in effect, gathers the Qi. This "closing" is the apex of this mysterious art and banishes all bad influences.

The rule is to fashion both the right and left hands into fists. Clench them firmly, with the palms facing Heaven and the backs, Earth. Then place the hands on the upper part of the knees, which will help maintain the body in being upright and centered. Quiet the mind, getting rid of all confused thinking. The primary idea here is to fully concentrate and then retain that presence of mind.

Knock the teeth thirty-six times.

[叩齒三十六, Kou Chi San Shi Liu]

To *knock the teeth* is to remove the fire from the heart and to collect the spirit within yourself, making a cohesion between body and spirit.

The procedure is to make the upper and lower teeth knock together thirty-six times, but producing only a slight sound. Do not be hurried in performing this, just exhaust the sound of the knock, and most importantly, do this slowly and lightly. If you become too anxious about this you could injure the spirit. Just exhausting the sound repeatedly is quite sufficient for removing the fire within the heart—it is otherwise without benefit. Pay attention to this.

The two hands embrace the Kunlun.

[兩手抱崑崙, Liang Shou Bao Kun Lun]

It is said that the Kunlun is likened to the head, because the Kunlun is the main peak of the Central Mountains, and the head is also the highest point of a person's body.

The procedure is to mutually interlace the fingers of both hands, with the ten fingers of both hands equally and alternately separated. Once they are securely interlaced, grasp the back of the brain—this is to *embrace*. The palms are placed directly over the base of the ears, with the thumbs pointing downwards. The two elbows are bent forming a triangle, with the elbows on line with the shoulders.

Left and right sound the Heavenly Drum.

[左右鳴天鼓, Zuo You Ming Tian Gu]

In this position you should inhale and exhale slowly and calmly, with nine complete respirations through the heels and then pause. Allow the breath to become completely full when inhaling, and completely empty when exhaling. There must be no audible sound produced. If there is, the Qi will then disperse. Through mind-intent, this procedure, without question, will gather the Qi.

The Heavenly Drum is the region both to the left and right, and back of both ears, the Hearing Gate [聰門, Cong Men]. *Beating* is to produce a drum-like sound internally by tapping the fingers on these areas. This beating can bring about good hearing faculties and also prevent the encroachment of external malignant spirits.

The proper method here is to place the two hands directly over the ear openings, the Ear Gates [耳門, Er Men]. Place the middle fingers on top of the index fingers, then with some force snap the middle fingers down. It is essential to be certain that a full echo sound is produced within the ears. Tap left and right alternately twenty-four times each. Start with the left and then do the right side. Collectively tapping forty-eight times and then stop.

Listening twenty-four times.

[二十四度聞, Er Shi Si Du Wen]

The ear openings are likened to the Gate of Life [精門, Jing Men]. The number twenty-four is contained within the secret of the hands: the Illimitable [無極, Wu Ji], the Two Powers [兩儀, Liang Yi], the Four Images [四象, Si Xiang], the Eight Diagrams [八卦, Ba Gua], and the Nine Palaces [九宮, Jiu Gong]. These represent the twenty-four breaths [Qi].

Both the left and right ears must be internally sounded twenty-four times. These twenty-four breaths are to be directed thoroughly though the body via the ears, using the Essence Gate [精門, Jing Men] as the source of holding the sound—this is the secret of prolonging the years. The sound produced is the ultimate of sounds and purifies the fire [Qi].

Gently shake the Heavenly Pillar.

[微擺撼天柱, Wei Bai Han Tian Zhu]

The Heavenly Pillar is the spinal column and the connective neck bone. To gently shake [to wave to and fro] means to sway the shoulders. *Gently shake the Heavenly Pillar* means to crick and move the neck. Properly, the neck is cricked to the left and right sides along with a gazing procedure. The two shoulders are followed by the gaze when swaying. Left and right sides are counted separately, with each side being performed twenty-four times, and collectively forty-eight times.

This cricking of the neck, swaying of the shoulders, and gazing in accordance with the movements in effect removes the fire of the heart and eliminates any invasions or disturbances of external malignant spirits.

The Red Dragon stirs up the saliva.

[赤龍攪水津, Chi Long Jiao Shui Jin]

Red Dragon is a name for the tongue. The tongue is the tool by which the saliva is produced and therefore functions as the source of good health. It is said that a bright red tongue is a sign of good health. Here it functions as the collector and stimulator of saliva.

The correct procedure is to place the tongue up against the cheeks. First follow a leftward rolling motion[10] towards the right side; alternate and follow a rightward rolling motion towards the left side.[11] Continue like this, to and fro, rolling and stirring, collecting the saliva within the mouth.

If during this procedure you should become unsettled or disturbed, you should pause to compose yourself and get rid of any anxiety, otherwise the source of your good health may well become damaged.

Rouse and rinse the saliva thirty-six times.

[鼓漱三十六, Gu Shu San Shi Liu]

Rouse and rinse means to gather the saliva within the mouth. The Qi is stimulated during the in and out motions of rinsing. Thirty-six is the number of revolutions. This procedure in effect causes the circulation and stimulation of Qi so that it can penetrate deeply.

---

10 This means to make a clockwise rotation of the tongue.

11 Counterclockwise turning of the tongue.

The method is to use the tongue to stir-up and produce saliva and to accumulate it into a single batch. Then, press it forward as if to spit it out. When it reaches the tip of the tongue this is the completion of issuing the saliva; when reaching the base of the tongue this is the end of withdrawing the saliva. One out [issuing] and one in [withdrawing] is counted as one full cycle. When having completed thirty-six cycles, stop.

Evenly fill the mouth with Divine Water.

[神水滿口匀, Shen Shui Man Kou Yun]
The term *Divine Water* refers to the saliva. With the mouth full of saliva after having performed rousing and rinsing thirty-six times, the saliva becomes a uniform mixture and spreads evenly throughout the mouth. At this time the breath and Qi will also be uniformly spread throughout the body.

Each mouthful is divided into three parts and swallowed.

[一口分三嚥, Yi Kou Fen San Yan]
Each mouthful means the mouth full of saliva. *Three parts and swallowed* means that the mouthful of saliva is divided into three equal parts and swallowed down successively. It is completely unintentional that this is analogous to the Three Powers [三才, San Cai].

When the dragon moves, the tiger naturally flees.

[龍行虎自奔, Long Xing Hu Zi Ben]
The terms *dragon* and *tiger* are metaphors for Yang and Yin energy, respectively. There is no truth to the idea that there is actually a dragon or tiger residing in the body. The dragon referred to in the *dragon moving* is the Spirit within yourself; the tiger referred to in the *tiger flees* is the Qi within yourself.

217

Now, just like collecting the saliva, rousing and rinsing, mixing and dividing, and swallowing down, the results are a fullness of Spirit and Qi, harmony of the Yin and Yang energies, and your entire being united peacefully like Heaven and Earth.

Close the breath and rub the hands until hot;

[閉氣搓手熱, Bi Qi Cuo Shou Re]

Close the breath means that the internal Qi is preserved within and not dissipated externally. *Rub the hands until hot* means, in effect, that the pulses are united during the motions of both hands moving back and forth.

Closing the breath and *rubbing the hands* results in the Qi being collected and the pulses harmonized. Internal impurities can be driven off and external malignant spirits cannot encroach.

On the back, massage the kidneys.

[背摩後精門, Bei Mo Hou Jing Men]

The proper procedure starts, in a seated and cross-legged posture, with the two palms placed together. First, with the left hand on top and the right below, circularly rub in a leftward [counterclockwise] motion twenty-four times. Then both palms change positions, with the right on top and the left below, circularly rub in a rightward [clockwise] motion twenty-four times. This concludes the procedure.

On the back, massage the Essence Gates [精門, Jing Men] means placing the hands behind on the back and massaging the kidney area. After having previously rubbed the hands together forty-eight times or to the point where the hands become very hot, place the hands securely over the Essence Gates. Perform the massaging motions simultaneously with both the right and left hands. Each hand is circled outwards and inwards, twenty-four times.

Entirely exhaust one breath. Afterwards close the hands firmly, just like in the above procedure of the same name, place the back of the hands on the knee areas. The true master of a person is the breath. The explanation given for completely exhausting this one breath is, "to exhaust is to accumulate the Qi within yourself and is called gathering from within."

Imagine the heat aflame at the Navel Wheel.

[想火燒臍輪, Xiang Huo Shao Qi Lun]

To *imagine the heat* means that your own imagination produces the fire—the fire is given imaginary form, but is not real fire.

To *imagine the heat aflame at the Navel Wheel* means that your imagination internally perceives that there is a fire burning below in the Navel Wheel region.

When the Qi [breath] is concentrated, use the mind to contemplate on this fire. Circulate the True Yang by fixing the mind-intent downward into the Dan Tian and on the flame.

This, however, is still not the True Fire [Qi], for people's eyes are incapable of seeing it. Nevertheless, in regards to circulation, the result will be a sustained awareness of warm Qi in the Elixir Field, as if there were a real fire burning. However, when the Field of Elixir is first heated there will be an overanxious attempt to accumulate more, but this will only cause it to dissipate. It can be restored again by "darkening the heart in a seated posture."

Left and right turn the Windlass.

[左右轆轤轉, Zuo You Lu Lu Zhuan]

To *turn the Windlass* is expressed through the hands, arms, and shoulders. First, bend the left arm and then in unison with the shoulder revolve them leftward thirty-six times. Afterwards, the right arm is likewise revolved towards the right thirty-six times.

This circling is the method for mobilizing the blood. After a total seventy-two times on the left and right sides, as before, return to closing the hands firmly and the original seated posture.

Stretch out both feet loosely.

[兩 脚 放 舒 伸, Liang Jiao Fang Shu Shen]
After having performed each of the previous seated exercises, having endured them for a long period of time, the lower limbs can experience tiredness and if they are not readjusted they will certainly become exhausted. For this reason they should be allowed to *stretch out.* The method is to simply uncross the folded legs and let them down, then gradually stretch them out towards the front, straightening them completely.

These exercises should not cause excessive tiredness, but if the legs do become very weary after sitting cross-legged for a long period of time, they must be stretched out. Otherwise the result will be that the veins and arteries of the lower limbs could possibly undergo some sort of injury.

Interlace both hands to support the Void.

[叉 手 雙 虛 托, Cha Shou Shuang Xu Tuo]
Both hands means that the fingers are mutually interlaced, so that all ten fingers are equally separated.

To *support the Void* means, even though the hands do not really raise anything substantial upwards, you imagine as you raise them upwards that emptiness above is being supported.

The correct procedure is to interlace both hands at the level of the chest, with the back of the hands facing heaven. Turn the palms face up when raising them. Make use of some imaginary resistance in supporting. The back of the hands should be directly over the topmost gate [泥 丸, Ni Wan, Muddy Pellet]. After having raised both arms completely, gradually lower them. Each movement, upwards and downwards, is counted as one time. Perform these actions nine times. Then, as before, close the hands firmly and place them on top of the area of the knees.

Repeatedly bend the head over and seize the feet.
[低頭攀足頻, Di Tou Pan Zu Pin]
This is the method for unifying the sinews and arteries of the whole body. This so-called *bending the head over* means it is not enough to just bend the cranium forward, but the entire upper torso must equally be bent forward and down.

Begin by separating the fingers of the hands, extending both arms to the front with the palms facing one another. Gradually bend the torso downwards.

Wait for the spiritual water to arrive.
[以候神水至, Yi Hou Shen Shui Zhi]
Both hands follow down along the sides of the legs while simultaneously drawing the feet back and inwards, then seize the bottoms of the feet [湧泉, Yong Quan cavities]—pause momentarily.

Next, using the head and Tail Gateway [尾閭, Wei Lu] in conjunction, slowly rise and withdraw to an upright position, finishing on line with one another.

One bowing-like motion and one rising action constitutes one gesture. Perform this gesture a total of twelve times and then rest momentarily.

Repeat rinsing and repeat swallowing.
[再漱再嚥吞, Zai Shu Zai Yan Tun]
Just like the previous method of the *Red Dragon stirs the saliva*, use the tongue to excite and stir-up the saliva until the mouth

is full. Accumulate the saliva and then repeat the method of rousing and rinsing, and swallowing it down.

Dividing it into a total of three parts.

[如此三度畢, Ru Ci San Du Bi]

The meaning of *one time* is to rouse and rinse thirty-six times each, then swallow the saliva in three parts. Repeat this process three times, rousing and rinsing one hundred and eight times total and swallowing nine times total.

Altogether swallow the Spiritual Water nine times.

[神水九次吞, Shen Shui Jiu Zi Tun]

In performing the previous method three times, *swallowing the spiritual water nine times* symbolizes the Four Seasons [四時, Si Shi] and Five Elements [五行, Wu Xing]. This is the reason for the number nine.

Swallow it down with the sound of gu gu.

[嚥下汩汩響, Yan Xia Gu Gu Xiang]

By what means can the saliva produce a divine sound? Through the rousing of the Qi. As water by itself cannot of its own accord make waves, it needs the wind to do this. At the time of swallowing the saliva, you must make the *sound of "gu gu."* Why? Because through the rousing of the saliva this sound is produced, the Spirit and Qi will thereby influence the saliva. Likewise, the Spirit and Qi will be brought to fullness. From the ears above to the Elixir Field below, and throughout all in between, the Spirit and Qi will circulate everywhere and the mind itself will likewise settle.

Then the hundred pulses will be naturally harmonized.

[百脉自調匀, Bai Mo Zi Tiao Yun]

The source of the *hundred pulses* is in the blood and Qi, of which the Spirit is the true master. If the Spirit is not tranquil, the blood and Qi will most certainly be injured. If the blood and Qi are injured, the hundred pulses cannot be harmonized. If the hundred pulses are not harmonized, the entire body is weakened and death awaits in secret ambush.

Complete the motion of the River Cart.

[河車搬運訖, He Che Ban Yun Qi]

If you are able to perform the previous methods correctly, the Spirit and Qi will then circulate throughout the entire body. The blood will naturally follow and circulate without obstruction. The hundred bones[12] will also acquire good health if the hundred pulses are naturally harmonized. Therefore, the stanza, *then the one hundred pulses will be naturally harmonized.*

The meaning of the *River Cart*[13] is that in Daoism you seek the refinement of True Mercury [真汞, Zhen Gong]—True Mercury is a representation of water. Hence, this explanation gives a more subtle meaning to the term *divine water.*

The meaning of *the motion* of this is, in application, like that of "drifting with the current in a row boat."

Each of the previous methods, *Rouse and Rinse* and *swallowing the saliva,* are the initial catalysts for this method. The reasons then for the expressions *excite the saliva, rouse* and *rinse,* and *swallow the saliva* are so that afterwards the Jing, Qi, and

---

12   The use of the terms the *hundred bones* and *pulses* is to denote all the bones and pulses, not that there are exactly one hundred.

13   *River Cart* is a term referring to circulating the elixir up the spine (Du Mai) and down the front of the body (Ren Mai).

Shen will circulate throughout the entire body and through each of the hundred pulses, thereby completely restoring the Primordial Qi [元氣, Yuan Qi], Stabilizing the Mind [心定, Xin Ding], and Quieting the Spirit [神寧, Shen Ning].

The term *complete* means that the Spirit and Qi are directed to circulate one complete orbit [周天, Zhou Tian].

Direct the fire to circulate and heat the entire body.

[發火偏燒身, Fa Huo Bian Shao Shen]

The *fire* is only an imaginary form of fire, void of any true external appearance, and the fire internally is likewise formless—this is Pure Yang True Fire [純陽眞火, Chun Yang Zhen Huo].

To *heat the body* means the Pure Yang True Fire penetrates entirely into each region of the body, which is brought about through the disciplining of your senses. This is a matter of directing the imagination within, in order that the Pure Yang True Fire can be produced to naturally heat the body. This is called, "forgetting your own form" [忘形, Wang Xing].

My master once told me long ago that "learning the Dao does not lie in just making the body hot. But if we can speak of the imagination heating the body, then we can get to what is called, 'forgetting your own form.'"

There are heterodox schools of thought which have this false view and so do not practice correctly. Therefore, I purposely present this correct view to all those of the various other schools so that this secret doctrine will not be misinterpreted and cause them to enter upon a divergent path.

Not Venturing Too Close to Evil Influences.

[邪魔不敢近, Xie Mo Bu Gan Jin]

The term *evil influences* does not necessarily mean hobgoblins and sprites, because first of all there is a saying, "The lot of all the mortals in your environment are quite sufficient enough to injure your body and mind." We merely expediently call it evil influences or malignant spirits. However, if you are able to discipline yourself according to the above procedures, these will surely result in a natural way of warding off harmful influences.

Do Not Become Muddled Even When Sleeping and Dreaming.

[夢寐不能昏, Meng Mei Bu Neng Hun]

Dreams are a constant cycle of false thinking, which is more than adequate in regards to confusing your spirit. But if you were to learn to control your mind, naturally dreams would vanish, making the spirit free of all confusion.

Heat and Cold Are Unable to Enter.

[寒暑不能久, Han Shu Bu Neng Jiu]

Cold and heat are external influences. In people, heat usually results in perspiration, and cold, in shaking. If these occur, it means that external influences have not yet been done away with and you have yet to discipline yourself. Through discipline, over a long period of time, with these elemental skills [行功, Xing Gong], the body will become stronger and more energetic. The mind will become peaceful and the spirit tranquil, the internal harmful influences driven off and the external influences cannot affect you—all with the result that *cold and heat will be incapable of having any influence on you.*

Pestilence and Illnesses Cannot Encroach.

[災病不能侵, Zai Bing Bu Neng Qin]

Pestilence comes from the arising of internal impurities, whereby external harmful influences can then appear. The source of these truly begin within the mind and are caused by the deep influences of the external senses, namely the Seven Passions and Six Desires.[14] It is because of these that disease can avail itself. *Sickness* also avails itself through internal tensions and anxieties created by the passions and of the desires of the stomach and mouth, which are bound by a sense of satisfaction—these also bring about illnesses.

But all types of illness begin with and depend upon the individual. Supposing these exercises are practiced for a long time, then all the muscles will be unaffected by cold and heat. However, if emotional lust for gain and profit still exists, then the result will be disease—all because of improper living habits.

Practice After Zi and Before Wu.

[子後午前作, Zi Hou Wu Qian Zuo]

When Zi [子] passes, Yang arises; when Wu [午] passes, Yin arises. *After midnight and before noon,* these are the proper times for the intercourse between Yin and Yang, because at these times you can begin to clearly distinguish between the pure and turbid.

The practice of these skills should be done at these times, for it should be considered as though resembling very intimate friends enjoining. Accordingly, when the Qi and Spirit intertwine within yourself it is then easy to obtain the function of the Dao.

---

14   Seven Emotions (七情, Qi Qing) and Six Sense-Desires (六慾, Liu Yu).

Initiate the Transformation by Uniting Qian and Kun.

[造化合乾坤, Zao Hua He Qian Kun]

Qian [乾] and *Kun* [坤] are the images of Heaven and Earth. In the beginning these two cosmic forces, Yin and Yang, were separate. This is why it is said, "after midnight and before noon," as these are the best times for practicing these skills. Creating a harmony between Heaven and Earth is the principle for engaging peace, and these time periods are the superior times for bringing harmony between the body and mind.

Revolve the Required Times Like Connecting the Rings of a Bracelet.

[連環次第轉, Lian Huan Zi Di Zhuan]

Connected together means to go full circle and return to the original position. *Cyclic arrangement* refers to the idea of something that is chronological and without interruption. This is what is said of people who practice these skills according to "after midnight and before noon." Moreover, after a time, join the exercises together so that every day you connect them to complete six rounds. The mind will then become ruler of the body, calm and composed.

Reversions and Revolutions Are With Excellent Reason.

[還返是良因, Huan Fan Shi Liang Yin]

Reversions and Revolutions are referring to the Three Restorations [三還, San Huan] and Nine Revolutions [九返, Jiu Fan]. In Daoism, the subtleties of the Dao are in the refinement of the elixir, and in Buddhism in youthfulness and long-life

There is is a reference to this type of kung fu. Because all the Ten Thousand Things have an effect, but first they must have a cause. Acquiring a good effect comes from having a good cause; a bad cause brings about a bad result. This is the principle of a cyclic arrangement, which is an expression of righteousness. Therefore, diligent practice of these skills will bring about youthfulness and long life, and the way to immortality—both come about from this cyclic arrangement.

Excellent reasoning, in regards to these skills, acts as substantial proof of the fundamentals of the Dao. How did other masters awaken to the Dao? What was their initial method? These are questions that I asked myself in the beginning. The Dao of strengthening the body is the origin of long life. Even though I do not consider myself an immortal, I have lived for nearly 250 years and have not experienced the ill effects of old age, disease, and death because I adhered to the practice of these skills.

The Methods of Walking, Moving, Sitting, and Lying Down

[行動坐臥亦當有法, Xing Dong Zuo Wo Yi Dang You Fa]

The movement and actions of people should be regular. Sitting and lying down should have regular timing. If we sit and lie down irregularly without right timing, this is not the healthy way. Everyone knows and talks about this. However, walking, sitting, and lying down all have their certain rules. Follow the rules, then life can be prolonged. To go against these rules will shorten life. But these are not things ordinary people would know about. We see turtles and cranes often, and when talking about their ages, we always call them a "thousand-year-old turtle" and a "thousand-year-old crane." This shows that everyone knows that they are long-lived. But the reasons they can live for so long, are rarely discussed. Turtles are reptiles and cranes are birds, but, why is their lifespan longer then a human's, and what are the reasons of this? I will explain it roughly and so everyone can understand. Turtles have a heavy shell. It moves pretty slowly and sluggishly. When it is in a hiding position, it withdraws its six body parts [head, four legs, and tail] into its shell. Concealing, quiet and motionless, even if there is a foreign matter to offend it, it will keep still, not feeling angry and not moving. It keeps to its hiding position, as quiet as before [the offensive action]. These are the signs of its Qi being clear and its Spirit peaceful.

This is why turtles can live longer. After a long walk or hard work, when we are sitting and resting, we should follow the principles of a turtle's quiet hiding position. Do not bring about any distracting thoughts, even if we are distracted. Don't get angry and don't move, then the mind will be peaceful, the

Spirit will be stable, and the Qi will be clear. These are the signs for achieving longevity.

Cranes live among the quiet and secluded mountains, pecking the tuckahoes[15] and ginseng flowers for food. This is what enables its Qi to be clear. Also, its actions show signs of longevity. When other birds walk on the land, they do not lift their feet and just dash forward, and their whole body is shaking. Only the crane does not act in this way. When the crane walks, it lift its foot first and opens its claws, keeps the head high and looks up when moving forward. Right before the foot touches the ground, it withdraws its claws and puts its foot down to the ground, lowers its head and then looks down naturally. Because the crane lifts up its foot and opens its claws, it can make the mind calm and step steady. Keeping the head high and looking up, lowering the head and looking down are to manage the Qi and to smooth the meridians. When the mind is calm, the Qi is regulated, and the meridians are smooth, then the life will be long.

Among other birds, only pigeons act similar to cranes, and this is why although the lifespan of the pigeon is shorter than the crane, it is still longer than other birds. So I say, "People should learn the way that cranes and pigeons walk." Dogs are animals, but when a dog is lying on the ground, it knows to lay its body on its side, stretch the front feet, bend its back feet, and straighten its neck. By doing these movements, the internal organs will be stretched, the meridians will operate smoothly, the circulation of Qi and blood will be without obstacles. The Qi can circulate well when it is clear. When the Qi is clear, the Spirit will be calm. When the Spirit is calm, then the mind will be stable. In this way, when falling asleep, there will be no

---

15   *Tuckahoes* are the underground roots of a ginseng plant.

interference from external matters. This is one of the points. The dog's character is also very alert, and keeps its alertness while sleeping. So even if it just hears a tiny noise, it would get up and bark right away.

When people sleep soundly, it is often as if they are dead, and this allows the Six Thieves[16] to invade. Because of sleeping so soundly, people can have nightmares, which will likely cause them to get sick. So we should lie as a dog lies and learn the dog's alertness while sleeping. But it not to actually learn to be like a dog, getting up and barking as soon as hearing a tiny noise. Everyone should keep these words in mind: *sit like a turtle, walk like a crane, lie down like a dog.* Actively follow these methods, then longevity is a sure thing.

---

16   *Six Thieves* (六 賊, Da Zei) refers to eyes, ears, nose, tongue, body and mind.

A Summary of Names for Acupuncture Points and Meridians of the Entire Body

[全身關竅脉絡總名, Quan Shen Guan Qiao Mo Luo Zong Ming]

[The Eight Extraordinary Meridians]

The *Book of Changes* [易經, *Yi Jing*] says, "Qian and Kun can be regarded as the gateway of the *Book of Changes.*" The Qian [乾] is Yang. It's an odd number when it rests in a circle. When it moves, it is straight, so it creates Great Production [大生, Da Sheng]. The Kun [坤] is Yin. It's an even number. When it rests, it is closed and capacious. When it moves, it opens up, so it creates Wide Production [廣生, Guang Sheng].

Ziyang Zhenren[17] said, "What is the Gateway of the Mysterious Female [玄牝, Xuan Pin]? This is rarely understood."

Daoguang [18] annotated *Mysterious* and *Female* as being two different things, saying, "How can these be regarded as one aperture? Without these two distinct things, how can the myriad of things and transformations be created?"

Ziye [子野] annotated, "The place of access and contacts, the Earthly intersection of Yin and Yang, this is the Gate of the Mysterious [玄門, Xuan Men] and the Door of the Female.[19] Kunlun [the brain] and Heavenly Root [天根, Tian Gen] both mean Gate of the Mysterious. The Flower Pool [華池, Hua Chi], the Bend in the River [曲江, Qu Jiang], the Fallen Moon Stove [偃月爐, Yan Yue Lu] all mean the Door of the Female. People think the mouth is the Mysterious and the Female respectively. People also think the

---

17   Ziyang Zhenren (紫陽眞人) is Zhang Boduan (張伯端, 984–1092 CE).

18   Daoguang (道光, 1078–1191 CE).

19   Door of the Female (牝戶, Pin Hu), vaginal opening.

aperture between the two kidneys is the Mysterious Female. Both are wrong. In front of the kidneys and behind the umbilicus [navel], at a little more than three inches [between them], is the Supreme Center of the Ultimate [太中極, Tai Zhong Ji], also known as the Golden Embryo Spirit Chamber [金胎神室, Jin Tai Shen Shi], Original Barrier [關元, Guan Yuan], Ocean of Qi [氣海, Qi Hai], Collecting Yin [會陰, Hui Yin], and the Constant Strength [長強, Chang Qiang].

At the end of the Ren Mai and Du Mai [Qi meridians], the left side belongs to liver, color blue; the right side belongs to the lungs, color white; the upper side belongs to the heart, color red; the lower side belongs to kidneys, color black; the middle part belongs to spleen and stomach, color yellow. The Yang Preserver [陽維, Yang Wei] is in front of the Topmost Gate [20] by one inch and three fen.[21] The Yin Preserver [陰維, Yin Wei] is in back of the Topmost Gate by one inch and three fen. The Thoroughfare Meridian[22] starts in the Tiger Wind Cavity [風虎穴, Feng Hu Xue, an acupuncture point] towards the pubic hair by one inch and two fen, and the Belt Meridian [帶脉, Dai Mai] is on both sides of the navel. It is like a waistband.

The Ren Meridian [任脉, Ren Mai] starts at the Central Mortal [人中, Ren Zhong, base of the pubic bone], descending and stopping at the Collecting Yin [會陰, Hui Yin, perineum].

The Du Meridian [督脉, Du Mai] starts at the Tail Gateway [尾閭, Wei Lu, tailbone area], runs upwards to the Muddy Pellet

---

[20]   Topmost Gate (頂門, Ding Men) is the Muddy Pellet (泥丸, Ni Wan), top of the head.

[21]   One fen is equal to 0.13 inches.

[22]   Thoroughfare Meridian (衝脉, Chong Mai), sometimes called the Thrusting Channel.

[泥丸, Ni Wan] and stops at the intersection of the teeth and gums.[23] The Strong Yang [陽蹻, Yang Qiao] is at the second bone behind the Tail Gateway. The Strong Yin [陰蹻, Yin Qiao] is in front of the Grain of Dao [穀道, Gu Dao, anus] for about one inch and two fen from the Strong Yang.

Among the Eight Extraordinary Meridians [八脈, Ba Mai], when the Strong Yin moves, the whole body will then move. The Ren Meridian and Du Meridian are the commanders of the Yin and Yang in the human body. The Ren Meridian is the central control of the Yin Meridians of the whole body. It starts at the Assembly of Yin [會陰, Hui Yin], then to the Bent Bone [曲骨, Qu Gu], Central Ultimate [中極, Zhong Ji], Original Barrier [關元, Guan Yuan], Stone Gate [石門, Shi Men], Ocean of Qi [氣海, Qi Hai], Intertwined Yin [陰交, Yin Jiao], Spirit Watchtower [神闕, Shen Que], Divided Water [水分, Shui Fen], Lower Wrist [下腕, Xia Wan], Established Village [建里, Jian Li], Middle Wrist [中腕, Zhong Wan], Upper Wrist [上腕, Shang Wan], Large Watchtower [巨闕, Ju Que], Turtledove Tail [鳩尾, Jiu Wei], Central Room [中庭, Zhong Ting], Central Flock of Goats [膻中, Shan Zhong], Jade Hall [玉堂, Yu Tang], Purple Hall [紫宮, Zi Gong], Flower Umbrella [華蓋, Hua Gai], Jade Pearl [璇璣, Xuan Ji], Protruding Heaven [天突, Tian Tu], Side Stream [廉泉, Lian Quan], Holding Serum [承漿, Cheng Jiang], then enters and stops at Central Mortal [人中, Ren Zhong].

Up to the hairline, there are a total of twenty-four acupuncture points. *Ren* [任] means to conceive [姙, to become pregnant], because it encircles the abdomen.

---

23   *Intersection of the teeth and gums* (齒交齦, Chi Jiao Ken). This is actually the Intersecting Yin Cavity (齦交穴, Yin Jiao Xue).

[The Importance of the Du Meridian]

Therefore, the reason Tortoise Breathing [龜息, Gui Xi] is received through the nose, is so the Crane Breathing [鶴息, He Xi] can nourish the embryo [胎, Tai], and so these [two breaths] can extend the lifespan. The meridians are all connected to the Du [督] Yang Meridian [陽脉], and so this foremost Du Meridian leads to the Ocean of Yang [海陽] Meridians. It begins from Lower Ultimate [下極, Xia Ji], ascends to Double Spine [夾脊, Jia Ji], goes to the Strong Elder [長強, Chang Qiang], then to the Vital Point [要腧, Yao Shu], Essence Gate [精門, Jing Men], Yang Barrier [陽關, Yang Guan], Gate of Life [命門, Ming Men], Mysterious Pillar [玄柱, Xuan Zhu], Central Spine [脊中, Ji Zhong], Central Pivot [中樞, Zhong Shu], Highest Yang [至陽, Zhi Yang], Binding Sinews [筋束, Jin Shu], Spiritual Terrace [靈臺, Ling Tai], Spirit Way [神道, Shen Dao], Spirit Pillar [神柱, Shen Zhu], Kiln of Dao [陶道, Tao Dao], Great Push [大推, Da Tui], Second Gate [亞門, Ya Men], Wind Mansion [風府, Feng Fu], Door of the Brain [腦戶, Nao Hu], Powerful Room [強間, Qiang Jian], Behind the Top [後頂, Hou Ding], One Hundred Assemblies [百會, Bai Hui], Front of the Top [前頂, Qian Ding], Assembly Chief [總會, Zong Hui], Highest Star [上星, Shang Xing], Spirit Chamber [神庭, Shen Ting], and then goes down to Plain Glue [素膠, Su Liao], Water Ravine [水溝, Shui Gou], and arrives at the Origin of the Valley [兌端, Dui Duan] and to the gums [齦, Ken], going through thirty acupoints.

The Du Meridian is the Governor [督] and it runs along inside the back, just like a running deer lifting its tail, and operates the Tail Gateway. This causes Essence to Revert and Repair the Brain [還精補腦, Huan Jing Bu Nao]. Therefore it is foremost in increasing the lifespan, because the Du Meridian is directly connected [to the Tail Gateway].

[Palaces of the Body]

The Palace of the Heart [心宮, Xin Gong] is the Master Ruler [君主, Jun Zhu]. Spiritual Illumination [神明, Shen Ming] is generated from here. It is the Supreme Yang [太陽, Tai Yang] among Yang and its most vigorous time is in summer. It has sufficient blood, but insufficient Qi. The blood and Qi flow into it during the hours of 11:00 a.m. to 1:00 p.m.

The Palace of the Lungs [肺宮, Fei Gong] are the Oral Transmitters [相傳, Xiang Zhuan]. They manage the Qi and regulate all the sections of the body. They are the Supreme Yin [太陰, Tai Yin] of Yin and their most vigorous time is during the autumn. They have sufficient Qi, but insufficient blood. The blood and Qi flow into them during the hours of 3:00 a.m. to 5:00 a.m.

The Palace of the Liver [肝宮, Gan Gong] is the Military General [將軍, Jiang Jun]. Scheming thoughts are expressed from here. It is Young Yang [少陽, Shao Yang] and is the most vigorous during the spring. The blood and the Qi flow into it during the hours of 1:00 a.m. to 3:00 a.m.

The Palace of the Spleen and Stomach [脾胃宮, Pi Wei Gong] are like the Public Granary [倉稟, Cang Bing]. The five flavors and nutrition rely on their functions to digest, absorb, and transport. These are Foremost Yin [至陰, Zhi Yin], and are connected to the Earth Qi. They have sufficient Qi, but insufficient blood. The blood and the Qi flow into the spleen during the hours of 9:00 a.m. to 11:00 a.m., and flows into the stomach during 7:00 a.m. to 9:00 a.m.

The Palace of the Gallbladder [膽宮, Dan Gong] is the Central Regulator [中正, Zhong Zheng]. Judgements and decisions come from here. It belongs to Young Yin [少陰, Shao Yin], the Kidney Meridian and appended to the Liver Meridian. It has sufficient Qi, but insufficient blood. The blood and Qi flow into here during the hours of 11:00 p.m. to 1:00 a.m.

The Palace in the Chest Center [膻中宮, Dan Zhong Gong] is like an Ambassador [使臣, Shi Chen]. Goodness and joy come from here. It belongs to the Pericardium [厥陰, Jue Yin] Meridian in the heart of the hand. It has sufficient blood, but insufficient Qi. The blood and Qi flow into here during the hours of 7:00 p.m. to 9:00 p.m.

The Palace of the Large Intestine [大腸宮, Da Chang Gong] is the Conveyor [傳導, Zhuan Dao]. It can convey the dregs of food and make it change into feces and move out from the body. It belongs to the Bright Yang [陽明, Yang Ming] Meridian of the hand. It has sufficient blood and Qi. The blood and the Qi flow into it during the hours of 5:00 a.m. to 7:00 a.m.

The Palace of the Small Intestine [小腸宮, Xiao Chang Gong] is like a Receptor [受盛, Shou Sheng]. It receives the food coming downwards from the stomach, absorbs its essences, then assigns them to the various organs. It belongs to the Supreme Yang [太陽, Tai Yang] Meridian of the hand. It has sufficient blood, but insufficient Qi. The blood and Qi flow into it during the hours of 1:00 p.m. to 3:00 p.m.

The Palace of the Kidneys [腎宮, Shen Gong] are like Soldiers [作強, Zuo Jiang]. They deliver strength and a variety of skills. They are centered on Young Yin [少陰, Shao Yin]. Their most vigorous time is in winter. They have sufficient blood, but insufficient

237

Qi. The blood and Qi flow into them during the hours of 5:00 p.m. to 7:00 p.m.

In the Palace of the Triple Warmer [三焦, San Jiao] is the Watercourse Way [水道, Shui Dao]. Its function is to clean out the waterways. It belongs to the Young Yin [少陰, Shao Yin] Kidney Meridian. It has sufficient blood, but insufficient Qi. The blood and Qi flow into it during the hours of 9:00 p.m. to 11:00 p.m.

The Palace of the Bladder [膀胱宮, Pang Guang Gong] is like a Reservoir. It stores up body fluids and through transformation of the Qi it then excretes the body fluids. It is the Supreme Gateway [太閭, Tai Lu] cavity of the foot.

[The Nine Pathways]

The Confucians call this *The Nine Bright Crooks of a Pearl*. The Buddhists call it *The Nine Balanced Iron Drum*. The Daoists call it *The Nine Bends of the Yellow River*.[24] All of these proclaim the right path to transport the Qi to the top of the head. People who study the Dao have to open the Tail Gateway first. If this point is not open, the Qi of Yin and Yang cannot move up or down, and the Qi of the Spirit cannot flow—but this is still a long way from the Dao.

---

24 *The Nine Bright Crooks of a Pearl* (九曲明珠, Jiu Qu Ming Zhu) refers to a pearl with a string hole that bends or curves nine times. *The Nine Balanced Iron Drum* (九重鐵鼓, Jiu Zhong Tie Gu), the drum is balanced on nine legs. *The Nine Bends of the Yellow River* (九曲黃河, Jiu Qu Huang He).

[The Importance of Marrow]

All marrows belong to the brain, from the top of the head, the Muddy Pellet, and down to the Tail Gateway. The kidneys are the master of the bones, and bones produce marrow.

[The Three Bodily Function Regulatory Points]

The Central Chest [膻中, Dan Zhong] is midpoint between the two nipples, it is a reservoir of Qi, distributing Yin and Yang, and is the source of the vital functions, so it is also called the Ocean of Qi [氣海, Qi Hai].

The Diaphragm [隔膜, Ge Mo] is under the lungs. It is connected around the flank and lateral regions of the abdomen. It acts like a membrane to block the dirty Qi from fumigating the upper part of the Triple Warmer.

The Secret Gate [幽門, You Men] is within the large intestine. The body fluid seeps into the bladder, the dregs get into the large intestine, changes to feces, and moves out of the body.

[Hours of Qi Movement in the Body]

The following lists the hours of Qi movement in the body with their corresponding *Book of Changes* [易經, Yi Jing] image[25] and Qi center.

---

25   In the *Zhou Yi Cantongqi* (周易參同契) by Wei Boyang (魏伯陽) appears the construct and explanation of what are called the "Twelve Sovereign Images (辟卦, Bi Gua)." These hexagram images, as Wei Boyang relates, are associated with the movements of the sun and moon throughout the year, and he likewise illustrates that there are six trigram images relating to the days within a month showing the ascent and descent of the sun and moon. Herein, Li is relating the hexagrams associated with the movement times of Qi within the human body.

During the day [24-hour cycle], the Qi in humans moves as follows:[26]

#24
Returning

From 11:00 p.m. to 1:00 a.m., the Returning Qi [復氣, Fu Qi] is at the Tail Gateway [尾閭, Wei Lu, inside of the tailbone and up 2.5 inches].

#19
Approaching

From 1:00 a.m. to 3:00 a.m., the Approaching Qi [臨氣, Ling Qi] runs to the Spiritual Hall [神堂, Shen Tang, the cavity between the two kidneys, the Gate of Life].

#11
Peacefulness

From 3:00 a.m. to 5:00 a.m., the Peacefulness Qi [泰氣, Tai Qi] runs to the Mysterious Pivot [玄樞, Xuan Shu, equal distance between the kidneys and the Spine Handle].

#34
Great Strength

From 5:00 a.m. to 7:00 a.m., the Great Strength Qi [大壯氣, Da Zhuang Qi] runs to the Spine Handle [夾脊, Jia Ji, middle of the spine].

#43
Decision

From 7:00 a.m. to 9:00 a.m., the Decision Qi [夬氣] runs to the Kiln of Dao [陶道, Tao Dao, upper-most vertebra of the spine].

#1
Creativity
of Heaven

From 9:00 a.m. to 11:00 a.m., the Creativity of Heaven Qi [乾氣, Qian Qi] runs to the Jade Pillow [玉枕, Yu Zhen, the occiput].

---

26   The twelve hexagram images and the drawing of the *Three on the Front, Three on the Back* were added for this edition.

#44
Pairing

From 11:00 a.m. to 1:00 p.m., the Pairing Qi [姤氣 Gou Qi] runs to the Muddy Pellet [泥丸, Ni Wan, top of the head].

#33
Retreating

From 1:00 p.m. to 3:00 p.m., the Retreating Qi [遯氣, Dun Qi] runs to the Illuminated Hall [明堂, Ming Tang, midpoint between the eyes].

#12
Adversity

From 3:00 p.m. to 5:00 p.m., the Adversity Qi [否氣, Pi Qi] runs to the Central Chest [膻中, Dan Zhong, midpoint between the two nipples].

#20
Contemplation

From 5:00 p.m. to 7:00 p.m., the Contemplation Qi [觀氣, Guan Qi] runs to the Middle Wrist [中腕, Zhong Wan].

#23
Removing

From 7:00 p.m. to 9:00 p.m., the Removing Qi [剝氣, Bo Qi] runs to the Spiritual Pass [神關, Shen Guan, navel].

#2
Receptivity
of Earth

From 9:00 p.m. to 11:00 p.m., the Receptivity of Earth Qi [坤氣, Kun Qi] runs to the Ocean of Qi [氣海, Qi Hai, below the navel].

[Three on the Front, Three on the Back]

The *Three Passes on the Front* [前三關, Qian San Guan] are:

The Upper Pass [上關, Shang Guan], the Muddy Pellet [泥丸, Ni Wan]. It is the aperture of the source of the heart and the Sea of Original Nature [源性, Yuan Xing].

The Middle Pass [中關, Zhong Guan], the Yellow Court [黃庭, Huang Ting]. It is the aperture of the correct position and the central yellow.

The Lower Pass [下關, Xia Guan], the Crystal Water Palace [水晶宮, Shui Jing Gong]. It means the aperture of the Elixir Field [丹田, Dan Tian] and Ocean of Qi [氣海, Qi Hai].

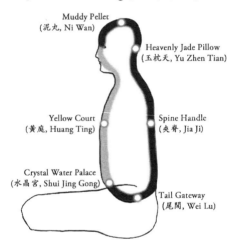

Muddy Pellet
(泥丸, Ni Wan)

Heavenly Jade Pillow
(玉枕天, Yu Zhen Tian)

Yellow Court
(黃庭, Huang Ting)

Spine Handle
(夾脊, Jia Ji)

Crystal Water Palace
(水晶宮, Shui Jing Gong)

Tail Gateway
(尾閭, Wei Lu)

The *Three Passes on the Back* [後三關, Hou San Guan] are:

The Lower Pass [下關, Xia Guan] is the Tail Gateway [尾閭, Wei Lu]. It is the aperture of the Du Meridian, Supreme Mystery [太玄, Tai Xuan].

The Middle Pass [中關, Zhong Guan] is the Spine Handle [夾脊, Jia Ji]. It is the aperture of the Life Gate [命門, Ming Men] and Double Pass [雙關, Shuang Guan].

The Upper Pass [上關, Shang Guan] is the Heavenly Jade Pillow [玉枕天, Yu Zhen Tian]. It is the aperture of the Valley of the Muddy Pellet [谷泥丸, Gu Ni Wan].

[The Ancestral Cavities]
Life up to the singular sound of crying out at the moment of birth is called *Before Heaven* [先天, Xian Tian, prenatal], everything after the umbilical cord is cut is After Heaven [後天, Hou Tian, postnatal]. Heaven's Destiny and True Nature are attached to the ancestral cavities. They reside in the two eyes during the day and hide in the Muddy Pellet. They reside in the two kidneys during the night and are stored up in the Elixir Cauldron [丹鼎, Dan Ding, another name for the Lower Elixir Field].

[Three Gates]
So the Manipura[27] is called the Gate of Birth [生門, Sheng Men]. Between the two kidneys is the Gate of Life [命門, Ming Men]. Below the navel, one inch and two fen, it is the lower Elixir Field. At one inch and five fen, it is called the Original Pass [元關, Yuan Guan] and Ocean of Qi [氣海, Qi Hai].

[Nine Qi Apertures]
The top of the head is Mt. Sumeru [須彌, Xu Mi]. In the head there are Nine Palaces [九宮, Jiu Gong], the center of which is the Muddy Pellet, and becomes the Green Woman [青女. Qing Nu]. The mouth is the Elixir Pool [丹池, Dan Chi]. There are two throats, the left side is the esophagus, the right side is the trachea, and these are part of the Twelve Storied Pagoda [重樓, Chong Lou]. The heart aperture is the Bright Palace [絳宮, Jiang

---

27   Manipura (Sanskrit), third chakra in Hindu Yoga, the solar plexus region.

Gong]. The eyes are the Eyes of the Loins [腰眼, Yao Yan], called the Secret House [密户, Mi Hu], also called the Inner Kidneys [内肾, Nei Shen]. The anus [糞門, Fen Men] is the Grain Path [穀道, Gu Dao]. In the front [of the body], there is the Jade Stove Cavity [玉爐穴, Yu Lu Xue, another name for the Ocean of Qi]. The Yang becomes the Heavenly Root [天根, Tian Gen, penis], and the Yin becomes the Moon Cave [月窟, Yue Ku, vagina].

[Orifices]

There are two orifices [in the genitals]. The top one is the water orifice, and the lower one is the route for Essence[28] and from where the blood arrives and departs. There is also the Stone of Supporting Root-Power[29] and the two short leaves of the West River,[30] and this is the orifice for the sword [the penis]. It is the Gate of Birth, but if going too deep into it, it then becomes the Gate of Death. The Upper Magpie Bridge[31] means the tongue; the Lower Magpie Bridge means the Jade Stem.[32] The backbone [spine] has twenty-four sections and is called the Milky Way [銀河, Yin He]. The center of soles [on the feet] are called the Bubbling Well [湧泉, Yong Quan].

---

28 Essence (精, Jing) refers to male's semen and female's secretions.

29 Stone of Supporting Root-Power (支機石, Zhi Ji Shi), refers to the clitoris.

30 West River (西江, Xi Jing), refers to the labia minora.

31 Upper Magpie Bridge (上鵲橋, Shang Que Qiao), a symbolic bridge formed by magpie birds.

32 Lower Magpie Bridge (下鵲橋, Xia Que Qiao) and Jade Stem (玉莖, Yu Jing) refer to the penis.

The Diagram of Human Body Acupoints [33]

泥丸: Niwan [Muddy Pellet]

天庭: Tianting [Heavenly Court]

明堂: Mingtang [Illuminated Hall]

山根: Shangen [Base of the Mountain]

準頭: Zhuntou [The Head of Certainty]

上丹田: Shangdantian [Upper Elixir Field]

中丹田: Zhongdantian [Middle Elixir Field]

神關: Shenguan [Spiritual Pass]

---

[33]   This section appeared in the back of Yang Sen's book, but it fits here. The image was edited to include Pinyin and English.

Please note the difference in the locations of the Upper, Middle, and Lower Elixir Fields. In most Internal Alchemy (內丹, Nei Dan, Internal Elixir) works, the Upper Elixir Field is located in the Third Eye region of the head and is usually termed as the Mysterious Pass (玄關, Xuan Guan) or Upper Yellow Court. The Middle Elixir Field is located in the solar plexus region of the chest and is usually referred to as the Bright Palace (炯宮, Jiong Gong) or Middle Yellow Court. The Lower Elixir Field is located behind the navel in the abdomen and is usually referred to as the Gate of Life (命門, Ming Men) or Lower Yellow Court.

The illustration used here comes from the Physician's School of acupuncture (外丹, Wai Dan, External Elixir), what is now called Medical Qigong. Here, the Upper Elixir Field is located in the middle of the breast, the middle in the solar plexus, and the lower is three inches beneath the navel. The difference between these Internal and External systems is that in the External Elixir School, the qi points and qi meridians are those which are active in every human body. The Internal Alchemy school is referring to those areas that a person opens up through the cultivation of "Refining the Three Treasures" of Essence (Jing), Vital-Energy (Qi), and Shen (Spirit).

下丹田: Xiadantian [Lower Elixir Field]

玉枕: Yuzhen [Jade Pillow]

命門: Mingmen [Gate of Life]

尾閭: Weilu [Tailbone Gateway]

湧泉穴: Yongquan Xue [Bubbling Well Points]

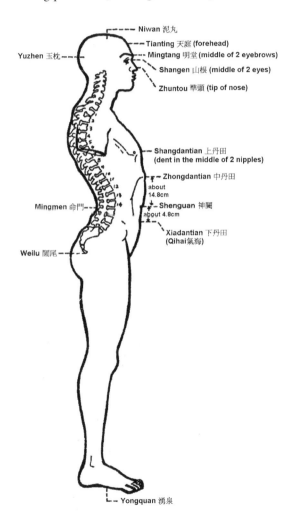

Part Three
The Way of Achieving the Dao

[達道章, Da Dao Zhang]

Someone asked Li Qingyun, "Regarding the root-power [1] of the Great Dao, are we possibly at the end of anyone achieving it? Is there still something we are lacking?"

Li Qingyun said, with a sigh, "In the past, Confucius asked Laozi, 'What is the Dao?' Laozi responded, 'Dao is very difficult to be put in plain language.' Some have asked me for a brief or rough explanation of Dao. Without understanding the true meaning of Dao, it's difficult to express this in words. I have quoted the old philosophers' conversations, as one of the many examples. These are hints of the answer. Presently, you have now asked me for the meaning of Dao, so I would like to explain it with the words of the ancient philosophers."

---

[1]   *Root-power* (機勢, Ji Shi) is a term used to describe the very energy behind everything in the universe, the Great Dao.

Huainanzi [2] [淮南子]

So Dao supports Heaven, carries Earth, extends into
all the Four Directions, and reaches the Eight Poles.
It is too high to be reached, too deep to be measured.
It covers the whole universe, creating everything from
nothing. It springs from the source like a fountain; it is
weak at the beginning and then becomes plentiful and
strong, flowing torrentially and turning clear from
turbid. Hence, when standing up, Dao can bridge the
space between Heaven and Earth; when lying down,
Dao can suffuse everywhere within the Four Seas;
being used, Dao becomes unlimited and will never
exhaust itself. When it extends, it pervades everywhere
within the Six Directions; and when it shrinks, it
becomes less than a handful. It is tiny, but it can
expand, it is dark but can become bright, it is weak
but can turn strong, it's soft but can harden. It
traverses the Four Directions and contains Yin and
Yang, commands Heaven and Earth and makes the
sun, moon, and stars shine. Dao is very soft and
gentle. Dao is very slim and tiny. Because of Dao,
mountains are lofty, abysses are deep, wild animals
can run, birds can fly, the sun and moon can shine,
stars can move, the female Unicorn [麟, Lin] can roam
and the male Phoenix [鳳, Huang] can soar.

---

2   Huainanzi lived in the second century BCE, the Han dynasty.
He wrote a Chinese classic called the *Philosopher of Huai Nan*
(淮南子, *Huai Nan Zi*). The book blends Daoism with Confucianism, Legalist thought, along with Yin and Yang Theory and Five
Element (or Phases) Theory.

The first origin of Dao created and fostered things and creatures, but didn't keep them to itself. It facilitated myriad of things but didn't put them under its own control. All the creatures were born because of Dao, whether it has legs to walk, or has a mouth to breathe, or those that can fly or crawl. But none of these realizes it should be grateful to Dao. Things die by complying with Dao, and nothing could or know to blame Dao for it. Those that benefited from Dao cannot praise it, and those that are devastated due to the effects of Dao cannot slander it. Dao collects and accumulates, but it does not become richer; Dao distributes and gives but does not become poorer. It is very thin and tiny, but it won't be exhausted; it is very slim and weak but will continue without an end. When being piled up, it doesn't become higher; when being cast down, it doesn't drop; when being increased, it does not get more; when being diminished, it does not become less; when being hacked, it does not become thinner; when being destroyed, it is not damaged; when being dug, it does not become deeper; and when being filled, it does not become shallower. Being faraway and dreamy, it cannot be forced into a shape. Being dreamy and faraway, it will never be exhausted. Being deep and dark, it reacts to external things with its shapelessness. Being profound and empty, it does not act without any reason. It extends and crimps along with the soft and the rigid, and it ascends and descends along with Yin and Yang.

Laozi[3] [老子]

The Dao that can be told is not the real and Constant Dao. The name that can be named is not the real and Constant Name. Nonexistence [無 , Wu, non-being] is the origin of Heaven and Earth. Existence [有 , You, being] is the mother of all things. Always try to observe the abstruseness of Dao with nonexistence in mind, always try to find clues of Dao with existence in mind. Even though nonexistence and existence have different names, they are both from the same source. Together we call them the Mystery. The Mystery of all mysteries, the gateway that all mysteries and wonders came from.

There was something evolved from chaos. It was formed before Heaven and Earth. It was inaudible. It was invisible. It stood independently and was unchanging. It operated continuously and never failed. It could be regarded as the Mother of all things. I do not know its true name. I call it *Dao* just as its designation. If I have to name it, I call it the Great. *Great* also means passing. *Passing* means going far away. *Going far away* means returning. Therefore, the Dao is great, Heaven is great, Earth is great, and the King [ruler of human beings] is also great. In the universe are the Four Greats, and the King is one of them. Humans follow the laws of Earth. Earth follows the

---

3   Laozi is the attributed founder of Daoism. Living sometime during sixth century BCE, his name means "Old Philosopher." He is said to have written *The Scripture on the Way and Virtue* (道德經, *Dao De Jing).*

laws of Heaven. Heaven follows the laws of Dao. Dao follows the laws of the "naturally just so."

Look at it, it cannot be seen. It is called invisible. Listened to, it cannot be heard. It is called inaudible. Try to grasp it, but do not get hold of it. It is called intangible.

These three [characteristics] are beyond comprehension, so they could be blended into one. It is not bright above it. It is not dark below it. It has no boundary and cannot be named or described. And then it again returns and becomes nothing. This is so-called "the form of the formless," and "the semblance of the invisible"; it is called "the indistinctness." When confronting it, one cannot see its front; when following it, one does not see its back. Use the Dao which exists since long ago to steer the affairs of the present days. Knowing the origin of the universe is knowing the rules of Dao.

Zhuangzi [4] [莊周]

Nanbozi [南伯子] of Kui [葵] asked Nuju [女踽], "You are old, Sir, but your complexion is like a child, how is this so?"

Nuju replied, "I have become acquainted with the Dao."

---

[4]   Zhuang Zhou lived sometime during the fourth century BCE. He and his writing, *Zhuangzi,* translates as *Philosopher* or *Philosophy of Zhuang.* So this title has a double meaning of signifying him, as a philosopher, and the work as one of the three major founding philosophers and works of Daoism.

Nanbozi of Kui then asked "Can Dao be learned?"

Nuju said, "No, it cannot, and you are not one to do so. Liangyi [梁倚] had the abilities of the sage, but not the Dao of the sage. While I had the Dao of the sage, I did not have the abilities. I wished I could have taught him the Dao so he might become a complete sage. But it was not quite so. I assumed it would be easy to communicate the Dao of the sage to a person who is already possessing the abilities of the sage. I did and proceeded to teach him the Dao. After three days, he was able to dispel all worldly matters out of his mind. After this was accomplished, I continued my course with him in the same way; seven more days later, he was able to dispel all the objects out of his mind. After this was accomplished, and my instructions continued, in nine more days he was able to dispel his own body and life out of his mind. After this was accomplished, his mind became as clear as the sunshine in the morning. He was able to see his own individuality. After the individuality was perceived, he was able to banish all thought of past or present. After this, he was able to penetrate the truth that there is no difference between life and death. A person who overturns the attachment of life is not dying; a person who attaches to life as it is, is not really living. Dao accompanies everything and welcomes everything. Dao destroys everything and completes everything. Its name is Yingning [攖寧]. Yingning means that after all the disturbances pass, it will lead to perfect tranquility."

Nanbozi of Kui said, "And where did you learn all this?"

Nuju replied, "I learned from the son of Fumo [副墨, implying literacy]. The son of Fumo learned it from the grandson of Luosong [洛誦, recitation]. The grandson of Luosong learned it from Zhanming [瞻明, insight]. Zhanming learned it from Niexu [聶許, word of mouth]. Niexu learned from Xushe [需設, diligence]. Xushe learned from Ou [謳, chant]. Ou learned from Xuanming [玄冥, profundity]. Xuanming learned from Shenliao [參寥, emptiness], and he learned it from Shiyi [始疑, suspected origin].

Dao is real and genuine. But it does nothing and it's formless. It can be taught by the heart but cannot be learned by words. It's real, so it can be taught; it's shapeless, so it cannot be learned through words. It may be acquired by heart [mind] but cannot be seen by the eyes. Dao is its own source and Dao is its own root. Dao existed before Heaven and Earth. Dao exists securely since ancient times. It gave birth to demons and gods. It created Heaven and Earth. It is above the zenith but doesn't seem high. It's below the nadir but doesn't seem low. It existed before Heaven and Earth but does not seem long ago. It was there since time immemorial but does not seem old. Xiwei [豨韋] got it and used it to govern Heaven and Earth. Fuxi [5] got it and used it to adjust his Qi. Plough got it and thereby has never changed its position. The Sun and Moon got it and thereby they never stopped operating their course. Kanrang [堪壞] got it and became the God of Kunlun Mountains. Fengyi [馮夷] got it and became

---

5   Fuxi (伏羲, circa 2800 BCE), the first mythical emperor of China.

the God of the Yellow River. Jianwu [肩吾] got it and became the God of Mount Tai. The Yellow Emperor[6] got it and he could soar to Heaven surrounded by clouds. Zhuanxu[7] got it and became the King of the North. Yuqiang[8] got it and became the God of the North Sea. Queen Mother of the West[9] got it and received the Palace of Mount Shaoguang [少廣]. Nobody knows when it began and nobody knows when it will end. Peng Zu [彭祖] got it and lived a very long life from the time of Emperor Shun to the period of the Five-Princesses. Fuyue[10] got it and became the prime minister of King Wuding[11] and helped him rule the kingdom. And since then, he mounted the stars of Ji and Wei[12] and then he was ranked among the stars.

---

6   Yellow Emperor (黃帝, Huang Di, 2697–2597 BCE). The third mythical emperor of China.

7   Zhuanxu (顓頊), grandson of the Yellow Emperor.

8   Yuqiang (禺強), a descendant of the Yellow Emperor.

9   Queen Mother of the West (西王母, Xi Wang Mu). Matriarchal Daoist immortaless.

10   Fuyue (傅說, 1335–1246 BCE).

11   King Wuding (武丁). King of the Shang dynasty, 1600–1046 BCE.

12   Ji and Wei (箕尾), the sixth constellation, the Winnow Basket.

Among Laozi's disciples, there was Gengsang Chu,[13] who had learned all the knowledge of Dao from Laozi. He went north and lived in the Weilei [畏壘] mountains. He dismissed those servants who were pretentious and showing off their cleverness; he stayed away from those maids who boasted about their benevolence and righteousness. He stayed with those who were simple and innocent, and only employed those knowing nothing but work. There was a great bumper crop in Weilei mountains three years after he lived there. And the people said to one another, "When Mr. Gengsang first got here, we all thought he was eccentric and we didn't trust him. If we estimate our income by day, we may not have enough; but count the total income by the year, we have more than enough. He might be a sage indeed. Why don't we pay tribute to him as our ancestor and build a temple for him?"

When Gengsang heard of this, he sat facing south and was displeased. His disciples were wondering why, and he said to them, "Why, my disciples, should you wonder about my reaction? When the vital energy grows in spring, the plants begin to flourish. When the autumn arrives, the fruits and crops begin to ripen. How can spring and autumn act this way without any adequate cause? They do not, and the processes of the Great Dao have been in operation. I have heard that the perfect man dwells quietly in his small house while

---

13   Gengsang Chu (庚桑楚), lived during the Zhou dynasty, is the attributed author of the *Perfect Numinous Grotto Scripture* (洞靈 真經, *Dong Ling Zhen Jing*).

the others are free to follow their natural bent and get wild. Now the people of Weilei are whispering among themselves that I should be deified and placed along with other sages. Doesn't it mean I will be the center of attention? This is the reason that I am not happy, when I think of the instructions of Laozi."

Zengzi [14] was residing in Wei [衛]. He wore a robe quilted with hemp, and had no outer garment. His face looked rough and emaciated; his hands and feet were covered with thick calluses. Sometimes, he would go without cooked food for three days and no new clothes for ten years. Any slight adjustment to make his cap straight would cause the tassel to fall off. Any slight pull on his lapels would expose his elbows. When putting on his shoes, the heels would become loose. He didn't mind, and dragged his broken shoes along while he sang the *Hymns of Shang* [歌 商]. His voice sounded as if it came from some bell constructed of metal and stone. The king was not able to get him to be his minister; no prince was able to associate with him. So, it is that he who seeks to cultivate his mind forgets his physical form; that he who seeks to preserve his health ignores wealth; and that he who is devoted to the Dao forgets his own mind.

---

14   Zengzi (曾子, 505–436 BCE) was a Chinese philosopher and disciple of Confucius

Guanyinzi [15] [關 尹 子]

Dao cannot be described in human language. After overcoming the burden of language, then one can achieve Dao. Dao cannot be realized by mortal thinking. After jumping out from human thought and mind, then one can achieve Dao, and the universe still operates continuously.

Human society develops in the cycles of birth, growth, decay, and death, without ending. People fight with each other, sometimes winning, sometimes losing. Such scenes come and go. These scenes look similar but they are quite different. People fight for it, wish to be part of it, hate it and like it, want to remove it, and want to master it. To describe Dao with language is like using the mouth to blow on the shadow; to imagine Dao with one's brain is like using a knife to carve on a handful of dust.

Some eminent thinkers and wise people were actually spreading superstition. They do not understand Dao, nor do they understand demons and gods. Dao cannot be made, Dao cannot be achieved, Dao cannot be measured, and Dao cannot be divided. Therefore, it is called the Heaven, it is called the faith, it is called the god, it is called the origin of all things, and it is called Dao.

---

15   Guanyinzi was the gatekeeper of the Northwest Passage (leading to the Himalayas) in China. He was responsible for encouraging Laozi to write the *The Scripture on the Way and Virtue* (道 德 經, *Dao De Jing*) before leaving China. He lived during the sixth century BCE in the Han dynasty.

The Dao that I am talking about is like the great ocean. Dumping in hundreds of millions kilograms of metal in it, we won't see those in it. Dumping in hundreds of millions kilograms of stone in it, we won't see those in it. Dumping in hundreds of millions kilograms of garbage in it, we won't see those in it. It can carry small fishes and shrimps. It can also carry giant whales. The grand ocean accepts water from all the rivers and streams, but it doesn't seem it's getting too much. To take much of the water from it, it doesn't appear to obtain less.

Heaven cannot make the lotus to bloom in the winter or chrysanthemum to bloom in the spring. Therefore, sages do not work against the timing of the seasons. The Earth cannot make oranges grow in Luo [洛, northwest China] or badgers to survive in Min [汶, northeast Shangdong]. Therefore, sages do not work against the working traditions. Sages cannot walk on their hands and hold things with their feet. Therefore, sages do not work against their own strengths.

Sages cannot make fish fly or birds run. Therefore, sages do not work against other people's strengths. These are the reasons that objects move and stop naturally. The sky becomes bright and dark naturally. Don't try to gain control of everything, that's how to achieve Dao.

Those who are craftier than a thief can capture a thief. The one who is more powerful than the tiger can catch the tiger. Those who can control themselves can make themselves successful. Those who don't attach to things or objects can get the benefit from things and objects. Only those who can forget the fact they are pursuing the Dao have a chance of achieving it.

A person talking about the Dao is like talking about one's own dreams. People discuss their dreams as though they were gold and jade, or fine dinnerware, or wild exotic animals. They can only talk about it. They cannot show it to you and give it to you. Those who listen to the talk can only hear it, but cannot get the truth about it. Of those who are listening to it, only those who really understand won't attach themselves to it and won't argue about it.

Using a small tub to contain water as the lake and then place a stone in the center as an island. A tiny fish will swim in a circle around the island. After swimming for a thousand miles it still doesn't know the end. Why is it so? The water in the tub has no beginning and no end. The sages' Dao also has no beginning and no end, therefore it creates many things and everything is without end.

The sage's Dao sometimes seems independent and has no connections to anything. Sometimes, it seems linked to everything, and everything contains Dao. Sometimes, it seems so obvious. Everybody can see it. Sometimes, it seems it's hiding in a very deep place, and can't be found.

Only Dao can manage to arrange the myriad things like controlling dolls, but nothing can touch Dao. So, Dao is on top of all the things. A bud sprouts from a seed and a plant produces seeds. This cycle is repeated countless times. As wide as Heaven and Earth, it cannot sprout a bud from an empty seed. Eggs hatch and become birds. Female birds produce eggs. This cycle repeats countless times. As clever as Yin and Yang are, they cannot hatch eggs that are not fertilized.

An object that becomes an individual life obtains its consciousness via breathing. Not a single life can be without the consciousness of itself. Knowing that my real body is the body in my dream: follow one's own feelings, one can see various of things. Then one can fly their spirit and be their true self roaming in the fields of Supreme Purity [太清, Tai Qing]. Knowing that things in reality are the things in the dream: follow one's own feelings, one can see numerous of things. Then, one can Congeal Essence [凝精, Ning Jinq] and gallop into the Unknown [入荒, Ru Huang]. This is the Dao, where the Spirit of Vitality is seen and one can live long, and where the Spirit forgets all about death.

Persons who do not talk too much would not be envied and hated by others.

Persons who do not do things beyond theirs duties would not be blamed by others.

Persons who do not show off their cleverness would not be commanded by others.

Persons who do not boast what they can do would not be assigned extra works by others.

Behave with honesty, do things with a simple mind, treat people with leniency, deal with conflicts in silence. Your Dao should have no limit and no end.

Do things with good planning and judge things with principle.

Let people do what they can do and let the spirits make the final judgments. Learn how to do things from people who really know, then learn rules and principles from the ancients.

Work with other people, but achieve the Dao alone and by yourself. It's difficult to give away precious gold and jade, and easy to dump useless dirt and stone. So for those pursuing the Dao, keep in mind to be unattached to profound and abstruse statements, and things encountered.

You can try to realize and achieve [Dao], but don't be attached to it. If attached to it, it's a disease of the mind and inner body, which no medicines can cure.

Ordinary people do not understand that the most important matter is to achieve Dao; instead, they work in multiple businesses, unimportant businesses, and strange businesses. Therefore, they often spend their entire life with indigence and disaster. They do not realize that the Dao is everywhere. Yet they seek something else that is far from their reach. The so-called principles nowadays are like replacing close friends with strangers, chasing the inferior instead of the primary, employing ordinary people instead of a sage, and neglecting what actually lies near them. Such [decisions] may show some good results over time; however, it is detrimental to your life in the long term.

Some in the past who talked about Dao said the Dao is coagulated and lonely, some said the Dao is deep and profound, some said the Dao is bright and spotless, some said Dao is hollow and empty, some said the Dao is obscure and dark. Don't be scared away by these words, as the real Dao cannot be described by words. If you understand the state of Dao is way above what can actually be put into words and what can be explained by language, then you can understand my words.

Heaven covers everything, some things are living and some are dead, but it is not that Heaven likes some things better than the rest. The sun shines on everything, some are beautiful and some are ugly, but it is not that the sun prefers some rather than the rest.

The sage's behavior and methods are naturally complimented with the Dao, but it's not that the sage follows the Dao intentionally. The sage has moral character and conduct naturally complimentary with the Dao, but it's not that the sage wants to be a noble and moral person. The way sages deal with human affairs is based on humanity, and this is also naturally complimentary with the Dao, but it's not that sages deal with these in their own way. Thus, the sage does not have Dao, does not have integrity, and does not have social experience. Sages know the real "self" is selfless, has no gap between themselves and others, and therefore treat people with humaneness. Sages know there's no difference between their affairs or the affairs of others. So, they deal with all affairs with righteousness [義, yi].

Sages know a person's mind is constantly changing, there is no consistent mentality or desire, so they contain it with propriety [禮, li]. Sages know that knowledge is not constant, it transforms over time, so they verify it with their great wisdom [智, zhi]. Sages know statements can be taken back or denied, so they keep their promises with integrity [信, xin]. Sages understand the Dao, so they are not selfish. They are benevolent [仁, ren] because they have benevolence in their mind. They are righteous because they have benevolence in their mind. They can have propriety, are wise, and be sincere because they have benevolence in their mind. Benevolence, righteousness, propriety, wisdom, integrity, sages have all five, but these are actually all the same for sages. They are named differently by other people.

The Dao I am talking about is like a sharp sword. It's a good tool to use for cutting things. It is hurtful if holding the blade by hands. Bamboo sticks do not ask for peas, and peas do not answer bamboo sticks. Tiles do not ask stones. Stones do not answer tiles. Yet, the Dao is there among all of them. The questions and answers are just the voice passing through the air. Nothing to do with whether the Dao exists or not. Those who admire the Dao are like a walking creeper, those who understand the Dao are like galloping upon a horse. People know the phenomenon of Dao, but do not know the essence of Dao. Thus, sages do not look up to Dao and then belittle themselves. Sages do not show off because they achieved the Dao. Sages do not ask for the Dao from other sages. Sages do not trade the Dao to ordinary people for material possessions.

Sages work hard and are not lazy, but don't think that Dao can be achieved by just working hard. The sage doesn't vacillate, but also doesn't think the Dao can be

achieved by just persisting in it. The way sages act is
like an arrow which has been shot, the arrow travels
along a trajectory which follows the laws of the
universe. It does not change course with its own desire.
The perseverance of sages is like holding an arrow on
a stretched bow. They hold it as long as it's necessary.
They do not hold it with their own desire. If trying
to achieve the Dao through pursuing knowledge and
good behavior, and if people explain the Dao to each
other, no one will ever achieve the Dao.

People should know that speech is similar to the
sound of flowing spring water, know that action is
similar to a bird flying, know that learning is similar
to capturing shadows, know that knowledge is similar
to dreaming at night. When there is nothing in mind,
it's coming very close to the Dao. To make or create
an object is difficult, but with the Dao, it's easy to
abandon everything. Everything is difficult to make
and easy to destroy. The heart can form a date tree,
liver can form an elm tree. I can communicate with
Heaven and Earth. I can dream of water on a cloudy
day. I can dream of fire on a sunny day.

Heaven and Earth can communicate with me.
I and Heaven and Earth appear in harmony and yet
seem divided at the same time. We appear blended,
but we still have our own tune.

Zihuazi [16] [子華子]

Kindness cannot be forced. Yao said, "If this is so, how is this good for giving devotion to others? Shun also said, "If this is so, how is this good for giving devotion to others?" This is both the upper level and lower level contending for the good. Upper level and lower level contending for good works is two seeds. When there are two seeds, it's not balanced. When the balance cannot be achieved, then it won't be straight. Without the balance and the straightness, then Yao wouldn't be Yao, and Shun wouldn't be Shun. My students should keep Yao and Shun in mind all the time, and be good to other people.

Yangzi [17] [陽子]

Someone asked my master, "When you were young, were you good at poetry [賦, Fu]?"

He then answered, "Yes. When I was a child, I practiced carving bronze, making seals, and scripts." Soon after, he exclaimed, "Adults do not do that."

Someone else asked, "Can poetry not be used for remonstrating through satires?"

He responded, "Satirizing! Once we realize it's a satire, it should be halted. If it is not halted, I am afraid it couldn't be prevented from encouraging others to do the same."

---

[16] *Zihuazi* was written by Cheng Ben (程本) in the Zhou period, 1046–256 BCE.

[17] Yangzi is Yang Zhu (陽朱, 440–380 BCE), who appears in the *Book of Liezi*. One of the first freethinkers and naturalists in Daoism, his school of thought was termed as *Yangism*.

Another person asked, "Like the misty gauze in a piece of fine silk cloth?"

Yangzi said, "Yes, like worms working in women's fabric."

Another said, *The Swordsman's Treatise* [18] says, "The sword can be used to protect and strengthen your body."

Yangzi said, "But can the skills of a swordsman make people act more morally?"

Someone else asked, "Was the poetry of Jing Cha [景差], Tang Le [唐勒], Song Wang [宋王], and Mei Cheng [枚乘] not valuable?"

Yangzi said, "If they were, then they were also using excessive flowery language more than necessary."

Another said, "What do you mean by 'excessive' and what could be wrong with it?"

Yangzi said, "The beautiful words in poetry made by poets should be based on the principles of Dao. The flowery language in poetry made by poetasters are just excessive flowery words with no real content. If the Confucian school had used poetry to teach its theories, and was judged by the skill of making poetry, Jia Yi [19] would have been just an entry level Confucian scholar, and Xiangru [20] would have gained mastery of Confucianism. However, the Confucian school didn't

---

18   *The Swordsman's Treatise* (劍刻論, *Jian Ge Lun*).

19   Jia Yi (賈誼, 200–169 BCE), Chinese poet and political leader during the Han dynasty.

20   Xiangru (相如), poet during the Han dynasty.

use poetry. So how is poetry important concerning Jia Yi and Xiangru?"

Someone asked about if there are some people who can reverse black and white and dazzle the people's eyes with unorthodox colors.

Yangzi said, "Look carefully and clearly."

Another said, "How about the music of Zheng [鄭] and Wei [衛], these are very similar?"

Yangzi said, "Listen carefully and clearly."

Another person said, "Zhu and Kuang [21] have left this world. What can be done?"

Yangzi said, "Just concentrate your mind while you are seeing and listening. That's all you need."

Someone else asked, "All music is based on the five tones and the twelve-note scale, yet some music is ceremonial, and some is like the kind of music by Zheng and Wei. Why is that?"

Yangzi said, "If it is proper and correct, then it is ceremonial. If it is excessive and unrestrained, then it is like that of Zheng and Wei."

Someone asked about the fundamentals of making music.

Yangzi said, "If the Yellow Bell [黃鐘, Huang Zhong] is used as the root for producing the twelve-note scale, and if one uses moderation and a correct attitude to make the notes of properly equal pitch, this will ensure that the Zheng and Wei sort of music will not be able to enter and defile one's music."

---

21   Zhu (朱), famous for his sharp eyes, and Kuang (曠), famous for his sharp ears.

Someone said, "Women have beauty. Do books also have beauty?"

Yangzi said, "Yes, they do. Women hate cosmetics that would ruin their beauty. Books hate excessive words that create chaos in laws and institutions. When sailing on the big ocean, one then realizes how muddy the water of rivers are, not to mention the water of a drying swamp. Abandon the boat and yet want to cross a great river, there has never been anyone who could do this. Throwing away the Five Classics [22] and yet want to achieve the Dao, there has never been anyone who could do this either! For those who discard the regular delicacies but are fond of strange food, do you think they can recognize tastes? For those who abandon the great sage and prefer other various philosophers, do you think they can recognize the Dao? A trail down into a mountain ravine cannot be followed to the end; a door facing a wall cannot be entered."

Another said, "From where can one enter?"

Yangzi said, "Confucius! Confucius is the door."

Another said, "Have you also passed through Confucius's door?"

Yangzi said, "The door! The door! How could I be the only one who has entered through the door?"

Vast! Vast is the grand Dao! In the past the sages completed it. If one goes too far, they pass the target.

---

22   *Five Classics* (五經, *Wu Jing*). The Five Canons of Confucianism: *Book of Changes, Book of Odes, Book of History, Book of Rites,* and *Spring and Autumn Annals*.

If one doesn't go all the way, they don't reach the Dao that cannot be defiled or maligned.

Someone asked about the Dao.

Yangzi said, "The Dao is pervading, there is nothing it does not penetrate."

Another said, "Is Dao working for people in other countries?"

Yangzi said, "That which leads to Shun, Yao, and King Wen[23] is the correct Dao. Those which do not lead to Shun, Yao, and King Wen are the other Daos. The Wise Person follows the correct one and not the others."

Someone asked about the Dao.

Yangzi said, "The Dao is like a road or a river. The carts and boats are passing through on it, nonstop day and night."

Another said, "How does one get on the straight road [correct Dao] and follow it?"

Yangzi said, "Although the road curves, if it reaches Xia,[24] then follow it. Although the river winds, if it reaches the ocean, then follow it."

Another said, "So, although some affairs may seem to have a crooked path ahead, if it reaches the sage's Dao, then we follow it?"

---

23 King Wen (文王, 1152–1056 BCE) of the Zhou dynasty, attributed author of the *Book of Changes*.

24 Xia (夏) is the kingdom of Yu the Great.

Xuanzhenzi[25] [玄真子]

Tongzhen of Bo met with Zeng Qiguan of Jun and
Zuowang of Hou at Kui [暌].[26] They were all good
cultivators of the Mystery, yet they had varying
opinions. During their conversation, they talked about
Dao, and existence and nonexistence. They discussed
for a whole day and didn't feel it was enough.

Guan of Jun said, "When I was in the Pavilion
of Contemplation [觀亭, Guan Ting], I realized that
Dao couldn't be seen but it was there."

Wang of Hou said, "When I sat upon the Stage
of Forgetting, I could see the Dao but knew it did
not exist."

Tongzhen of Bo said to them, "Regarding the
Foremost Dao, it is of no difference if it exists or not.
Couldn't you tell that the sun, moon, and stars see
Heaven differently than those seeing it from the Earth?
It's difference is due to the high and low positions. Sun
and moon are different in size, and the space between
the stars are different. Some are narrower and some
are wider.

"If we judge the size by the distance, we know it's
not correct, as the sun is hot and the moon is cold. If

---

25   *Xuanzhenzi* (玄真子, *Xuan Zhen Zi*), Master of Mysterious Perfection,
is a Daoist book written sometime during the Tang dynasty (618–
907 CE) by the scholar Zhang Shihe (張志和). His manner of
writing is very similar to that of *Zhuangzi.*

26   Tongzhen (通真, Penetrating the True) of Bo (伯). Zeng Qiguan
(曾起觀, Contemplating Establishing the Past) of Jun (君).
Zuowang (坐忘, Sitting and Forgetting) of Hou (后, the
Empress).

we judge the distance by the hot or cold, we know it's not correct, as the sun is big and the moon is small. So, there is no absolute distance. Some see it from the side, some see from the bottom, it all depends on from where you see it. It is similar that the True Dao can only be seen by the heart.

"It doesn't matter if in the Pavilion of Contemplation or on the Stage of Forgetting, some believe that Dao does exist and some that Dao does not exist. Believing that Dao does exist, Guan of Jun may not see Dao on the Stage of Forgetting; believing that Dao does not exist, Wang of Hou may see Dao in the Pavilion of Contemplation. These are what's in Guan of Jun's and Wang of Hou's hearts, there is not a difference between existing or not. It's the preconception in one's mind. So that those who argue about the distance of the sun, the moon, and the stars, don't realize it's dangerous to judge things by the eye; those who argue about the existence of the Dao, don't realize that the preconception is already in their mind."

After listening to Tongzhen of Bo, both of them stopped arguing.

The Master of Penetrating the Mystery [27] said, "In the meeting at Kui, the distance to the sun, moon, and stars and the existence of the real Dao were concluded. It straightened the unknown and settled the undecided argument. It was Zhen of Bo's effort that settled the argument between Qiguan of Jun and Zuowang of Hou."

---

[27]   The Master of Penetrating the Mystery (達玄夫子, Da Xuan Fu Zi).

Yingzhanzi [28] said, "The Great Dao has no shape. One cannot see it, doesn't mean it cannot be seen. The great Dao is silent. One cannot hear it, doesn't mean it cannot be heard. The so-called 'can be seen' or 'can be heard' is not by the eyes or by the ears. It's to see by your heart and realize by your mind. Take the strong wind as an example, it cannot be seen by it alone. But when it reaches the mountain, it shakes the trees; when it reaches the water it creates waves on it. Can one say it cannot be seen? You cannot see it, you cannot hear it, how can you say it does exist?"

Lumenzi [29] [鹿門子]

The sun is so bright in the sky, how could it be eclipsed? The mountain is so solid on the Earth, how could it collapse? People say summer is the season when plants grow, but wheat doesn't; people say winter is the season when plants have leaves falling, but a pine tree doesn't. People say water is cold, but there are hot springs in the mountain valleys. People say fire is hot, but there is the cold fire on the Su Qiu [蕭丘] Island. These are the things we don't understand, but these are what we have to understand.

---

28   Yingzhanzi (瑩蟾子) means Master Gazing Upon Bright Gems.

29   *Lumenzi* is a work written by the Daoist scholar Liu Guimeng, who lived sometime during the Tang dynasty (618–907 CE). Liu also wrote a commentary on *The Yellow Emperor's Yin Convergence Scripture* (黃帝陰符經, *Huang Di Yin Fu Jing*).

Nanshanzi [30] [南山子]

Can you not be captious to others and conceited about yourself? Can you not keep silent, not expressing the right things just to please people? Can you not be too aggressive like the birds of prey flying? Can you not flinch like chickens hiding in the grass when finding difficulties? Can you hold your mind steady? Can you resist seductions from the outside? Can you stand tall and still like mountains? Can you be lenient like the oceans accepting water from all the rivers and streams? If you can do all this, you are close to Dao.

Hengtongzi [恆通子]

The Supreme Beginning [太初, Tai Chu] is the origin of the natural sciences. The Supreme Void [太虛, Tai Xu] is the origin of Qi. The Supreme Simplicity [太素, Tai Su] is the origin of the images [Eight Diagrams]. The Supreme One [太乙, Tai Yi] is the origin of calculations, and the Supreme Ultimate [太極, Tai Ji] is the origin of all of them—natural sciences, Qi, images, and calculations.

Dao is spread by language and word of mouth. However, Dao is also puzzled by language and word of mouth. It's not that the language or word of mouth can puzzle Dao. They are misleading. When misled a little, it becomes lectures. When misled more, it

---

30   Nanshanzi is possibly Zhuangzi, who also went by the name of Southern Mountain Immortal, as Zhuangzi is thought to have lived on Hua Shan (華山, Flower Mountain), which was also known as Southern Mountain.

becomes just a regular article or speech. When people talk and talk too much, it's a sign that the Dao is declining. Thus, the scholars do not talk too much.

Fangshuzi [31] [方叔子]

Fuxi carried on from Heaven to create the Poles. He was the origin of the *Book of Changes* [易經, Yi Jing] and the founder of the Chinese culture and civilization. When these were passed on to the Zhou dynasty, the sixty-four hexagrams [卦, Gua] and comments on each of the lines of the hexagrams [爻, Yao] were created, forming the *Book of Changes*. And then Confucius wrote the *Ten Wings* [十翼, Shi Yi]. After that, some followed the tracks of sages and some had their own inventions, but those are all far away from sages and much inferior than the original.

Then, Lianxi [32] was the only one who got the real secrets after one thousand years. The Supreme Ultimate [太極, Tai Ji] was born from the *Book of Changes*. After the Supreme Ultimate was born, the Two Powers of Yin and Yang [兩儀, Liang Yi], the Five Elements [五行, Wu Xing], and all the creatures and beings were born from it. It's that the Supreme Ultimate delivered the Two Powers of Yin and Yang, which delivered the Four Symbols [四象, Si Xiang],

---

31   Fangshuzi is Lizhi (李廌, 1059–1109 CE), a recluse living on Mt. Hua from the Northern Song dynasty period.

32   Lianxi (濂溪), a sobriquet for Zhou Dunyi (周敦頤, 1017–1073 CE), a neo-Confucianist, cosmologist, and creator of the Tai Ji Symbol.

which then delivered the Eight Diagrams [八卦, Ba Gua].

The Supreme Ultimate divided the Five Elements and Four Seasons. The purpose was to create creatures and beings. And since then, the heart of the human is the most spiritual. The sage in creating the Poles was similar to the Supreme Ultimate creating and categorizing phenomena. Heaven and Earth can move, and the Supreme Ultimate is the most exquisite of either motion or stillness. And this was how the Yin and Yang, hard and soft were categorized. The sage perceived the Supreme Ultimate, it was complete in either motion or stillness.

So, it was said, "The Dao of humanity is propriety and benevolence. These are the motions of the Six Yao and the method of the Three Poles.[33] In the macro view, the Three Poles are equal to the Supreme Ultimate; however, in the micro view, each Pole could be the Supreme Ultimate individually. So it was concluded that the *Yi*[34] is grand! It was also the purpose of Zhouzi[35] creating the Tai Ji diagram. For those people who understand I would agree that the Supreme Ultimate diagram and the *Book of Changes* is similar to the exterior and interior of the same thing.

---

33 *Six Yao* are the six lines of a hexagram in the *Book of Changes*. The *Three Poles* refer to Heaven, Earth, and Humanity.

34 Abbreviated form of the *Yi Jing (Book of Changes)*.

35 Zhouzi (周子), a reference to Zhou Dunyi.

Du Zheng[36] said, "The Supreme Ultimate understands the usefulness of the mind. Those who perceive "I" understand the usefulness of Supreme Ultimate. This statement is right on the target. The Dao became decayed over time, then the Pavilion of Examinations [考亭, Kao Ting] filled the gap. The Dao passed down from the immortals and sages and the Chinese Classics were actually all surrounding the Supreme Ultimate. After Zhuzi[37] elucidated and propagated it, it got much more clear again. He had benefited greatly the generations of scholars and posterity. He explained in every detail like minutes and second to time, this was Zhuzi's great skill. He also cherished other opinions like those of the brothers of Lu [陸] and Lin [林], and those of Zhang [張, Daoling].

Linchuanzi[38] [臨川子]

When studying Dao, one should set a high goal, but practice in detail, including all the small factors. Setting a high goal is to understand the origin of the Dao, practicing in each detail is to understand how the Dao is gradually achieved. Dao has an origin like water

---

36 Du Zheng (度正) is from Guanghuan, birth and death dates unknown. He served under the warlord Liu Zhang (劉璋) of the late Eastern Han dynasty, 206 BCE–220 CE.

37 Zhuzi (朱子), is Zhuxi (朱熹, 1130–1200 CE), one of China's greatest and most influential philosophers and scholars.

38 Linchuanzi is quoted from *The Collected Works of Linchuanzi,* the 9th scroll "A Portrait of Du Fu," a Tang dynasty poet living from 712–770 CE.

has its source. When studying Dao, like Yu the Great[39] who controlled the waters to prevent floods, one should trace it from the lower reaches. He started from Yanzhou [兖州, in the southwest of Shandong province] then traced back up to Yizhou [冀州, in the northwest of Shangdong province]. The Yellow River has three hundred major upper reaches and three thousand minor lower and upper reaches. He traced and controlled all of these, including irrigation ditches in the land fills. He managed these small ditches like controlling big rivers, and did not ignore these just because they were unimportant. Isn't this to be complete and unprejudiced? Start from the lesser virtue and that will add up to the great virtue, and this is similar to tracing the source of the Dao.

The sages teach Dao, but they start from a common language and easy practices, focus on the ordinary and simple things, and do not think these are unimportant. This is indeed the origin of the Dao. Therefore, Confucius seldom explained benevolence in language that couldn't be understood and practiced easily. This was also why Chengzi [程子] kept the Supreme Ultimate Diagram in private and didn't publish it out to the public. It was too complicated to explain. When talking about filial piety [孝, xiao], brotherliness [悌, ti], rites [禮, li], and music [樂, yue], Chen Qianshi [陳潛室] said, "To climb to the top of the hill, we must start from the foot of the hill; to reach a far away place, we must pass through the

---

39 Yu the Great (大禹, Da Yu), founded the Xia dynasty, 2070–1600 BCE.

near place first. This is the practical principle from
the sages.

Yinguangzi [陰光子]

Is Dao real or far away from us? When a person
witnesses it, they know Dao is real and it could be
everywhere. Is it difficult to become a sage? When one
realizes what a sage really is, then they know everyone
could be a sage. Once destiny arrives and the right
moment is achieved, one can see how wonderful the
Dao is. The only way is to dismiss the desires in one's
mind, and there is no method nor do you need secrets
from the sages. For those to understand this, they
already know the will of the founder without him
mentioning it; for those who do not understand,
even if they think very hard, they are still like a
thousand mountains away.

Ranghuizi [壞慧子]

Confucius said, "Am I indeed possessed of knowledge?
No, I am not."

Yan Yuan [顏淵] said, "I really couldn't find the
Way to do so."

Mengzi[40] said, "Is there no one to transmit
Confucius' doctrines?"

Mencius was so humble that he didn't think he
achieved the Dao and could transmit Confucius'
doctrines. For those who boast they have achieved
Dao are those who do not understand the True Dao.

---

40   Mengzi (孟子, 372–289 BCE), romanized as Mencius, is a famous
      Confucian philosopher.

Who really understands Dao? A vulgar person. Why? Because vulgar persons do not have preconceptions. Their minds are empty. With an empty mind, one could reach the further two ends. Who really understands Dao? A naive person. Why? Because naive persons do not have worries and do not worry about learning the Dao. They could reach everywhere in the world.

Yangmingzi[41] [陽明子]

Does Dao really exist. Can this be discussed? Some say yes, but it doesn't mean it can be proved it exists. Some say no, but it also cannot be proven that it doesn't exist. However, how can we see it and prove it? People say Dao can be seen and yet never seen; the Dao exists, but this may not be true, which means it really does exist. It does not exist, but this may not be true, so this means it really does not exist. It can be seen, but it can't really be seen, and this means there really is a seeing. For those just believing it doesn't exist, they do not use their mind. Their mind is roaming without a harbor. For those just believing it does exist, they use their hearing and perceive the wrong things, and their efforts end in vain. Therefore, between existing and not existing, or what can be seen and cannot be seen, the subtle difference cannot be distinguished by language.

---

41   Yangmingzi is Wang Yangming (王陽明, 1472–1529 CE) of the Ming dynasty, a neo-Confucian.

Qianmingzi [乾銘子]

Does Heaven have an origin? Some say it does not.
If Heaven had an origin, it means that Dao had an
origin. Does Heaven have an end? Some say it does
not. If Heaven had an end, it means Dao has an
end, then Heaven and Dao are two different things.
We see the sky [Heaven] every day, but we do not
see Dao. We talk about Dao every day, but we
do not talk about sky.

This is because we are confused. When
the spiritual Muchangli met a bird with nine
characteristics,[42] it lost its beautiful colors. When
the auspicious Qilin [43] met with the beast having
soft antlers, it confused itself admiring the beast
with antlers. Roaming within the sky and Heaven
aside spiritual beings, everything is right in front of
the eyes, but if trying to verify them clearly by just
guessing, the more you guess, the further away you
are from the true answers. Some say Dao is the origin
of the Heaven, this would mean there is a Heaven
outside of the Heaven. Some say Heaven is the origin
of Dao. This would mean there is a Heaven inside of
the Heaven. There is only one Dao. For those who
said there were two, what are those two?

---

42 *Muchangli* (慕長離) is another name for the mythological phoenix
(鳳, Feng). *A bird with nine characteristics* implies Feng as well.

43 *Qilin* (騏麟, Qi lin) is a mythical creature like a unicorn. *The beast
having soft antlers* implies Qilin as well.

Mingliaozi[44] [冥寥子]

Those who understand the Dao can keep their mind peaceful in any environment. Dao is not inside some particular person, thus it's not correct to argue about Dao through certain persons.

For those who achieve Dao, even when on a busy street, they can still keep their mind calm and are not bothered by the traffic at all. Alone in a remote place, they still have a clean mind, and do not feel lonely.

For those who do not understand the Dao, when in the busy street or market, their heart feels disturbed, and their mind is not calm. When alone on a remote mountain, their heart feels lonely, and their mind wants to find some activity.

Fuyuanzi[45] [復元子]

My Dao is an all-pervading oneness. "Oneness" means centered and concealed. Those of Great Virtue[46] get it and use it to benefit all the people and beings. It rules as a united Supreme Ultimate [太極, Tai Ji]. Oneness is concealed, but is used to benefit others.

---

44 Mingliaozi lived in the Ming dynasty (1368–1644 CE). He was an official who tired of speaking against his heart in his official duties, so he became a Daoist. The book *Mingliaozi on Free Roaming* was composed by Tu Long (屠隆).

45 Fuyuanzi is a Daoist who wrote *Morning and Evening Lessons of the Great Qi on the Secrets of Nourishing Life* (早晚課大啟的養生秘訣, Zao Wan Ke Da Qi De Yang Sheng Mi Jue), composed by Jiang Hongyang (姜泓阳). Dates unknown.

46 *Great Virtue* (大德, Da De), usually implies an emperor or king.

"All-pervading" means mixed together and spreading. Those of Small Virtue [47] get it and benefit where they rule like a river irrigating the land where it flows. On its own, the all-pervading Dao is like a Supreme Ultimate, where the Dao is the sovereign [of Yin and Yang].

This all-pervading oneness is spreading the form of benevolence. To understand thoughtfully the real meaning of the principles, then everything is clear and can be seen. To practice benevolence with propriety is the base, so one can realize the true meanings. The emperor has nothing to hide, because the emperor cannot hide anything. You want to keep silent, because you are not allowed to speak. If one sees this, but didn't follow it, they are like an unfilial son. If one sees this and steals it for their self, then they are like a thief from Heaven.

Laozi [老子]

The Great Dao doesn't have a visible form or shape, but it created Heaven and Earth. The Great Dao is without impulse, but it keeps the sun and moon operating continuously. The Great Dao has no name, but it nourishes all the creatures and beings. I do not know its name, but if pressed to give it a name I would call it "Dao." So, the Dao contains everything, could have clarity, could have turbidity; could be motional, could be motionless. Heaven has clarity and Earth has turbidity. Heaven is motional and Earth is motionless.

---

47   Small Virtue (小德, Xiao De), usually refers to a local ruler or prince.

The male is clarity, and the female is turbidity; the male is motional, and the female is motionless. These are the foundational rules upon which the universe and all the creatures and beings were created. Clarity is the origin of turbidity. Motion is the foundation of the motionless. Once people can keep clarity in the mind and be motionless,[48] all of Heaven and Earth would blend with clarity and tranquility of mind.

The human spirit tends towards clarity, but the mind disturbs it. The human mind tends towards tranquility, but desires drag or draw it away. When desires are dispelled, the mind will be motionless. When the mind is settled, the spirit will be clear. Then, naturally, the Six Desires [六慾, Liu Yu] won't be induced and the Three Poisons [49] will not be dispatched.

Thus, for those who cannot achieve clarity and tranquility, it means their mind is not settled and their desires are not dispelled. Those who can dispel desires, when observing their minds internally, still cannot find their minds. When observing external forms, they still cannot see the form. When observing objects from far away, they still cannot find objects.

When these three poisons are dispelled, then there is only the emptiness of the true self left. It's empty when looking at emptiness, but when it's really empty, there is nothing more to be emptied. If it's really empty, then there is nothing left. If there really is

---

48 *Motionless* here means to keep the mind from moving.

49 *Three Poisons* (三毒, San Du) are greed, anger, and ignorance.

nothing left, then even nothingness does not exist. Until reaching this stage, it's contentedly and deeply quiet. When it's quiet to the limit, there is no way the desires could be induced. When the desires cannot grow, then it is the real silence and motionlessness. Using the real and unchanging Dao to deal with things, it will lead to the true understanding of the natural characteristics of things.

Things come and go. When things come, deal with them with the Dao. When things go, then the mind goes back to the silent stage. If this can be achieved, the mind will be always be in the silent stage and motionless.

Keeping to clarity and tranquility, then it will gradually lead towards the path of achieving the True Dao. After going through the gate of the True Dao, it can be called, "Obtaining the Dao." Although it's called Obtaining the Dao, there really is nothing to obtain. It is only because of the transformation of the person it can indeed be called achieved Dao. Those who realize the Dao can carry and spread the sage's Dao.

The Exalted One Venerable Sovereign said,[50] "Persons of virtue do not contend. Common people do. Persons of integrity do not mention the good they do. Common people brag about what they do for other people. Those who brag do not understand the meaning of the Way and Virtue [道 德, Dao De].

---

50   The Exalted One Venerable Sovereign (太上老君, Tai Shang Lao Jun) is a deified name for Laozi.

The reason common people cannot achieve the Dao is because they are presumptuous and have desire in their hearts. Once there is presumptuousness and desire in the heart, these will disturb the spirit. Once the spirit is disturbed, it will attach to objects. Once it attaches to objects, greed and desire will follow. Once greed and desire are generated, all kinds of worry will come. When worry and extravagant desire come together, a human's physical body and mind will suffer. Then disgrace and humiliation will mount and the life will be vagrant until sinking into the sea of bitterness and lose the True Dao forever. People who have intuition could realize the true meaning of Dao. And those who have realized it, their minds are clear and always tranquil.[51]

Guanyinzi [關 尹 子]

So a fruit yields seeds until water, fire [light], and soil are completely present, then the life continues nonstop, seeds grow to plants and plants produce seeds. If these are compromised, such as from a drought, flood, or hardening of soil, then life could not come forth. Therefore, Essence Water [精 水, Jing Shui], Spirit Fire [神 火, Shen Huo], and Mind-Intent Soil [意 土, Yi Tu], if these didn't have a central point of origin where the foundations all come together, then there could be no birth of human life.

---

[51] This passage is from *The Exalted One's Clarity and Tranquility of the Constant Scripture* (太上清靜常經, *Tai Shang Qing Jing Chang Jing*), a text attributed to Laozi.

This is analogous to sorcery and metaphysics, seeing things from emptiness. The Spirit lies in the category of Wood. Wood grows roots with Winter Water [冬水, Dong Shui], and becomes vigorous with Summer Fire [夏火, Xia Huo]. Therefore, a human Spirit hides its Essence [精, Jing] during the nighttime, and exhibits its Spirit [神, Shen] during the daytime. While hiding in Essence, dreams at night are unique, only the person sees them. Thus, Essence has senses of other people.[52]

While exhibiting the Spirit during the day, everybody sees the same world and the same thing. Thus, Spirit does not have the concept of self. Knowing that my real body is the body in my dream. Follow one's own feelings, one can see various of things. Then one can fly their Spirit and be their true self roaming in the fields of Supreme Purity.[53] Knowing that things in reality are the things in the dream. Follow one's own feelings, one can see various of things. Then one can collect their energy and gallop in the lands of every direction. Achieving such a state of the Dao, one can have longevity via the Spirit, and one can be above life and death by forgetting about the Spirit.

Breathing in the Vitality [氣, Qi] to nurse the Essence, it's similar to that of Metal generating Water. Breathing in the wind to nourish the Spirit, it's similar to that of Wood generating Fire. These are to prolong

---

52 *Essence has senses of other people* means we can have senses (all five) of other people in our dreams, making them seem real when we dream.

53 *Supreme Purity* (太清, Tai Qing) is the Void.

the Essence and Spirit from the external. Drinking water to nourish the Essence is how the Essence doesn't become destitute. Rubbing the Elixir Field to nourish the Spirit is how the Spirit doesn't become exhausted. These prolong the Essence and Spirit from the internal. If one can forget about the Essence and Spirit, one can detach the self from death and life.

I once said this can be done. Someone asked me, "What is your race? What is your surname? What is your name? What is your stylized name? What do you eat? What do you wear? Who are your friends? Who are your servants? What kind of Qin [琴, musical instrument] do you use? What kind of books do you read? What is your past? What is your present?" I was silent at the time and did not say a word.

The person pursued me relentlessly, I had no alternative but to answer, "I still cannot see myself, how could I answer these questions?"

During the process a farmer trains a cow to till the field, he himself also gets stronger. During the process a hunter fights with a tiger, he gets braver. During the process a fisherman dives to fish seafood, he is able to stay under water longer and longer. During the process a soldier learns to ride a horse, he gets more vigorous. All things on Earth could be me. Like my own body, pinworms and roundworms can live inside. Outside of my body, it can feed louses and fleas. When I have a breathing disorder, I can be like a turtle or a fish. When I have a tumor, I can be like a mouse or an ant. I could be all or any of the myriad things. Maintain the breath to nourish the harmony of the body, one would not feel hungry. Preserve the Spirit to nourish the body temperature, one would not feel cold. Based on Five Elements [五行, Wu Xing] to take care of Five Viscera [五藏, Wu Zang], the Five Viscera won't be harmed, so one will not have diseases. Restore position of Five Viscera per the Five Elements, then they don't have feelings, then they don't feel hurt. Humankind's ability can be mighty, they could change the nature created by Heaven and Earth. Such as to create thunders in winter, to make snow in summer, to make a dead body walk, to make a dried tree bloom.

To use a small bean to absorb spirits, to catch a fish in a cup, to draw a door on a wall which can be opened, to use clay to make a doll that could talk. These are all possible because of Qi, it can change all the things on Earth. All of the fondness and affection are also because of Qi. The way Qi makes things, it can converge, it can also diverge. The reason I practice Qi, is not to converge, nor to diverge. Those who converge live, those who diverge die.

Tanzi [54] [譚子]

The Dao's extrinsic appearance is: emptiness generates Spirit and Mind, Spirit and Mind generate Qi, Qi generates the elements. Then the elements turn into all the myriad things. These myriad things have very different shapes in appearance. The Dao's intrinsic essence is: elements generate Qi, Qi generates Spirit and Mind, Spirit and Mind turn back to the emptiness. Everything is connected and there is no

---

[54] Little is known of Tanzi except that he was a public figure, a monarch, from the Xing Clan.

difference with emptiness. Thus in the past, the sages observed and analyzed the facts about cycles and realized the principle of how things and beings were created and transformed. Forget about the bodily form and nourish the Qi, then forget about Qi and nourish the Spirit and Mind, then forget about Spirit and Mind and nourish emptiness. Then emptiness will connect to the body, and enter a stage of Great Harmony. Therefore, the sage who achieves harmony with the Dao preserves the Essence and Spirit inside the body. When using or presenting it, it could be anything in any shape. When it is hidden, it's the stage of the Supreme One.[55] When it is released, it becomes Supreme Purity [太清, Tai Qing]. Yin and Yang, Water and Fire grow and decline inside the body. The wasted Qi vents through the Seven Apertures.[56] The Qi of Spirit and Vitality steam and warm the body, thus the body is affected by the outside temperature. The Qi of Pure Yang flows and fills the whole body, then the body will be full of energy and will not decay. It's the way to immortality.

When a snake transforms into a turtle, or the sparrow transforms into a clam. The snake suddenly forgets how to wriggle and wind its body, and moves very slowly and staggeringly. The sparrow suddenly doesn't know how to fly or how to sing and gets a soft body inside a shell. Even using a knife or an axe to

---

[55]   Supreme One (太一, or 太乙, Tai Yi), meaning a stage of emptiness.

[56]   *Seven Apertures* (七竅): two eyes, two ears, two nostrils, and the mouth.

chop doesn't increase its abilities, even using an inked marking string or a ruler cannot define its shape. The question is what causes these rapid transformations.

Moreover, the piece which is supposed to be empty, we only see the piece but we cannot see the emptiness. Smashing the piece to see the emptiness, then we can only see the emptiness and the piece is no longer existing. The shape of the piece does not impede the existence of the emptiness. It is that human beings impede by themselves to realize the meaning of the emptiness. It does not hold up when the piece transforms from and into emptiness. It is that human beings hold up the process in their mind. This is sad!

Canzi [57] [璨子]

The True Dao is not difficult to realize. Nevertheless, do not attach the mind trying to distinguish what is good and what is bad. Keep the heart away from hate and love, then the door is wide opened, everything is clear and realized. However, the method is very important, the results may be far apart like the sky and the Earth if only missed by a tiny bit. If we want to see the Dao realized in sight, do not have the thought of what is in the same direction as us and

---

[57]   Canzi was a collaborator on *A Mirror for the Wise Ruler* (资治通鉴), a vast chronological general history written by Sima Guang (司馬光,1019–1089 CE) and other collaborators during the Northern Song dynasty in 1084. The work, totaling 294 scrolls, covers the period of 403 BCE to 959 CE. Canzi's work appears in the 83rd scroll.

what is against us. It is a disease of the heart to persist in figuring out what is good and what is the method. If we don't understand these basic principles, our practice of meditation and reciting will be in vain. Our original heart is like the Supreme Void, it is complete, it does not lack of anything, or contains too much of anything.

People judge things with biased preconceptions, that's why their mind is not emptied and cannot understand the true nature of True-Thusness [真如, Zhen Ru]. Do not persuade those to have a relationship with our fate. But don't overly constrain our thought either, as it's not the real meaning of emptiness. Maintain the common heart, then all the thoughts of right and wrong, good and bad, and all the worries will be dispelled naturally. If you don't understand this and just want to force the improper thought to stop, then the more you force it, the stronger it becomes. When one gets stuck in wanting to force the mind to be calm, this will only confuse the two ends, such as reality and emptiness, and one won't be able to realize these two ends are actually the same thing. If we do not understand thoroughly, we are just circling around between these two ends. All your efforts will be in vain. Starting with the desire to dispel all improper thoughts is itself an improper thought. The pursuit of emptiness is actually an act against emptiness. The more you talk, the more worries you will have, and the more you will increasingly become incompatible with the Dao. Forget about language and thinking, then one can find the Dao everywhere.

The way to obtain Dao is to return to the fundamentals of life. Following people to pursue the Dao from the surface is like losing the direction to find destiny. However, when one realizes it only needs a short moment to get back to the right track and achieve Dao, it's even better than the stage of emptiness. Hearts are born with emptiness. The emptiness turns into all the things because of the acquired arrogance. No need to chase the true nature of reality, it resides in the heart. Only if all the desires are dispelled and the heart is truly calm can we see the true nature of reality. The relative aspects of two ends [such as good and bad] are not realistic. Do not try to compare or see which end is real or correct. If there is a thought of defining good or bad in the mind, then the mind will never calm. If there is "one" in the heart, the relative thought of two ends will be created. So, even "one" shouldn't be kept in the heart. As long as "one" doesn't reside in the heart, everything outside can neither disturb nor affect the heart. Since the heart cannot be disturbed, the improper thought will not be created. The improper thought in the heart follows the outside scenes to dispel. The outside scenes follow the thought in the heart to sink also.

Outside scenes are reflecting what is in our heart; the thought in the heart is generated from the scenes we see. Both outside scenes and the inner heart, in fact, are empty. Although both are empty, they are the source of all things and beings. Therefore, the fundamental of everything is empty. Thus, everything is no different from anything else. This has nothing to do with likes or hates. The key to Obtaining the Dao is to calm the heart and comprehend [the Dao]. It can be easy, it can be difficult, but it all depends on the heart. For those who perceive the Dao as external and don't believe the Dao is within their own heart, the result is that the more eager they are to achieve the Dao, the further they are away from it. Persisting in only a certain way of practice is actually not following the right track. Confidence is established based on a constant belief [of the Dao within]. This then is true and constant confidence. With this confidence, the Dao that cannot be described or explained by plain language [can be realized].

Benjizi⁵⁸ [本寂子]

The monk Shi Yin [師因] asked the master, "What are the key principles of the Five Relations⁵⁹ between the ruler and the minister?"

The master said, "The center position is the Arupaloka [Void Realm]. Originally there was nothing there. The side position is Rupaloka [Form Realm], where there are tens of thousands of shapes. At the side of the center position is the irrationality of engaging in principles and affairs. On the other side of the center position is the rationality of engaging in affairs and principles. To accommodate [engaging in the Five Relations] is the middle position, wherein everyone's needs are catered to quietly, everything is considered

---

58 Benjizi (840–901 CE) was a Buddhist monk.

59 *Five Relations* (五位, Wu Wei): ruler to minister, father to son, husband to wife, elder brother to younger brother, and friend to friend.

and not abandoned, and nothing is infected but not perfectly clean either. It's not in the center position, but not in the side position either.

The unreal and abstruse Dao doesn't have an orthodox origin. From the beginning until now, there is only one position that is most incredible and exquisite. The ruler is the center position, and the minister is the side position. The minister devoting to the ruler is the side leaning toward the center. The ruler treating the minister well is the center leaning toward the side. If the ruler and the minister cherish the same ideals and have a common goal, this then is the accommodation.

The monk Shi Yin then asked, "How can one be a good ruler?"

The master answered, "The ruler has the great virtues and is respected by the whole country. It is like the sun shining in the sky."

The monk Shi Yin asked again, "How can one be a good minister?"

The master said, "Promoting the ruler's Dao with excellent methods intelligently, and helping the ruler to benefit the people of the country with real wisdom."

The monk Shi Yin asked, "What does the 'minister devoted to the ruler' mean?"

The master said, "Don't have any wrong thinking in mind and look up to and be loyal to the ruler."

The monk Shi Yin asked, "What does the 'ruler treating the minister well' mean?"

The master answered, "The emotion is not showing on the appearance and, like the sun, shines on everything without bias."

The monk Shi Yin asked, "What does the 'ruler and the minister cherishing the same ideals' mean?"

The master said, "Blended into one and no difference of outside and inside, the ruler and the minister are in harmony and respect each other."

The master then said, "To explain the relationship of the ruler and the minister as the position of the center and the side is not to damage the harmony. Thus, when ministers mention the ruler, they won't use the language of rebuke. This is essential to our theory."

Later, the master made a gatha [chant], which says, "The learners should understand their own clans first. Don't confuse your heart and temperament with false emptiness. Once the heart can be comfortably calm, then we won't diverge away from the right path to the Dao. And we don't need to rely on the outside force to help achieve it. To use language that is not against Dao, then you won't be burnt by the fire of prajna. The learners should follow the way that the sages seek for Dao. Once we can forget the temperate body that our spirit resides in and spend our efforts looking for the True Dao, then we are already on the right track. Once the Dao is achieved, then there is no self-body nor things we should seek. No difference between the beginning and ending."

Chongxinzi [崇信子]

The master had been living in the Heavenly Emperor's Temple [天皇寺, Tian Huang Si]. One day, he asked the emperor, "Since I arrived here, you haven't given me any instructions about improving my nature and temperament."

The emperor said, "Since you arrived here, I have been giving you instructions."

The master asked, "Where and when did you give me instruction?"

The emperor said, "When you handed me a cup of tea, I accepted it from you. When you served me a meal, I ate it for you. When you bowed to me, I nodded my head. Aren't these instructions to you?" The master then lowered his head and thought for quite a while.

The master said, "If you see it, you see it right away. If you need to think about it, then it means you are not seeing it." The master then realized suddenly and asked again, "How do I maintain the natural characteristics and utilize them?"

The emperor answered, "Let nature lead the way and function as it wills. Do not force anything. Let it follow its fate. Also, do not add too much thought and color to these ideas, just treat everything with a common heart.

After the master realized the Dao at Dragon Pool [龍潭, Long Tan], he would like to disseminate the Dao to the people as much as possible. One day, he preached at Dragon Pool, and said to the assembly, "Among us, there is a man. His teeth are sharp, like a tree of swords; his mouth is big, like a blood bowl. He wouldn't even turn his head if somebody hit him with a club. He should go to the top of the lonely mountain and disseminate my Dao there."

Master Xuan Jian [宣 鑒] then placed the Clearing Away Money Obstructions [60] talisman in front of the Buddha Hall. Holding up a torch he said, "I thoroughly studied these abstruse Buddhist scriptures, however, they are only like a hair out of the universe. Analyzing the key points of anything in the world is like putting a droplet of water into a big ocean."

He then burnt scriptures on the Virtue Mountain [德 山, De Shan]. After Xuan Jian realized the Dao, he preached to the crowd and said, "If there are no affairs in the mind, don't pursue things by forcing it. Even if you obtain it by force, it does not really belong to you. You only need to keep the affairs out of your mind and do not attach to the affairs, then your heart will be calm and spiritual, empty with nothing attached to it. Even if there is a tiny bit in the mind, we are lying to ourselves if treating it like it is as unimportant as a tiny scratch. Why is that? Because attaching to even the tiniest of affairs, we become trapped in the three bad paths [suffering, illusion, and mortality]. The affairs arise in the mind periodically and become like shackles forever. The fame of a sage or just a regular person, after all, is just the sound coming from a hollow. Either the handsome figure or the ugly shape is just an imagined scene. If people pursue these, how can they not end up tired. Afterwards, such pursuits become hate in the heart. They are harmful and of no benefit at all."

---

60   *Clearing Away Money Obstructions* (青 龍 疏 鈔, Qing Long Shu Chao) is a Daoist talisman, a spirit writing usually written on ochre paper, to invoke various spirits to lend aid for protection or to bring about good fortune to a situation.

Longanzi [龍安子]

If there were one thing that could be extended to preside over all the myriad things, then there would be nothing which is not the True. If all the turbid myriad things could be Returned to the One [歸一, Gui Yi], then the True would be in everything. Extending out would then not really be extending out, so there could be no presiding over. Turbidity would then not really be turbidity, therefore there could be no returning.

When [cultivating] alone, people are hurried, even if for just ten days, they only [cultivate] what is called Exhibiting the Function.[61] But if they can expediently identify with worldly matters, they can ultimately flow with the movement, and this is called the True and Constant [真常, Zhen Chang]. True Nature [眞性, Zhen Xing] is profound and void, without even a single thing, and this is called the method of Clarity and Purity [清淨, Qing Jing]. When the body contains all the adornments from discipline, this is called the Complete Reward Body.[62] When the body follows the root-power [天機 Tian Ji] and establishes the teachings, various virtues will be acquired without limit, and this is called One Hundred Thousand Flowers [百千億花, Bai Qian Yi Hua].

---

61 *Exhibiting the Function* (施用, Shi Yong) means the cultivator only goes through the motions of cultivation, but does not have the long-term discipline needed.

62 *Complete Reward Body* (圓滿報, Yuan Man Bao) is a term from the Buddhist *Flower Adornment Sutra* (華嚴經, Hua Yan Jing).

Delusion means that those who only see the external world are bound to follow in the footsteps and quarrels of others. Being bent on harboring animosity, disregarding following on dangerous roads, so that the mechanism for offensives and misfortunes come about, they are foolishly unaware of where they are headed.

Realization means those who see the internal world, they are heading to the place of prosperity and longevity. When living by the True and Nature through nourishing the Great Harmony, then life will be free and easy, and self-satisfied.

Huizhongzi [63] [慧中子]

A Buddhist monk [僧, Seng] asked, "What is the Buddha?"

The master answered, "The mind is the Buddha?"

The monk then asked, "Where does the mind dwell?"

The master said, "The light of the spirit shines by its own, far away from the vulgar world, realizes and reveals the true natural humanity."

The monk asked, "Is the common mind the right way?"

The master said, "Trying to approach it is against the Way."

The monk asked, "If I do not approach it, how do I know it is Dao?"

---

63   Huizhongzi (638–713 CE) is Hui Neng (慧能), the Sixth Patriarch of Chan Buddhism. He is one of the most important figures in Chinese Buddhism.

The master answered, "Dao is not something that could be understood, nor is it not something that could not be understood. If someone claims they understand the Dao, then they do not really understand, because it is their Nature they have not yet understood. If we can achieve the Dao with this doubt, it is like we arrived in Heaven."

The monk asked, "How about if I study Chan [Zen]?"

The master said, "Emptiness asks of the manifestations, and the manifestations answer through emptiness. Who can hear it? You are right here."

The monk asked, "How about if the mind refuses to pass down the classics? The salt in the water and the black dye in the paint, although we know they are there, we can't see their shape. The mind king [心王, Xin Wang] is similar. It is inside our body and it controls us, going in and out at will. It runs freely with no obstructions."

Somebody asked, "The master said, 'If the heart is empty, the wisdom sun would shine.' If you think, you will understand. If you analyze, you will perceive. A lonely lamp under the bright sunshine cannot show its light."

Someone asked, "Should we use the natural mind to treat people in the daily life?"

The master said, "I have a special pearl. It was blocked by the dusts, but this morning, the dusts are all gone and it is bright again. It is so bright that it shines on the mountains, rivers, and thousands of plants."

Someone asked, "Because I have a body, I have all sorts of needs. In order to extinguish the desires in the mind, should I extinguish the body first?"

The master replied, "The ancient people said, 'It is called seeing, because there is use of the eyes. It is called hearing, because there is use of the ears. It is called smelling, because there is use of the nose. It is called talking, because there is use of the mouth. It is called feeling, because there is use of the body. It is called attaching, because there is use of the mind.'

"Although truthful, these observations are like only seeing the sharp tip of an awl, and not seeing the other end of the square body of the awl. If [the body] were in Gold Mountain [金山, Jin Shan], then all this is different. But having eyes, do not see; having ears, do not hear; having a nose, do not smell; having a body, do not feel; having a mind, do not attach. Then suddenly the Chan [Zen] is realized and the Six Roots [六根, Liu Gen] will all be released."

Someone asked, "How do I release myself?"

The master said, "You were not tied up originally, you do not need to look for a release. The only thing you need is to realize you are not tied up."

A monk asked, "Is the Void of the Ten Directions [十方虚空, Shi Fang Xu Kong] the True Body?"

The master said, "What you received from the mind of desire is reversed. The green vine grows along the branch all the way to the top of pine trees. The cloud is white and clean and moves in the sky.

The things of the world are originally calm and free. It is people that stir things up."

Kuangzi [64] [鄺子]

It had been more than ten years since Kuang Ziyuan [鄺子元] was originally transferred to become a member of the Imperial Academy and hold a position in another part of the country, and he was not to be transferred back to the capital. He was neither happy nor bored, but then eventually he suffered an illness of the heart [mind]. When the illness broke out, he felt he was in a dream, and would speak deliriously. But when the illness was in remission, he acted like a normal person.

Somebody told him at True Void Temple [眞空寺, Zhen Kong Si] about an old monk who can cure heart illness without magic figures, incantations, or medicines. So Ziyuan went to the temple to see the old monk.

The old monk said, "Sir, your illness originates from your worries. The worries are born from vexation [煩惱, Fan Nao] and false thoughts [妄想, Wang Xiang]. There are three kinds of extravagant thoughts or hopes based on the periods of time.

"Recalling the past events of tens of years ago. The past glory and dishonor, gratitude and revenge, sorrows, joys, and vicissitudes of life, and various personal affections. These are vexations of the past.

---

64   Kuangzi was a master in the One Hundred Schools of Thoughts. He lived during the Song dynasty, 960–1279 CE.

"The issues that are right under our nose, we can conform to and deal with. However, some might be overcautious, change their mind many times and can't make up their mind. These are vexations of the present.

"People expect in the future they will be rich and honorable. Everything will fulfill as they wish. Some may wish they will achieve success and win recognition, and be welcomed by cheers when returning to their hometown. Or they wish descendants will pass the imperial examination and become government officials. Or they wish for any other outcome that has no guarantee of being achieved or acquired. These are extravagant thoughts of the future.

"These three kinds of vexations appear suddenly and disappear suddenly. Buddhists call this the 'Illusionary Heart' [幻心, Huan Xin]. If a person can see the vexations and cut those off, Buddhists call this, 'Awakened Heart' [覺心, Jue Xin]. So, do not worry about vexations appearing; worry about being aware of them too late. If the heart is like the Supreme Void, nothing inside, then where could worries find a foothold?"

The old master then said, "Your illness is also related to fire in your heart and water in the kidneys. These do not get along well. But what are the reasons? For those who indulge in sexual pleasure, and behave licentiously, Buddhists call this the 'desire induced by the outside world.' When sleeping on the bed at night still thinking about the beautiful girls, and who sometimes come into the dreams. Buddhists calls this the 'desire induced from the inside.' When attaching to these two kinds of desires, it consumes a person's Jing and Qi. If we can keep away from these attachments, then the water of the kidneys will nourish the body, and get along with the fire of the heart smoothly. As for people who overly ponder things, and who can't eat and can't sleep, Buddhists call this the 'noumenal hindrance' [理障, Li Zhang]. Working very hard for one's own career and business and not feeling tired, Buddhists call this the 'phenomenal hindrance' [事障, Shi Zhang]. Although these two kinds of hindrances are not categorized as selfish desires, they still cause injury and hinder one spiritually. If we can remove all these obstructions, then the fire of the heart would not rise too much and cause illness. Instead, the fire of the heart will get along with the water of the kidneys and nourish the body. So it is said, 'When the Six Dusts are dispelled, the roots of them will not function, they then flow back to the Original Nature, and all Six Roots become non-functional.'"

The old monk then said, "The sea of bitterness has no boundaries, only if you turn around can you find the other shore."

Ziyuan then followed these words and stayed alone in a room. He swept away all disturbances and desires, sat in meditation for a month, then his illness was cured.

Huzi [胡子]

Laozi talked about nonexistence [無]. He said it is profound, dark, and obscure, but things and essences are inside it. Within the eluding sight are their semblances. Thus, so-called "nonexistence" is not really non-existing. The Buddhists talk about emptiness, and they also say humanity is naturally between Heaven and Earth. It is not alive, and it will not die, and is outside of the cycle of rebirth. Thus, the so-called "emptiness" is not really empty. When us Confucianists say, if it's there, then it's really there; saying it's empty and it really has nothing; saying it's solid, then it really is solid; saying it's hollow, then it really is hollow: this is because our theories, they are precious and realistic. If we judge by the reason, then the reason follows the laws of the universe and the characteristics are determined. How can it be empty or not existing? If we judge the Qi when Qi gathers, it does exist; when Qi dispels, it does not exist. There are reasons when things gather. There are reasons also when things dispel. What can one say, there is no cause? When Qi gathers and forms a shape, then it is solid; when Qi gathers but does not form a shape, then it is hollow. Reasons are not hollow. Laozi said the "Existence was born from Nonexistence." Buddhists say, "After death we then return to our True Nature." Don't we know how our body was born? Why did [Laozi] say it was born from nonexistence? Don't we know how our body dies? Why did [Buddha] say that it returns to the True Nature after death? Thus, there must be reason for birth. It cannot be without reason. If death is the way of returning to True Nature, does this mean Life [命, Ming] is also not true, or even Nature [命, Ming]?

Part Four
Chapters on the Nature of Mind

[心性章, Xin Xing Zhang]

The principles for achieving the Dao has been explained in previous chapters. Where the Dao is located is also where the Nature of Mind is located. The following are then collected discussions about the reasons behind Nature of Mind from the One Hundred Schools of Thought.

The True Nature Dwells in the Constant
By Zhuangzi [莊子]

To rely on the hook and line, or the compass and square, to correct things only damages what naturally belongs to these things; to rely on the rope or glue to bind things together only hurts the natural quality of these things. By using etiquette and music to change and correct people's rigidness; by utilizing benevolence and righteousness to educate people in order to comfort their minds, doing these will lose the nature of the human constitution.

All things in the world have their normality. So-called normality is that a curved thing is not made so by using the hook; a straight thing is not made so by using the ruler; a circular thing is not made so by using the compass; a square thing is not made so by the need to be made by a square; the adhesion

307

effect between things do not rely on the glue or the varnish. Things that bond together do not rely on the rope to tie them together. Thus, all things in the world are unwittingly produced by a natural guide without knowing themselves how they are produced, and then equally unwittingly obtain results without knowing how these are so. This was true before and is so now. So it is unlikely any of these relationships appear deficient. Then why do benevolence and righteousness act as the connections, or like glue and varnish, ropes and bands, among the Dao and its characteristics? This is only making people bewildered! A small confusion will lead people into the wrong direction. The great confusion will make people change their natural characteristics. How do I know this? Since the time of the Yu Clan[1] called in his benevolence and righteousness and turned the world upside down. All the people in the world were competing to run for benevolence and righteousness. Isn't this to use benevolence and righteousness to change the people's original nature?

The Indignant Mind Is Not Benevolence or Righteousness

By Zhuangzi [莊 子]

Confucius visited Laozi and they talked about benevolence and righteousness. Laozi said, "If someone is blowing on a rice chaff, and the dust gets into their eyes, they then try to sense the four directions of Heaven and Earth, and are immediately confused. If mosquitoes or gadflies bite someone's skin, they will not be able to sleep all night long. For what you said, benevolence and

---

1   *Yu Clan* (虞 氏, Yu Shi). This is Emperor Shun, one of the Five Legendary Emperors.

righteousness only spur people into doing things that go beyond their nature. There is nothing greater than such confusion in the world. In fact, we just need to keep people of the world from losing their pristine nature. So long as we try to control the wind direction, the people will be like the grass, naturally moving towards the direction where the wind goes. So should everything just follow principles of morality, is that it? Why should you expend such an effort carrying a giant drum and beating it along the road, working so hard to find a lost child? The swan does not bathe every day to make itself white, a crow does not dye itself everyday to make itself black. The natural simplicity of black and white does not form a base for judging beauty and ugliness. The glory of fame and reputation does not do a man better than his natural characteristic. Benevolence and righteousness is like when the water of a pool dries up and fishes are stranded on land. They try to moisten each other with their humid breath and spittle to save their lives. It would be better to forget each other in the rivers and lakes!"

Benevolence and Righteousness Falsely Wandering in the Mind

By Zhuangzi [莊子]

Yierzi [意而子] met with Xuyou [許由]. Xuyou asked, "What did Yao [堯] instruct you?"

Yierzi said, "Yao told me, you must follow the guidelines of benevolence and righteousness, and be able to figure out what is right and what is wrong."

Xuyou said, "Then, why did you come to me? Yao already tattooed the benevolence and righteousness on your face and cut your nose with the straight of right and wrong. How can you wander in the way of free enjoyment, unregulated contemplation, and constant change?"

Yierzi said, "Nevertheless, I am still willing to skirt along the way."

Xuyou said, "It cannot be, the blind cannot see the beauty of the eyebrows, eyes, and other features. The blind cannot see the colorful patterns of embroidery on the cloth."

Yierzi replied, "The beautiful woman Wu Zhuang [無莊] forgot her beauty, the warrior Ju Liang [據梁] forgot his strength, the Yellow Emperor [黃帝, Huang Di] forgot his wisdom, these were all achieved in the furnace of practicing the Dao. How do you know that the creator will not erase the tattoo on my face and redo my nose, and let me have a complete form to follow you as my master?"

Xuyou said, "Alas! We don't know that yet, but I will tell you some reasons of the Dao. My master offered all things and yet did not think it was of any great righteousness. The benefits [of his offerings] stretched to the future generations and yet he did not think it was benevolence. He was born in ancient times but did not consider himself old. He carved the shape of all things but did not think he was skillful. What my master achieved is the realm that we should explore."

Obtaining Perfection in Heaven
By Guanyinzi [關尹子]

Liezi [列子] asked Guanyinzi, "The cultivated man who dives into the water does not feel obstructed, jumps into the fire but does not feel hot, walks high up on top of all things and does not feel fear, how can he achieve such a realm?"

Guanyinzi said, "It is because he can embrace pure Qi rather than his wisdom and bravery. Let me tell you, everything that has appearance, image, sound, and color is called an object, but why is there such a big difference between objects? What objects are actually superior to other objects? They are all just things with appearance and colors after all. So, actually a visible object does not truly exhibit form or color, and there remains nothing that isn't subject to change.[2] The persons who understand this truth are fully aware of its mysteries. How then could other things control or repress them? These kinds of people can stay in the instinct within their limits, hide in the gratuitous chaos. They wonder among all the things or the changing environment from the beginning to the end. They purify their natural temperament, raise their vitality, retain their virtue, so that they can communicate with the law of nature. For the persons who achieve this, they keep what was endowed and intact from their nature, and guard their spirits well without an opening, then from where can foreign objects invade?

"There was a drunken man who fell off a cart and got injured but not killed. His bones and joints were the same as a normal man, but he suffered less injury than a normal man would have. This was because his mind was not affected. He was unaware of getting on or falling off the cart. The fear of death did not enter into his mind. So he was not afraid at all when he encountered the danger of foreign objects. That person can keep the full nature of mind with wine not to mention maintaining the integrity of the mind with the laws of nature. Sages keep their minds in the nature, so there is nothing that can hurt them."

---

2   These statements agree with the Buddhist idea from the *Heart Sutra,* "Form is emptiness and emptiness is just form."

The Human Mind Is Like Water in a Dish
By Xunzi[3] [荀 子]

People's minds are just like water in a dish. Place it properly and not to stir, then the muddy dregs will fall to the bottom and clear water will appear on top. It is so clear that it can be used as a mirror to see the beard, eyebrows, and the texture of skin very clearly. But if a breeze blows on it, and the dirty dregs are disturbed and float in the water, then the clear water on top will also become muddied. It can no longer be used as a mirror to reflect the correct image of the human body. People's minds are also like this. If using correct reasons to guide it, cultivating it with noble character, then foreign objects cannot make the mind tilt. Then it can be used to determine right and wrong and to judge suspicions. Even with one minuscule false thought within the mind, a person's upright demeanor will be changed on the appearance, the mind is tilted, and it can no longer be used to determine various affairs.

Those With a Virtuous Mind, Master the Mind
By Guanyinzi [關 尹 子]

When people dream at night, the time of their dreaming may seem longer than the actual time. So it's not certain when the mind was born. For example, if living during the time in the state of Qi,[4] the mind would only see things about Qi. And

---

3   Xunzi (荀 子, 312–230 BCE), a Confucian philosopher of the Warring States period, was an important figure in contributing to the One Hundred Schools of Thought.

4   Qi was a state in Western Zhou and the Warring States 1122–265 BCE.

later, if born in the state of Song [宋], Chu [楚], Jin [晉], or Liang [梁], what the mind sees will be different. So although the individual [in those environments and times] is not the same, the mind has no boundaries of time and space. People who are good at archery can learn more from the bow itself than from Master Yi [羿師]. People who are good at sailing can learn more from the ship than from Master Ao [奡師]. People who are good at controlling their mind can learn more from mind than learning from sages.

The Mind Has a Great Constant
By Guanyinzi [關尹子]

People who cannot be single-minded, it's because their five senses are turbulent and exhausted. Their minds are not capable of being calm and having one-pointed concentration. People who cannot keep extraneous thoughts outside of their mind, the Five Elements [五行, Wu Xing] change without end. Their minds will never be emptied. People who cannot calm their minds, then ten thousand kinds of distracting thoughts will pass through, and their minds can never be quieted. Even if these people seem like they are single-minded, often different thinking pops up. Even if they appear to be open-minded, they often become complacent. Even if they seem like they can calm their mind, often it becomes disturbed.

Only sages can restrain all things into a breath. Nothing can deter their clear mind. Only immortals can make a breath into all things and nothing can disturb their realm of inaction. Knowing that the mind is nothing, then we know that all things are nothing. Knowing that all things are nothing, then we know the Dao is nothing. Knowing that the Dao is nothing, then we do not have to promote the noble and incomparable behaviors, and do not need to feel surprised by esoteric and mysterious reasons.

When a material thing and me are connected, then the desire will form in the heart. When two wood pieces are rubbed together intensely, fire will be created. It cannot be said that this is because of me, nor can it be said that it is because of the other end; it cannot be said that it is not because of me, and it cannot be said that it is not because of the other end. Persistently to make a distinction between me or the other end is such a foolish thing. All the things were born from the soil, and they all return to the soil eventually. All affairs were made from thoughts, and will return to the thoughts eventually. Depending only on thoughts, then it suddenly becomes right, suddenly becomes wrong, suddenly may be good and suddenly may be bad. The thought may be changed at any time, but the heart cannot change. The thought may have consciousness, but the heart does not have consciousness. Only my single-minded heart doesn't change. Thoughts, like dusts in the world, come and go regularly. All the affairs rise and end rapidly and suddenly. My mind is constant and it will last forever.

Detaining the Mind
By Guanyinzi [關 尹 子]

Using the mind to sense things does not produce the mind, it only arises the feeling [of things]. Objects communicate with the mind. This doesn't create objects, but generates cognitions. Not even sure that objects are real, let alone cognitions. Not even sure that cognitions are real, let alone the feeling.

Some people extravagantly think that something exists where there is absolute emptiness, and that it's constant for the things that keep changing. Stubbornly thinking this is normal.

Once a tiny bit of feeling has been recognized, it can accumulate to excessive feeling. All things come and go without an end, but my heart has a boundary. Therefore, my conscience is constrained by the feeling, my original feeling is constrained by foreign objects. Some can make it leave, some can make it come, and these things come and go, and it is not dependent on my will. It is the creator who controls these. This has always been endless. Even as big and wide as [are] Heaven and Earth, they can only control visible things but not invisible things. Although Yin and Yang are exquisite, they can only control the things that have Qi. They cannot control the things without Qi. Where the mind goes, the Qi will follow. Where the Qi goes, then the shape will form correspondingly. Just like the Ultimate Void, it can create a complete Qi from the emptiness, and from this Qi to create all things. But this Qi is not equal to the Ultimate Void. My complete heart can transform to be Qi and to other forms, but my mind has no Qi and is invisible. Knowing my mind has no Qi and is invisible, then Heaven and Earth, Yin and Yang cannot control my mind.

My Mind Creates the Transformation and Circulation
By Guanyinzi [關 尹 子]

The transformation of the Five Elements [五行, Wu Xing] is because of Essence [精, Jing]. There is then Heavenly Spirit [魂, Hun]. Because of the Heavenly Spirit, there is then Spirit [神, Shen]. Because of the Mind-Intent [意, Yi], there is then Earthly Spirit [魄, Po]. Because of the Earthly Spirit, there is then Essence.

The Five Elements circulate and transform nonstop, thus the consciousness of individual lives in a changing and circulating universe. It has been so for hundreds of millions of years, and it still hasn't seen an end. Just like a bud sprouting from a seed and a plant producing seed, this cycle has been repeated countless times. As wide as Heaven and Earth are, they cannot sprout a bud from an empty seed. The egg hatches and becomes a bird. Female birds then produce more eggs. This cycle has repeated countless times. As clever as Yin and Yang are, they cannot hatch an egg that was not fertilized. Matter that becomes an individual life obtains its consciousness via breathing. There is no single life without the consciousness of itself. Life results from the transforming of Five Elements. Nobody can change this law of nature.

The Mind Is Affected So Easily

[No listed author]

Zicheshi [子車氏][5] had a hog. Its color was pure black. It once delivered three piglets. Two were pure black. The other was black but the color was impure with white spots on its body. The hog saw the different looking piglet, and became very disgusted. So the hog gnawed the little pig, biting through to its kidneys and intestines, until the little pig died. The other two purebred piglets, the hog took good care of them and didn't want anything to harm them.

Zihuazi [子華子] said, "This is very extreme, and its mind [the hog's] was affected so easily. The eyes were bewildered by the difference of the appearance, and its mind was controlled by like and dislike. Although the piglet was born by itself, the hog still killed it and did not feel regret, not to mention other animals that are not its kind? Nowadays, people usually hold hands and whisper together. Seemingly, they have a good relationship.

---

5   Zicheshi (子車氏) was from an old and great family in the state of Qin.

However, when they need to protect their personal interests, they no longer see each other as friends, even though they appeared glued to each other before. When they see something profitable or feel something is not adequate, they become anxious and quickly turn hostile. They will even attack their friends. This is because the mind is fickle and affected so easily. These kinds of people are no different from Zicheshi's hog.

Doing Good or Bad Cannot Be Forced
By Zihuazi [子華子]

Beigongzi[6] went to the state of Wei [魏國] to become an official. Zihuazi said, "Welcome. How do you cultivate your mind, are you willing to tell me that?"

Beigongzi said, "I am not finished yet. I lived in poverty and I had to rely on other people's help to keep from starving. Although I was so poor, I kept in mind to do virtuous things and to go against doing sinful things. This is what I think I have achieved."

Zihuazi's face turned serious. After a while he then said, "Oh! Why do you say that? Why is it doing good things should be favored and doing so-called wrong things should be hated?

"Let me tell you, when sages do not appear, the world is chaotic and people become infatuated. They want to hold onto something, but eventually end up with nothing. Wanting to extend things and to affect other people to improve, but eventually those people will be lost. Therefore, a ruler who wants to revitalize the country and clear up the quarrels between people removes the benevolence from his formula so he may be able to

---

6   Beigongzi (北宮子) was a warrior of the ancient state of Qi (齊國).

achieve it. If benevolence is not removed, then chaos also will not end. So why should they use the benevolence to educate people!"

Beigongzi then said, "Hey, if there is such a thing? I hope you can describe in detail."

Zihuazi said, "The human heart is small but it is the residence of the spirit. It is where many things interact, and it likes to deal with many disordered things, as if walking in the surging water. Sometimes, it feels frightened, sometimes it feels taboo, sometimes punished. These could all happen within a day, or even just within a short period of time, and in this tiny place [meaning the heart], it can suddenly feel very hot like a burning fire, or it can suddenly become cold as ice. So, in regard to the Spirit, why should it bear such harsh conditions? The spirit does not dwell in such places, and if the place becomes decayed, the Spirit will not live in such [decayed] places, so then the place will become depleted.

"How then can a person manage to do good things well? In ancient times, people who understood the Dao were moderate just like a pot of thick soup with no seasoning. They acted cautiously as children sitting on a swing. When being pushed, they would follow the force, swinging up and back naturally. Their essence, though appearing left behind, was pure and intact. Their spirits were free and leisurely, and communicated with Dao frequently.

"Ordinary people only know how to admire [others and things], but who knows how they could ever accomplish acquiring them? What you just said, 'to cautiously keep virtue in mind and to only do good things,' but who is going to do those not-so-good things? And who should be blamed for those bad things you go against? You want to give it out, but others may not want to accept it; you want to blame, but others may not agree with you. These will cause resentment and create enemies who go against you. With my mind inflated with pride against other people, with only enmity in their minds, then what can you do to eliminate the conflict? If the conflict does not stop, it may start with minor verbal insults, then develop to serious and harmful acts or killing. Based on what you were saying, and completing what you think is correct, this will put you in dangerous situations."

The Snobbish and Confused Mind
By Zihuazi [子華子]

In the Song dynasty [宋, 960–1297 CE], there was a man named Chengzi [澄子]. He lost a black robe and looked back along the way he had been. He saw a woman wearing a black robe, and after stopping her he would not let her go, saying, "Please give my black robe back to me."

The woman responded, "Although, you lost a black robe, this one is mine, and I made it myself."

Chengzi said, "If this is so, then you should give your robe to me now. The black robe I lost is made of silk, and this one you are wearing is made of cotton. Using your cotton robe in exchange for my silk robe, you are indeed taking a big advantage of me."

Zihuazi said, "Private gains dull people's minds, and thus people only care about taking advantage, and forget about their own quality of nature and character. Becoming so, is there anything they won't dare to do as long as there is a private gain? Nowadays, it's rare to find people who do not act like Chengzi."

The Highest Spirit of the Human Mind

By Yangzi [楊子]

Someone asked about Spirit [神, Shen]. Yangzi said, "It's about the mind."

"May I ask about it?"

Yangzi said, "Immerse yourself into Heaven and you will understand Heaven. Immerse yourself into the Earth and you will understand the Earth. Heaven and Earth are unfathomable, yet their ways are ordinary. They can only be understood when immersing into them with the mind. Is it more so with people? Is it more so with the principles or affairs of the world?"

"May I ask about immersing in the mind of sages?"

Yangzi said, "In the past, Confucius immersed himself into King Wen [文王, Wen Wang] of Zhou and he reached him. Yan Yuan [顏淵, 1635–1704 CE] immersed himself into Confucius and almost reached him, only short by a marginal bit. Therefore, the Spirit is not far away. Just immerse yourself into it and you will get it. Heaven has deities and clarity to shine on the world. Heaven has the essence and the purity to cover everything and create all types of things. Are people's minds similar to the deities'? If you can hold them [in your mind], they will stay. If you let them go, then they will be gone. One who is able constantly to hold onto them and allow them to abide, but isn't this only what a sage can accomplish? Sages preserve their Spirit and explore the highest Dao, to achieve the great smoothly and bring great prosperity to the world. They bridge the space between Heaven and Humanity, connecting them without a gap."

Great People Are Not Robbers of Life
By Tanzi [譚子]

Heaven and Earth come from the Ultimate Void [太虛, Tai Xu]; humanity and animals come from Heaven and Earth; Yingding [橙虹, a tapeworm] come from humans and animals. Yingding is a wormlike bug that lives in the stomachs of humans and animals. This worm seizes the essence of my body, broils my soul, and it relies on the food that I swallow to survive. The human has a certain lifespan, and everybody dies eventually from this or from that. We know the world will perish eventually. When the world has perished, will humankind survive? When I am dead, will the Yingding still be alive? Just like a treacherous official who endangers the country, shattering the country, there is no way for the families to survive. Termites eat wood. When wood is depleted, then termites will die, too. Profoundly moral people take their own essence, and hide their own spirit. They are not enthusiastic about the flavors of food, they control their own hobbies and desires, they are indifferent to things of wealth. If such people persist, even Heaven and Earth will perish, but I will still survive. The Yingding in my stomach dies and I will have long-life, just like if the treacherous official is executed, then the country will enjoy peace.

Conceal the Qi and Accumulate Essence
By Tanzi [譚子]

The mountain pine trees are able to bear the frost because they are able to conceal the Vital Energy [Qi]. Beautiful jade is able to resist the flame because the jade has Refined Essence [Jing]. Therefore, Great Persons [大人, Da Ren] during the day command their consciousness like a commander waves the banner to direct the troops. At night, they act like a Spiritual Mushroom[7] to complement their body and consciousness. They have no awareness of the outside world, because their thinking also stops during the night. They do not feel cold when the wind chills in the winter, do not feel hot during the heat of summer days. Therefore, Wise Persons [君子, Jun Zi] who accumulate their own Vital Energy can keep ghosts away and vanquish crafty and fawning enemies. Those who accumulate a Great Essence can be of benefit to other people's lives by protecting their wealth and longevity. Why so? Because they have an abundance of Vital Energy and Refined Essence.

Forget Form, Seek Nature

By Tanzi [譚子]

Amber cannot be regarded as a rotten plant. Cinnabar cannot be mixed into melted metal. A magnet cannot attract rusted iron. The Vital Energy cannot be used to ignite a ceramic furnace. So Great Persons make good use of the Essences of the Five Elements and are good at capturing the Spirit of all things. They enjoy good fortune from celestial beings, and enjoy the honor of riding on the wind as a horse. The Dao, the key is to forget your form and seek your Nature.

---

7   *Spiritual Mushroom* (神芝, Shen Zhi), means absorbing Jing, Qi, and Shen from Heaven and Earth. Ganoderma lucidum, commonly called Ling Zhi (靈芝), the Divine immortal mushroom or Reishi mushroom.

The Harmony of Nature

By Liuzi[8] [劉子]

When a blacksmith forges a sword, if the sword is too stiff then it will break, if it is too soft then it will curl. If he doesn't want the sword to break, he must add tin. If he doesn't want the sword to curl, he must add chromium. Why? Chromium is hard and tin is soft, these reconcile the hardness and softness, and become good alloys for forging swords. When a painter is painting, if he runs the paintbrush too slowly then it will be difficult to dry; if he runs the paintbrush too hurriedly then it will not be solid. Not too slow and not too hurried, then the paint is reconciled, and the finished painting will be beautiful. The natural character of humanity is similar to this. King Yan of Xu[9] was too soft, so his country was destroyed. Qi Shanggong[10] was too cowardly, so his country fell into ruin. These are examples of the too weak leading to failure.

Yang Chufu's [陽處父] personality was too rigid, and he ended up being murdered. Zheng Ziyang's [鄭子陽] temperament was too strict, which led to his assassination. These are examples of people with too strong of a personality.

---

8   Liuzi (劉子, 729-794 CE) was a Tang dynasty Daoist philosopher and poet.

9   King Yan of Xu (偃王, Yan Wang) was the ruler of the country Xu, 徐, in Western Zhou.

10   Qi Shanggong (齊商公) was the ruler of the state of Qi, during 484 to 481 BCE.

The Chu Zixi[11] was too lenient and was killed by his own subordinate. Zhu Zhuanggong [邾莊公, 540–507 BCE] was too rash, and in the end failed because of his temperament. These are examples of a narrow and brash mind leading people to disasters.

Xi Menbao [西門豹] knew he was impatient so he wore a wide leather belt to remind himself to slow down. Dong Anyu [董安于] was slow in personality so he tied silk strings to encourage himself. These were people who knew how to use the strength of something else to make up for their weakness and shortcomings.

Nature Has Its Own Preferences

By Liuzi [劉子]

A beautiful multistoried pavilion, with enclosed private houses, decorated curtains of pearls, and houses decorated with fine jades, this is what people would like [to live in]. But when a little bird flies inside, it feel anxious. High mountains with steep slopes, plenty of trees with thick twisted branches interlacing each other, these are the places the apes and monkeys like. But people would shudder if living up in these steep mountains. The Five Notes and Six Tunes, and *Xian Chi* and *Xiao Shao*,[12] these are music that people enjoy. But birds and animals regard these as just sonic vibrations. Pools underneath a waterfall, deep green lakes, sea waves, and running streams, these are

---

11   Chu Zixi (楚子西) was the prime minister of the state of Chu in 479 BCE.

12   The *Five Notes* and *Six Tunes* are ancient Chinese musical structures. *Xian Chi* (咸池) and *Xiao Shao* (蕭韶) are song titles of ancient music.

places where fish and water creatures live safely. But people [who don't know how to swim] feel afraid when jumping into the water. Flying squirrels eat smoked woods, tapirs swallow metals, cloud chickens like to eat snakes, and people like to eat livestock.

Birds, animals, and humans are all different in their dispositions. Their shape and essence are also different. Therefore it is not a surprise at all that their place of residence and habits are also different. People are born with two forms of Qi [Yin Qi and Yang Qi], and hold Five Constant Virtues [benevolence, righteousness, propriety, wisdom and fidelity] in their natures. Although some are smarter and some are not; some have good virtues, some do not; but for the eyes to see the sun and the moon, ears to hear the thunder, feeling hot when close to the fire, feeling cold when stepping on the ice, these are common senses and it is nothing special among human beings. Hearing, sight, smell, and taste have their own natural characteristics. Distinguishing between good and evil is revealed naturally. We cannot regard the black as white, or regard the ancient Chinese notes of Yu as Jue, Jue as Gong, Gong as Shang, Shang as Jue, Jue as Zhi, or Zhi as Yu, or the same as the Do, Re, Mi, So, La.[13] We cannot regard bitter as sweet, or regard stinky as fragrant.

However, preferences are a different story. Someone may have a preference that is especially different, others may have exactly the opposite. Everyone loves to see the smile of a beautiful lady, but the Yellow Emperor chose Momu to be his wife

---

13   Yu (羽), Jue (角), Gong (宮), Shang (商), Zhi (徵);
       Do (宮), Re (商), Mi (角), So (徵), La (羽).

and was not impressed by Luo Ying's [14] good looks. Chen Hou set his affections on Dunqia, but remained indifferent to Yangwen's beauty.[15] Grilled lamb and fried goose, turtle soup, and cooked soft bear paws, these are delicious food that everyone likes to eat, but King Wen of Zhou [16] preferred to eat salted Chang Pu roots [菖浦, calamus/sweet flag] rather than various other delicious foods. *Yang Chun* [陽春], *Baixue* [白雪], *Jiaochu* [嗷楚], *Cailing* [採陵] are music [ancient song titles] that everyone loves to hear. Emperor Shun of Han [17] liked to listen to the chirping of mountain birds rather than orchestral music. Marquis Wen of Wei [?–396 BCE] liked to listen to the sound of the hammer and chisel more than the tuned sounds of musical instruments made of metal and stone. The tulips of the Xuandan [玄憺], spring orchids, and autumn cymbidiums, these are aromatic flowers recognized by everyone, but some people who live by the sea prefer fishy smells to the aroma of these flowers.

All these examples show that people have different preferences. However, if one's preference becomes overly obsessive, the preference can become opposite to everyone else, and it may have the end result of the person believing white is black, bitter is sweet, Jue is Yu, stinky is aroma, and not able to tell what is beautiful and what is ugly, what is love, and what is hate.

---

14   Momu (嫫母) was a legendary unattractive woman, and Luo Ying (落英), a legendary beautiful woman.

15   Chen Hou (陳侯) was a monarch of Zhou Dynasty. Dunqia (敦洽) was an unattractive woman from the Chen state, while Yangwen (陽文), from Chu state, was known for her beauty.

16   King Wen of Zhou (文王, 1152–1056 BCE).

17   Emperor Shun (順, 115–144 CE) of Han (漢).

Remove Sense-Desires and Nourish Nature
By Liuzi [劉子]

Sense-desires [六慾, Liu Yu] are like the smoke produced from a fire, but the smoke then works against it and suppresses the fire. Ice comes from water, but it blocks the water from flowing. So when the smoke is weakened, then the fire will be strong; when ice melts, the water will run again. If the nature of one's mind has virtue, then the feelings of sense-desires will dissipate; if people have strong feelings of sense-desires, then the nature of their mind will disappear gradually.

Dust cannot attach onto the smooth. Sense-desires cannot infect people whose natures and minds are bright. The tree stands still, but is moved by the wind. Water is clean, but it becomes muddied as dirt mixes with it. The human nature is pure, but becomes corrupt because of the temptation of the sense-desires. Sense-desires to a human is like a moth to trees. The tree houses moths, but these insects eat and decay the tree. Similarly, if people cannot control desires, they will generate a bad feedback and hurt them. So if there are too many moths, the tree will break. If the desire of a human is too strong, then he or she will die. If people want to control their affections and desires, the first thing to do is to restrain the Five Senses. The Five Senses are the ways of affection and desire, and a residence of addictions. Eyes like to see the beautiful colors. I call it the ax to hew human nature. The ears like to listen to vulgar sounds. I call it the battle drum attacking the mind. The mouth likes to eat delicious food. I call it the poison decaying the intestines. The nose likes to smell fragrant aromas. I call it the smoke fumigating the throat. The body likes to ride upon the carriage. I call it a crippling instrument. Knowing how to control these five senses can preserve good health, otherwise they can also hurt people's health.

Mind and Body Were Originally Ultimate Void
By Xuanzhenzi [玄真子]

Water droplets on lotus leaves are round in shape. They are round shaped naturally without the help of any tool, and they cannot be made square. [The droplets] can fall off the lotus leaf and not leave wetness on it. A dying fire always moves around. It does not leap or break off. This is because fire moves quickly. With the backing of the sun and rain dispersing about, a rainbow can be produced. If facing the sun, the dispersed water will just produce shadows. Getting water from a river to brew wine, one should follow the current because it cannot be stopped. Rain drops fall onto the ground and then merge into the deep blue sea, and the individual drops can no longer be recognized. The quiet mind returning to the empty space of the Ultimate Void, and can no longer be distinguished, merges with Heaven.

Cultivating Nature and Penetrating the True
By Tianyinzi [天隱子]

In the *Book of Changes* [易經, Yi Jing] is Gradual Movement [53rd hexagram] and in the *Lao Zi*[18] there is the "exquisite gate of all-knowing." People who want to cultivate and want to attain Nature [性, Xing], do not expect to achieve it suddenly. They must go step by step and improve gradually. Number one is Fasting.[19]

---

18   *Scripture on Dao and Virtue* (道德經, Dao De Jing).

19   *Fasting* (齋戒, Zhai Jie), to "abstain and guard against."

Number two is Living Leisurely.[20] Number three is Fixating the Mind.[21] The fourth is Seated Meditation.[22] The fifth is Perceiving Spirit.[23]

What is Fasting? It is bathing the body and cleaning one's virtue. What is Living Leisurely? It is to be secluded in a quiet place. What is Fixating the Mind? It is to restore Essence and Nature. What is Seated Meditation? It is forgetting the forms and releasing the self. What is the Perceiving the Spirit? It is to communicate with the spirits and gods.

Lessen Desires and Nourish the Mind

By Zhuzi[24] [朱子]

When Kongming[25] chose his wife, he decided to marry an unattractive woman. He devoted himself to his job and his country. This is what most people cannot bear. His spirit was just and honorable. His knowledge, broad and deep. Although part of his endowed [innate] talents, his wisdom continued to grow day by day. And the reason his prestige continued to accumu-

---

20 *Living Leisurely* (安處, An Chu) is "quiet abiding."

21 *Fixating the Mind* (存想, Cun Xiang), means "keep to the imagination."

22 *Seated Meditation* (坐忘, Zuo Wang), means "to sit and forget."

23 *Perceiving Spirit* (神戒, Shen Jie), seeing and manifesting the spirit within the Third Eye, or Mysterious Pass, as Daoists call it.

24 Zhuzi (朱子, 156–224 CE) was a Neo-Confucianist.

25 Kongming (孔明) is the stylized name of Zhuge Liang (諸葛亮, 181–234 CE), considered one of China's greatest strategists, scholars, and inventors.

late daily, I believe, was that he had little desires and he cultivated his mind. These are what helped him the most.

Do Not Forget to Study the Correct
By Chengzi[程子]

Heaven created human beings through the laws of nature. So if
we do not study or learn from the masters, how can we realize
reason and acquire knowledge? Identifying sages and worthies
has been difficult even in ancient times. Even those having had
the opportunity to meet and study from the great teacher Confucius became great men with high moral characters. Sages and
worthies of the Dao teach people with their knowledge. Their
ideology has influenced the inner thoughts for generation after
generation, enlightening those people in confusion.

In Queli [闕里], during the Zhou dynasty, Yan Hui [顏薈]
previously lived there. He lived in an alley covered with weeds,
and the water well was blocked and in ruin. Ignorant towns-
people didn't even bother to come or visit the place. But,
among Confucius' disciples, who is more excellent than him?
To recall the past and looking at the current scene of the alley,
people would feel compassion about what he had been
through. Later, after kind businessmen and Confucius' disciples
donated money and spent effort, the alley was renovated and
the water well is now clean and deep. People then lived in the
alley, had clear water to wash with and grow plants. The trees
in the alley formed nice shade. They built a kiosk there and
named it the Kiosk of Yan Le [顏樂].

The thoughts of ancient people, I can only now try to interpret or guess at. But one thousand years ago, Yan studied
and learned from Confucius. After hundreds of generations,
the former residence of Yan was rebuilt by the descendants of

Confucius. His noble character was full of light. His literary talent, merit, and great learning will last forever. People cannot bear that the water well was ruined, people cannot bear that the alley was abandoned. Alas! What a great righteous doctrine, and how can we forget it.

Honor Your Mind By Renewing It Each Day
By Zhangzi [26] [張 子]

The teeth are originally white. However, if we do not brush them, they will acquire stains in just one day. The face is originally white, but if we do not wash it, dirt will cover it in just one day. The body is white, but if we do not bathe, it will become dirty in just one day. Although the teeth have stains, after we brush them, the stains will disappear. Although there is dirt on the face, after we wash it, the dirt will be removed. Although the body is dirty, after we bathe, it will be bright and clean as jade.

In fact, the teeth have originally no stain, the stains were made on our own. The face originally has no dirt, the dirt is incurred on our own. The body is originally clean, it is we who make our own body dirty. Teeth were white and we caused the stains, so who should we blame? The face was white and we caused it to be maculated, so whose fault was that? The body was white and we made it dirty, whose sin does this belong to? For-

---

[26]   Zhangzi (張 子) is Zhang Sanfeng (張 三 豐), a shadowy figure in Daoism. Supposedly born in 1247 (Song dynasty) and died in 1417 (Ming dynasty), he is credited with creating the exercise of Taijiquan and writings on Refining the Elixir. For more information, see *Tai Ji Quan Treatise: Attributed to the Song Dynasty Daoist Priest Zhang Sanfeng* (Valley Spirit Arts, 2011).

tunately, after brushing the teeth the next morning, they will turn back to white. After washing the face, it will return to a fair complexion. After bathing the body, it will be clean just like jade again. Our external body is clean but the mind is already contaminated with vulgar things. In one day, we can thoroughly wash away past bad habits and reform ourselves.

From now on, we should fault ourselves repeatedly. The way officials maintained their moral characters was to act like a virgin. The way scholars should cultivate themselves should be like that of a warrior. A virgin's room should be clean and spotless, so to firmly and constantly maintain their moral integrity. In this way, it can be said that maintaining their moral character is like a virgin. When warriors face enemies, they must move forward without hesitation and maintain bravery. In this way, it can be said they cultivate like a warrior. It is not rare to see women who do not keep to their virtue, and so they are called "licentious." A warrior who does not fight bravely, his [reputation of] "cowardice" then spreads about quickly. People whose bodies are clean and still intact, should always take a woman who does not hold unto chastity just as a memory. People whose bodies are incomplete, should clean it to properly present it, just like a warrior preventing himself to be seen as a coward.

The Mind Methods of Sages and Worthies

By Zhenzi [真子]

Shun taught Yu [27] a sixteen-word verse, one of the earliest methods for cultivating the mind. What is the mind of a human? It was born from spirit. It has its own properness and cheerfulness;

---

27   *Shun* is Emperor Shun (舜, 2317–2208 BCE). *Yu* is Yu the Great, founder of the Xia dynasty.

it has its own hatred and furiousness. Desires flow into a human's mind easily. This is dangerous. Even if we just slacken for a little while, then all kinds of transgressions will follow. What is the mind of the Dao? It is the root of the life, and these are [the principles of] benevolence, righteousness, fairness, and honesty. These principles do not have fixed form. They are subtle. Erring even by a fraction, little of them would still be left in the mind. Between the two [mind and benevolence] is almost seamless. If we can be aware of them, then we will be able to obtain their subtleties. For example, to distinguish between what is right or wrong, we can use the mind to resolve it and use benevolence to maintain it. These are mutually the beginning and the end. Only when people sincerely concentrate and without the interference of self-righteousness of the mind then people's deeds will consistently be with their belief and keep on the way of the impartial. Sages and worthies rise one after another, they follow the example of these good manners and use them as guiding principles to cultivate one's moral character. They use these principles to teach future generations so they may remain mindful of them, to restrain the impure thoughts, and to be honest. This means to regulate anger and suppress desires. Even when an ancient king faced these problems, could he overcome them? Even in an ancestral temple in which nobody could see, would he feel guilty? People should defeat the Four Do Nots,[28] just like when fighting with the enemies. But if the Four Virtues of Benevolence [仁, Ren]; Righteousness [義, Yi]; Propriety [禮, Li];   and Wisdom [智, Shi] can move with the situation and expand the influence, then the germination of these ideas will blossom. When plants sprout new

---

28   The *Four Do Nots* (四 非, Si Fei): do not look when it is not proper, do not listen when it is not proper, do not speak when it is not proper, and do not touch when it is not proper.

leaves, the flourishing of spring will bring a thriving vitality to plants. Even people who lost their chickens or dogs, they know they should look for them and bring them back. When herding cows and sheep in the grasslands, even though the grass is flourishing, one should worry about the day when it might become bare. If someone just focuses on maintaining his fingers but ended up losing the functions of his shoulders and back, what do you think, is this loss big or small? It doesn't matter if we accept just one basket of cooked rice or ten thousand kilograms of rice, people must be able to identify whether it is of propriety and righteousness.

Those who just keep raising the mind of nature and restraining desires to be successful, was Shun this kind of person? One hopes capable people can be like him, keeping their moral mind and being owners of complete good deeds. Heaven is higher than me. It is the greatest. Restraining your mind, and keeping the Supreme Ultimate [太極, Tai Ji] in the body, applying these principles to everything makes one versatile. Treat these principles like a treasure of a divine tortoise, regarding them as a treasure and so taking good care of them, then they can be very powerful. The ancient sages valued the importance of respecting others, and to pass it from generation to generation. They conducted themselves simply but their influence was wide spread. Nowadays, nobody seems to have the same criteria for respect. In order to avoid confused thoughts, I organized these various aphorisms. Use them to wash the mind and practice during daily life. In a room with bright windows, a clean reading table, nice paintings on the wall, and an incense burner, then when people are reading books in the room, they feel admirable and serve their own mind as though serving a Heavenly ruler.

The Source Is the Original Body

By Zhangzi [張 子]

Ultimate Void is without form, and is the original body of the Qi. It gathers and disperses, exhibiting the changing of outside forms. It is the condition of absolute tranquility with no connection to the external world, yet it is the root of the human nature.

After the senses came to be, the external world came to life. It is these external feelings that made contact with external objects. External feelings and external forms, yet with no senses and no forms, this is how a person can return to their own nature and be able to master everything.

Clean Water as an Allegory for Nature

By Wuzi, [吳 子]

The clearest substance in the world is water. The ancient scholars used the clarity of water as an allegory on the goodness of human nature. However, how can dirty water from the Yellow River become clean again? To understand the cleanness of water, we must trace it back to its origin. The source of water is the origin of water. Water gets dirty because of dust and mud on the ground that it flows through, but its source is clean. This is the reason that dirty water can still be made clear. Nowadays, the scholars of the world, have dirty temperaments, and these get worse every day due to the influence of foreign influences. They are trying to go back to the source of clear water, yet, everyday they make the dirty water even dirtier. How is it that the sins of human nature are to blame? To understand that the source of human nature is the clean Heaven, it gets dirty in the world just like water does. If the people are able to restrain themselves, human nature can be as clear as Heaven again. Does this not show how much we must depend on the efforts we spend on cleaning our mind?

A Discourse on the Movement and Tranquility of Mind

By Haiqiongzi [海瓊子]

When the human mind becomes active due to desires, it is like smoke pouring out of six windows of our body room, and wind roars around the seven orifices of our body. The One-Inch Field [29] would feel thorns and brambles; the heart would be like a monkey jumping up and down. The dragon is sadly trapped in an ocean of desire. The tiger degenerates due to all sorts of affairs of the external world. The banks of life and death are spread widely apart. The distance between me and others is as high as a mountain. Even if someone's merit and virtue can fill up an entire forest, they can still turn into weeds. The family members that are now friendly may turn hostile to each other later. Even people who are worried and distraught by a calamity, and then saved from it, could still end up dead in a cave of fame and fortune. The *Book of Changes* [易經, Yi Jing] says, "Fortune and misfortune, regret and repentance," all arise from these movements.

If people can keep the mind quiet when thinking, then the mind will shine like a sunny sky. The sea of human nature will be calm with minimum waves. The Elixir Field [丹田, Dan Tian] will be energized like blooming flowers; the Hua Chi [30] will secrete a lot of water [saliva]. At that time, it will reach to the realm of forgetting outside objects and oneself, not caring

---

29　　One-Inch Field (寸田, Cun Tian), located between the eyes.

30　　Hua Chi (華池, Pool of Flowers), the mouth.

about honor or shame per the secular standard. The wind in the pines and the moon in the water can become our brothers, apes and cranes can become our friends. Feeling happy in a silent sky, strolling on a clear and bright seaside. This is why the *Scripture on Dao and Virtue* [道德經, *Dao De Jing*] says, "All things return to their origin. It's called the stage of tranquility." And tranquility is the sign that that they have fulfilled their cultivation of Life [命, Ming]. I would grind up mouse teeth and sparrow's horn[31] in a place where I don't care. I would put a bug's arm and a fly's head[32] in a place where I don't go. If I have a Qin [琴] that can be played, I would play it during the evening moon. Would it be better than the Sheng and Yu[33] that gush through the ears? If I have wine that I can drink, I would drink until sunset. Would it be better than a feast filling people's eyes? Social hermits [羣逸人, Qun Yi Ren] can be friends to cultivate literary excellence with, and learned Daoists[34] can be friends with whom to cultivate spiritual excellence. Why should we envy that egrets and mandarin ducks can fly in formations, or can walk on the roofs of temples? Why should we envy people who can carve up a small bug and work very hard at carving a wood bug onto a table top?[35]

---

[31] *Grinding up mouse teeth and sparrow's horn* implies litigation over trivial matters.

[32] A *bug's arm* and a *fly's head* imply worthless and annoying things.

[33] Sheng (笙) and Yu (竽) are ancient Chinese musical Instruments.

[34] Learned Daoists (羽人, Yu Ren), literally "winged men" meaning immortals.

[35] Again, *carving up a small bug* and *carving a wood bug* imply having meaningless skills.

The Perfect Human Mind

By Zhuzi[36] [祝子]

The world was originally imperfect, the human mind was originally perfect. We should use the perfect human mind to complete the imperfect world. We should not use the imperfect world to cause imperfection to the perfect human mind.

Self-Nature Is Difficult to Clarify

By Zhuzi [祝子]

Time is everlasting, but people only live in their present life. A life may last for a hundred years, but only today is the present. If you believe in "only today is today," you will still be in a good shape after all kinds of suffering and tests. If you hesitated and didn't catch the present, then even if you live for a hundred years it will still be just a dream. Life is precious and it's difficult to see one's natural instincts clearly. One should treasure every opportunity in every moment. Do not miss it.

The Delirious and Insane Mind

By Yangmingzi [陽明子]

Have you seen people that are crazy or have lost their minds? When people lose their minds, their eyes are confused. Even if they walk through fire or boiling water, trample on thorns, they do not feel pain. Yet, they are still confident they are going the right way. Until they meet a good doctor, who flushes their system with clear and cold fluid, or gives them medicine to cure their mind—they could suddenly awaken. Telling them

---

36   Zhuzi (祝子, 156–224 CE) is a Neo-Confucianist.

about their odd previous behaviors, they would be surprised and feel sadness. To instruct them with words and deeds to return to the right path, they are pleased and feel happy, and they would think they should have met with a doctor much earlier. However, those who did not recover to normality quickly may laugh at other people, and think that only they are the normal person.

Guard Your Mind Cautiously
By Yangmingzi [陽明子]

Guarding your mind cautiously begins with goodness and virtue, which will begin to sprout inside you, just like the natural instinct to eat [any kind of] food when we are hungry. Or like being [apprehensive] when holding a newborn baby or skating over thin ice and fearing the ice may crack. Or like holding a priceless jade while standing on the edge of a very high cliff, fearing that the jade may fall down at any time.

Conversely, to guard your mind cautiously without virtue and goodness begins from having false thoughts that sprout inside you. Guarding against these thoughts is like preventing someone from trying to poison your delicious soup. Or like tigers or fierce snakes gathered in a cave, we have to find ways to avoid them. Or like a thief intruding into your home, you should find ways to fight and defeat him.

Preserve the Origin, Revert to the Origin
[No author listed]

Is the beginning of the world chaotic? Is the beginning of a country naive? Does the beginning of humanity come from the baby? When babies grow into children, then to adulthood, and then become elderly, this is the law of nature. We should take appropriate actions based on the different timings and occasions. It is fine to preserve one's Original Nature, but absurd trying to go against it.

The Peacefulness and Purity of the Heavenly Sovereign
By Xinxinzi [新新子]

Hearing, sight, smell, taste, and comfort are the Five Enemies [五寇, Wu Kou]. Foregone conclusions, arbitrariness, stubbornness, and egoism are the Four Harmful Bugs [四蠹, Si Du]. Fame and fortune are the Two Tyrants [二豪, Er Hao]. The Four Harmful Bugs and Five Enemies attack the outside with assistance from the inside [people's minds]. The Two Tyrants occupy the master's house and bully the Heavenly Sovereign [the human mind]. Fortunately, the Heavenly Sovereign perceived the situation quickly. He then appointed the Five Senses[37] as the commander, used the Six Organs[38] as the rampart. All other organs followed and performed their respective duties. They were wearing the armors of loyalty and faith, holding the shield of propriety and righteousness, to eliminate the harmful bugs, defeat the tyrants, and clean up the enemies of the Heavenly Sovereign.

---

37 *Five Senses* (五宮, Wu Gong), literally the "Five Palaces," a term for the five senses of sight, sound, smell, taste, and touch.

38 *Six Organs* (六府, Liu Fu), literally the "Six Mansions," a term for the six bowels of the body: gall bladder, stomach, large intestine, small intestine, bladder, and Triple Warmer (San Jiao).

The True Mind Acts on All Things
By Tianhuzi [天湖子]

When the deceptive mind ceases, the moon [Yin] and the gentle breeze [Qi] arrive. [The tranquil mind] does not need to sink into the bitter sea and go through the difficulties of life. When the mind is high up, it isn't bothered by the noise of horses running or the dusts from traffic. Therefore, why do we need to yearn for a secluded life in the mountains? In everyone's mind, there is a genuine article. Unfortunately, people are closed and detained by corrupted books. In everyone's mind is wonderful music. Unfortunately, it's buried by flirtatious dances and showy songs.

Everything in Nature Is Good
By Fuyuanzi [復元子]

The moon is shining over tens of thousands of rivers, and every river [reflects] its own moon. Heaven gives birth to everyone, and all beings have their own nature. There is no moonlight that is dim; there is no human nature that is unkind.

Moonlight has different levels of brightness because the water of each river has different levels of cleanness. The human mind has different levels of kindness because the Qi of people has different levels of purity. By filtering and cleaning the water, the moonlight of all the rivers would be bright. By strengthening our efforts in changing Qi, all human minds would be kind.

Dao Mind, Human Mind
By Feixiuzi [飛修子]

Under Heaven there is no mind of Dao outside the mind of humanity. The mind of the Dao is the purest area of the human mind.

Under Heaven there is no mind of humanity outside the mind of the Dao. The mind of humanity is the application area of the mind of the Dao. At the purest area of the human mind we can see the mind of Dao, so we know the mind of Dao is subtle. The application area of the mind of Dao is entirely the human mind, so we know the human mind is in danger.

On the green slopes of Ox Mountain [牛山, Niu Shan], trees flourish with a plentitude of plants. It is a beautiful scene that everyone enjoys. If there was a dangerous storm and weather at sea, wherein not even a solitary boat could survive the storm, yet [we know] the bright sky will return and the winds will clear away, some people think this situation will never change. Just like someone living in a poor and mean alley, even when it is close to noon time, they do not feel they are part of these workings of Heaven, and only think the Dao is like a teenager loafing off.

Shut Off the External, Hold Fast the Internal
By Bidongzi [筆洞子]

When a rooster crows at dawn, then within the breast comes Yushun.[39] This is [an analogy of] the origin of nature's root arriving inside of us. People must strictly put an end to external temptations. When the migratory birds arrive, then we know autumn is almost gone. This is a shadow of the outside object

---

39   Yushun (虞舜) is an ancient sagely king of wisdom.

that we can see as an indicator or hint. We must cling to our inner mind and guard it.

My Mind Can Work in the Myriad of Things

By Guanyinzi [關 尹 子]

Guanyinzi said, "The ancient people who were good at using yarrow stalks and tortoise shells for divination, they could reference present events to explain past events, examine past events to predict current events. They could know how things in a high position would work when in a low position, and predict how things in a low position would function in a high position. They could predict major events from small events. They could predict small things from major things. They could determine many events from seeing just one event. They could predict the result of one event from viewing many disparate events. They could tell another person's fate from my circumstances, and they could see my fate from others' fates. They could see nature changing from human society, and another person's circumstances. This is because they have realized the Dao.

"Nothing will live longer than the Dao, and nothing is older than the Dao. Dao is so high, there is nothing above it. Dao is so low, there is nothing beneath it. Dao is so big, there is nothing outside its reach. Dao is so small that it cannot contain anything. There is nothing outside of the Dao; there is nothing inside the Dao. Looking closely into the Dao, I cannot see myself. Looking far away from the Dao, I cannot see others either. It cannot be divided and cannot be combined. It cannot be explained and cannot be thought though. It is in the chaos, and this is how it became Dao.

"Water excels in concealing, so it can nurture the Five Essences.[40] Fire excels in flying, so it can distribute the Five Odors [五臭, Wu Chou]. Wood excels in flourishing, so it can glitter the Five Colors.[41] Metal excels in solidness, so it can produce the Five Sounds [五聲, Wu Sheng]. Earth excels in harmony, so it can nourish the Five Tastes.[42] There are five normal elements, but the combination is countless. There are five normal objects to correspond with the Five Elements [五行, Wu Xing]. Their variety cannot be counted. No matter how many things there are in the world, we should not insist there are ten thousand, or insist that there are just five, or insist there is only one. Nor should we insist that there is not ten thousand, five, or only one. Or insist that all of it can be combined or all can be separated. Thinking it must be this shape, it must be this amount, it must be this Qi, all of these thoughts bring distress to oneself.

"Foreign objects do not know me, and I do not know foreign objects. Our mind can produce all sorts of things and beings. It is probably that the mind has wishes, then the desire will follow it. When the desire follows it, then the essence will follow it. Because the mind is bonding to something, it will condense into the water. When the mind covets something, one will drool. When the mind feels sad about something, one will shed tears. When the mind feels ashamed, one will sweat. If there is no short duration, then there is no long duration of time. Nothing lasts a long time and yet does not change. The Water generates Wood, the Wood generates Fire, the Fire generates Earth, the

---

40   *Five Essences* (五精, Wu Jing): saliva, tears, secretions, sweat, and blood.

41   *Five Colors* (五色, Wu Se): black, red, azure, white, and yellow.

42   *Five Tastes* (五味, Wu Wei): sweet, sour, bitter, pungent, and salty.

Earth generates Metal, the Metal generates Water—the Five Elements mutually promote and show restraint with each other. The outcome is countless. In the alchemy field, the Infant [mercury] and Maiden [cinnabar], a Golden Chamber [a furnace] and a Crimson Palace [a cauldron], a Green Dragon and a White Tiger, a Precious Vessel and a Red Stove,these all are the products of the transformation of the Five Elements. Only the Dao itself is outside of this."

Realizing the Dream of Life and Death

[No author listed, from the *Zhuangzi*]

Ququezi [瞿 鵲 子] asked Changwuzi [長 梧 子], "I heard Confucius said that 'sages do not engage in trivial matters, they do not seek private profit, nor do they not try to avoid what is harmful. They do not seek for gains. They do not care to follow the established routes. They speak without speaking; they do not speak when they talk. And they can wander around outside the secular world.' Confucius thought these are reckless and improper things to do, but I think these are practical and comply to the subtleness of the Dao. What do you think, Sir?"

Changwuzi said, "Even the Yellow Emperor would be puzzled if he heard these words. How could Confucius understand them? And you are too hasty in trying to understand them. It's like you see the egg and then immediately look for the grown cockerel to hatch from it; you see the bow, then immediately look out for the turtledove being roasted. I will give you a rough explanation, and you can listen to it roughly.

"Why do you stand by the sun and the moon, and hold the universe under your arms? In this way, do you think you will merge yourself with everything in the world? Will you be able to ignore confusions and conflicts, and so then be able to leave it all alone, and then be able to treat inferiors and superiors equally? People are always busy in arguing over what is right and wrong, yet sages seem very foolish to them because they have nothing to perceive, and blend ten thousand years into one. All things are the same in their eyes, so they can blend into harmony. How would I know that my like of life is not a delusion? How would I know that the dislike of death is not like young people fleeing their homes, without knowing ways of coming back? Li of Ji [麗姬] was the daughter of a border defender of Ai [艾]. When the state of Jin [晉] was defeated, she was captured, and she cried until her tears soaked her dress. After she got into the palace of Jin, slept with the Marquis of Jin, became his wife and enjoyed delicious food, she then regretted she had cried at that time. How would I know dead people do not regret they had a long life? Those who have a dream about drinking may cry when they wake up in the morning. Those who have a dream about crying may go out and hunt happily in the next day. When people are dreaming, they do not know it is a dream. While in a dream, people may also try to interpret the dream. After they wake up, then they realize it was just a dream.

"Only after people are totally awakened, do they realize that all this is one big dream. Ignorant people think they are awake, and they are aware of everything. Monarchs are honored and shepherds are humble, such a view is really shallow! Confucius and you are dreaming. I say that you are in a dream; in fact, I am also dreaming. The above remarks are strange and weird. But after ten thousand ages, if once we met a sage, and realize the truth of these remarks, it would seem we met him just within the day."

The Wanderings of a True Person

[No author listed, from the *Huainanzi*]

True Persons [真人, Zhen Ren] are in accordance with Dao. Although they have a body, they appear shapeless. They are substantial, but also seem insubstantial. Their spirits stick to Dao, ignoring all other things. They focus on inner cultivation of their mind without the temptation of external objects. They are clear and simple. They let things follow their own course and do not force things. Their true form maintains the spirit of Dao, traveling in between Heaven and Earth, wandering outside of the dusty and dirty regions, and not needing to worry about worldly affairs in the universe. Their minds are vast and mighty and free from any kind of artful trickery, so they are not influenced even by important events such as life and death.

Even though all matter and beings are created by Heaven and Earth, True Persons do not depend on or interfere with them. They understand the immaculacy of nature [Dao]. Thus, external objects cannot tempt them. When facing the chaos of world affairs, they can still guard the fundamentals of Dao. Persons like this can forget about their liver and gallbladder, and leave their eyes and ears behind. Their efforts then focus on inner cultivation, so that their spirit and Dao will be in sync.

They stay at home. Nobody knows what they do. When they go out, nobody knows where they go. They come and go at will and freely. They look like dead wood. Their mind is calm as burnt ashes. They forget their five internal organs, neglect their human body. They understand things without the need to learn. They see things without raising their heads to watch. They complete things without taking action. They convince people without arguing. They respond to situations only if necessary. They take actions only when pressed to do so. They move only when they have no choice. Like the light of illumination, like the shadow imitating the shape of the physical object. Holding the Dao as the principle, relying only on Dao, they can achieve what has to be achieved. They keep the natural law as the foundation, no indulgence is allowed, and thus external objects cannot disturb their minds. They maintain openness of mind, yet they are empty. Their minds are tranquil without thinking and without worry.

Even if a great lake were boiling, they would not feel the heat. Even if the Yellow River and Yangtze River were frozen, they would not feel the cold. Even if thunder devastated a mountain, they would not be frightened. Even if darkness and a violent wind blocked the sun, they would not be injured. Therefore, they regard the treasures of jade and pearl as regular stones, they see the supreme emperor as a random traveler, they regard Mao Qiang and Xi Shi [43] as no different from homely women. They consider death and life as no different from each other, and all things and beings as the same. Their spirit is in sync with the natural law [Dao], so that they can travel boundlessly. They have Essence, but they do not use it; they have Spirit, but they don't exhibit it. Harmonizing with the Vast Chaos [大渾], they stand strong in the universe.

---

43   Mao Qiang (毛嬙) and Xi Shi (西施) were two famous and beautiful consorts in ancient China.

Wang Liang Asked the Shadow

By Yingzhenzi [應貞子]

Wang Liang[44] asked the shadow, "You are a wise and smart person, proficient in the Six Arts[45] and the doctrines of the One Hundred Schools of Thought. You explored Daoist secrets and the Buddhist scriptures of profound purport. You respectfully prepare sacrifices to the ancestors and admire their history. You would not intentionally obey secularity just to obtain fame. You would not slander others to achieve your own goal. You have such wonderful ethics and good spirits that you can rely on. Why then do you look so haggard and depressed? Why do you lie on the bed and feel worried? Even your clothing looks pitiful. You only attach to the outside shapes, and yet your shape is very close to you. Why don't you encourage it with noble character, instead of teaching it to be degenerate? Not to mention that you differ from the virtuous woman who takes delight in life and is willing to stay in poverty with you. And you think that you have a chronic illness so you don't have to make a living and so nobody relies on you. You are getting so lowly, do you forget how precious life is? The season is

---

44 Wang Liang (魍魎) is a fictitious person, a hermit and figure mentioned in the work of *Zhuangzi*. Herein, Yingzhengzi has Wang Liang speaking to the shadow of an imaginary person. Interestingly, the term "Wang Liang" normally means a demon, monster, sprite, or goblin. So the allegory here is of a fictitious hermit-like person, Wang Liang, who is actually some sort of spirit, speaking to the shadow of some imaginary person that he made up.

45 *Six Arts* (六術, Liu Shu) refers to music, archery, riding, writing, mathematics, and propriety.

changing, the winter has ended and spring has come. Sunlight is shining in the outskirts, the warm weather makes plum flowers open up and willow branches sprout. The snow is thawing and flowing around the house, the breeze blows gently through the window. These can eliminate the sorrow and cure the disease, please your spirit, and prolong your life. Why are you still so quiet and doing nothing, but only making yourself upset?"

The shadow felt agitated and said, "You live in a place where there is nobody and you wander in desolate remote areas. Your figure was engraved on the Xia Cauldrons,[46] and your name was recorded in the *Meng Zhuang*.[47] How can you not be knowledgeable? How can your speech not be profound?

"The shadow exists because of the light and so shapes itself like a human. Can you fully understand what it [the shadow] says? Can you identify how it acts? It appears and disappears with the light and the dark. It changes shape with the human body. The foolish people fear the dark [shadow], so that the shallow side of the human nature is manifested. Wise people see and understand the dark [shadow], so that they could realize the real meaning of the nature [Dao]. Your likes and dislikes are determined by your own, how innocent the shadow to be condemned? I have heard that the real Dao is deep and obscure; the ultimate Dao is empty, silent, and impenetrable. Dignitaries use it trying to modify the length of their life. People with noble character employ it to adjust the social morals of their time. Remorse and regret cannot entangle it. Glory and honor cannot delude it. When losing something, it doesn't regard it as

---

46   Xia Cauldrons (夏鼎, Xia Ding), nine vessels made by Yu the
      Great in the Xia dynasty.

47   Meng Zhuang (蒙莊), another name for Zhuangzi (莊子).

a loss; when getting something, it doesn't regard it as a gain. So, why are you angry at me, is it because I did not appreciate the beauty of the spring or because you blamed me for not wearing more attractive clothing? Besides, with your wisdom, are you able to measure or predict my conducts?"

He didn't finish his words. Wang Liang was terrified and said, "I was born in a remote area and grew up in the wild, so I did not know how people with wisdom behave themselves in society, so I made up an imaginary person to ask its shadow about the ultimate subtleties of these mysterious affairs, and to please hide me for the rest of my life."

Obtaining Mind in the Foremost Pavilion

[No author listed]

Scholars of the past had previously spoken in this temple, saying, "Under the moonlight we drank in a thatched pavilion. We have drunk with all our hearts to Heaven and Earth since ancient times. Yi! [48] How can one thatched pavilion cover all the affairs of Heaven and Earth? Heaven and Earth are so big, how can we drink it up?" They discussed everything and so named it all as Heaven's Root-Power [天機 Tian Ji]. The lively realm of mind is the realm of Dao. However, if a person's mind could understand the Dao then their temperament and interests would certainly be rich and profound. Presently, all is quiet and comfortable. Even this small pavilion corresponds with Heaven's Root-Power, so we can see in our imagination these interesting ancients, as well as the fascinating humming birds of the pavilion.

---

[48]   *Yi* is a belching sound.

Is the realm of mind the way to approach the realm of Dao? I have observed aromatic orchids, green bamboo, and the dark greenery of the Jade Maiden.[49] Their tender and beautiful colors were given by Heaven and Earth. The scenery there is so green, and all of it is connected to Heaven and Earth. These sceneries and our mind meet together between Heaven and Earth, and these green plants of the world meet and connect with our mind. Use our lively mind and feel free to wander between Heaven and Earth, then we can feel the flowers blooming at Zheng Garden,[50] and the butterflies dance in the Qi Yuan.[51] We can feel that standing in Yu Lou,[52] seeing the moonlight shining on the ground, or traveling to Liang Garden[53] while snow falls and covers all the mountains. How can we reach this state of mind? Alas! The worldly things and the dusts are all disturbed by themselves. The Ultimate Void [太 虛, Taixu] is free and leisurely, all because of itself. As for me, living by a river with willows is fine, or living life in secluded mountains is also fine. In this scene, it seems possible to drink up all the old worldly affairs in a jug of wine. Being morally lofty and tranquil is so fun, that only being at the Pavilion of

---

49   Jade Maiden (玉女, Yu Nu), one of thirty-six peaks of the Wuyi Mountains.

50   Zheng Garden (鄭圃), an ancient place where Liezi supposedly lived.

51   Qi Yuan (漆園), an ancient place where Zhuangzi lived, and where he dreamed he turned into a butterfly.

52   Yu Lou (庾樓), a romantic and elegant place.

53   Liang Garden (梁苑), the East Garden (東苑), built by the prince Liangxiao of Western Han Dynasty.

the Zhou Clan [54] could compare to being in this thatched pavilion, where the mind of Heaven and Earth, the mind of the ancients can all meet and connect within this small green pavilion.

---

54   Pavilion of the Zhou Clan (周氏之亭, Zhou Shi Zhi Ting).

Part Five
A Record of Quotations
from the Old Man, Qingyun

[青雲老人語錄, QIng Yun Lao Ren Yu Lu]

The Old Man, Qingyun said: "Why do people worry about troubles coming from their own imagination and cannot realize their own self. They only envy the long lives of immortals, and in the end, while their own life will pass by in rapid time. They are like the mushroom, it is not rewarded the alternation of even a day and night, and the cicada doesn't know the alternation of spring and autumn. It is a pity their lives are so short! It is not impossible to reach the way of immortals, but first of all, it should be started with learning how to purify the mind and diminish harmful desires. For those people who complain that the way to immortality is hard to find, yet, they do not want to purify their mind and restrain their desires, then the harder they pursue it, the farther away they are from their goal. Finally, they end up with a sickened mind which is not curable anymore. These are real mediocre people!"

The Old Man, Qingyun said: "Do all of you know where is 'The Way Of Longevity?' Actually it is in our mind. If we do one good thing, the 'Dao' in our mind would gain one point. If we do one bad thing, the 'Dao' will fly away. It cannot be forced. My so-named 'The Way of Longevity,' you have to experience it on your own to understand!"

[The Old Man, Qingyun said:] "The Exalted One Venerable Sovereign[1] said, 'Primordial spirit of the human was pure and without stain but it was disturbed by the acquirable human ideas [of greed, anger, and ignorance].' The original human mind was desireless and quiet, but it was affected by greedy desires. If people are able to remove all lustful distractions, their minds would become naturally calm. When the mind is tranquil, along with the influences of clarity, the primordial spirit will naturally be clear and quiet. To observe one's own mind, be empty with no desire. To observe the outside appearances, be empty without form. To look far into the distance of things, there is nothing. If people can understand that the mind, shape, and things are nothingness, then they will see the void of their own mind. If people are able to do so and see the nothingness of the sky but this vanity, if we know that everything is nothingness, then what else can exist in our mind? This is all original illusion. If we know everything is illusion, then do not be obsessed with the illusion. When we are not obsessed with these illusions, then it is a state of tranquility.

"If everyone could understand the true meaning of these words, then we would forget all the things and even ourselves. The spirit is pure and the mind is calm. All of the inside wicked thoughts would be eliminated. Outside demons could not invade. Honor or disgrace cannot affect our mind. The spirit would not be bothered by life or death. This is the way to keep healthy and attain longevity!"

---

1   Exalted One Venerable Sovereign (太上老君, Tai Shang Lao Jun), honorific and deified title of Laozi.

The Old Man, Qingyun said: "The ancients said that only benevolent people could acquire the foremost longevity. Even Confucius rarely talked about it, because it was hard to talk about the great truth of benevolence. Benevolence [仁, Ren] is Greatness [元, Yuan].[2] As a season it is spring, as all things begin to grow in the spring. The *Book of Changes* [易經, *Yi Jing*] says, 'Creativity of Heaven [乾, Qian], it is Great [元, Yuan], Persevering [亨, Heng], Advantageous [利, Li], and Correct [貞, Zhen].' Before all things had a beginning there was Qian [乾]. The Four Aspects of Qian [refers to Yuan, Heng, Li, and Zhen], Yuan was revealed through Qian, and so it was called 'Benevolence.' Laozi embraced Yuan as 'Origination,' and so held it to mean 'Benevolence.'"

The Old Man, Qingyun said: "For thousands of years, Daoism used the middle principal of the constant changing Dao. This theory emphasizes too much on staying in a tiny middle pathway, so it becomes unusual for purifying the mind and keeping the mind stable and calm. In regard to the middle and changing Dao, the Grafting [採補, Cai Bu] with Leading and Guiding [導引, Dao Yin] is only a partial and unorthodox Dao. Within the Great Net of Heaven [大羅天, Da Luo Tian], there is not this kind of immortal! In the Way of Longevity, there is definitely no such kind of rule! If someone gets into this heresy, they will lose their natural instincts, and will fall into the animal domains and suffer the pains."

[The Old Man, Qingyun said:] "The *Scripture on Penetrating the Great* [大通經, *Da Tung Jing*] says, 'If one's nature is silent, then one's heart of desire is sealed inside it. If one's heart of desire is active, then one's nature is sealed inside it. When the heart of

---

2   *Yuan* means "origination" and "greatness."

357

desire arises, then one's inner nature is sealed. When the heart desire is eliminated, then one's inner nature appears. Nature is empty and has no shape, it is pure and complete. The Great Dao [大道, Da Dao] has no shape, therefore, it actually exists inside of itself. True Nature [眞性, Zhen Xing] does not force other things, therefore, it's mind doesn't go out from it. Great Nature [大性, Da Xing] represents the eternal presence of the highest rules and is boundless. Looking at the surroundings we may be involved in, we should ignore all of it. Then, we will not fall into the snare of Six Thieves.[3] Live in the world of dust, but stay out of the dust. Then we will not be drawn into the endless disturbances of worldly affairs. Therefore, if we can achieve this, then our mind is at the most quite stage. We will be able to see the true meaning of emptiness.'"

The Venerable, Qingyun said, "Desires arise from the mind. The breath goes with the mind. The mind and breath are interdependent. If the breath is tuned, then mind can be settled. People who are able to do so must have spent a good deal of effort in practicing breath."

"This is what *The Yellow Emperor's Yin Convergence Scripture*[4] states, 'The mind is born from all things and dies in all things. The eyes are the root-power of the mind.' It also says, 'Life is the root of death. Death is the root of life. Fortune is born from misfortune. Misfortune is born from fortune.' People who can come to understand this will then know that there is no death and no life, no fortune and no misfortune. This

---

3   *Six Thieves* (六賊, Da Zei), eyes, ears, nose, tongue, body and mind.

4   *The Yellow Emperor's Yin Convergence Scripture* (黃帝陰符經, *Huang Di Yin Fu Jing*).

conforms with what Buddhists call 'no birth and no death, no filth and no purity.'"

[The Old Man, Qingyun said:] "Laozi said, 'One who is contented will not be humiliated. One who knows when to stop will not encounter danger.' These words were for ordinary people, so it talks about disgrace and danger. So, for the mind of a human, those who know contentment will always be happy. Those who know when to stop will have no contention with others. Being happy and having no contention with others, this is the basis for maintaining good health and prolonging life. If ordinary people are able to be this way, then they will attain longevity."

The Old Man, Qingyun said, "My master had once admonished me, saying 'Grass and trees grow up from the root, without soil they would die; fish and turtles all live in water, without water they would die; humans live by their bodies, without Qi they would die. Do you understand the abstruseness of these [words]?'

"I replied, 'The sages, worthies, immortals, and Buddhas know how important Qi is and that it is a treasure. Buddhism calls it the Harmonious Qi [和氣, He Qi] that creates auspiciousness. Therefore, both Buddhism and Daoism understand that developing Qi is the first and most important lesson to learn.'

"After listening to my answer, my master smiled and said, 'The Great Dao is not far away, it is in the human body. The Ten Thousand Things mean nothing, only the Nature is real. If a person finds their True Nature, the Harmonious Qi will dwell within and will return to the Original Ocean of Long Life⁵ without end.

---

5   *Original Ocean of Long Life* (元海壽, Yuan Hai Shou), the Dan Tian.

'Seeking to retain the spirit within the body, do not leave visible things in the mind. Visible things in the mind cause the spirit to be unclear, and so the spirit is dissipated and this will hurt the bones and muscles.

'If the Original Spirit does leave, return it quickly, and when the spirit returns to the body, the Qi will come back. Every morning and evening practice this and then naturally the Mercury Child [6] will produce the True Embryo.'

"These three poems by Heavenly Master Tranquility in the Void [7] should be read and memorized. Through these poems a person can come to understand the purpose of Nature. He also said,

'Don't be afraid of having thoughts. Just be afraid of not being aware of having thoughts. Having wicked thoughts is sick. Stopping them is the cure. Once wicked thoughts are stopped, they will be cured and other wicked thoughts won't arise.'"

The Old Man, Qingyun said: "When the human mind is active, the Six Confusions [8] are like evening smog. The Seven Orifices [七竅, Qi Qiao] are like the roaring wind. The One-Inch

---

6   *Mercury Child* (赤子, Chi Zi); *True Embryo* (眞胎, Zhen Tai).

7   Heavenly Master Tranquility in the Void (天師虛靜, Tian Shu Xu Jing).

8   *Six Confusions* (六惚, Liu Hu), another term for the Six Sense-Desires.

Field [寸 田, Cun Tian] feels [like] thorns and brambles. The mind is like a monkey. The dragon will whistle through the ocean of desire. Tigers will fall into the Saila,⁹ and life and death become like the wide banks of a river. When people stand on top of the hill they think they are higher than a mountain. Even if a person's merit and virtue could fill an entire forest, it will turn into weeds. Peaceful coexistence of couples will turn hostile on each other; gloom will become the means of more affliction. [People will die] of old age in a cave of fame and fortune. All this is caused by an active mind.

"If people can keep the mind quiet, not over thinking, then the mind and sky will be sunny. The waves on the sea of natural instincts will be calm. The Elixir Field will be like flowers in bloom and bright. The Flower Pool¹⁰ will secrete water. At that time, we can reach to the realm of forgetting, of myself and all things, not caring whether being favored or humiliated. The wind in the pines and the moon in the water can become brothers, and even apes and cranes can become friends. One feels happiness as though under a silent sky or strolling along a clear and bright seaside. All this is brought about by tranquility. Observe the timing for activity and tranquility, then you will understand the Way of Longevity."

[The Old Man, Qingyun said:] "Ultimate Void has no form, and is the original body of the Qi. The Qi gathers and disperses, and so is connected with life and death. So nourishing the Qi is the first priority of these methods."

---

9   *Saila* is a Sanskrit term, meaning crags in the mountains.

10   *Flower Pool* (花 池, Hua Chi) refers to the mouth.

[The Old Man, Qingyun said:] "Life is everlasting, but a person only lives in their present life. A life may last for a hundred years, but only today is today. If you believe in only today is today, you will still be in a good shape after all kinds of suffering and tests. If you hesitate, even if living for a hundred years, it will still be like a dream. Life is precious and it's difficult to see one's Nature clearly. One should treasure the opportunity in every moment. Do not miss it. This statement is so true. It's all in our mind, and the mind is for achieving Dao through our lifetime. If someone missed out on the opportunity, they will be lost for a lifetime."

[The Old Man, Qingyun said:] "Daoists use the Four Preservations [四存, Si Cun] of Clarity [清, Qing], Purity [淨, Jing], the Unseen [希, Xi], and the Unheard [夷, Yi] as the gist of its doctrine. 'Clarity,' means the mind does not attach to dust. 'Purity' means the mind does not rush indiscriminately into action. The 'Unseen' means the mind does not look at external things. The 'Unheard' means the mind does not listen to external sounds. Even though these are specific Daoist terms, they are also the subtle and true essences of longevity."

[The Old Man, Qingyun said:] "When I was 129 years old, this was before I met my master, my body was spry and easy. I could walk with vigorous strides. Some people suspected that I was either an immortal or a swordsman. This made me feel funny at that time. Actually, it was because that after turning forty years old, my mind was always calm. With a calm mind, my spirit was peaceful. With a peaceful spirit, my body was strong and so kept all kinds of diseases way. So I was healthy and happy. In the year when I was fifty years old, I went into the mountains to collect herbs and met up with an elder. He could

362

run fast, and fly and leap between big rocks. I dashed forward and but couldn't catch up with him. Later, when I met him again, I asked for his secrets. This elder gave me some wild berries and said, "The only secret is that I eat this often." I took a look, and they were Gou Qi. After that, I started eating 3 qians of Gou Qi every day. After a while, I felt my body become lighter and I could walk much faster. I didn't feel tired after a 50km walk. My energy and foot strength were all better than ordinary people. I just take 3 qians of Gou Qi a day only. So, am I an immortal or a swordsman?"

[The Old Man, Qingyun said:] "For our daily life, we should note that in winter not to go hungry in the morning. In summer, don't eat too much at night. Don't wake up before the rooster is crowing. Don't get up after the sunrise. Keep the mind pure. Immortals stay in the places where they can keep the Qi steady, so wickedness and filthiness could not grow in their body. If we can get used to it, this is better than eating Ginseng and Fungus [Poria]. Lu Chunyang [11] said, 'No worry in mind for one day, is like being an immortal for one day. If the Six Vital Organs [12] are healthy, then the Qi in the mind will be at peace, and the Qi will fill the Elixir Field with treasures. From this, one doesn't need to be looking for Dao any more. If one keeps peace of mind, then when looking at himself in the mirror, one doesn't need to sit for meditation any more.'"

---

[11] Lu Chunyang (呂純陽) is Lu Dongbin of the Eight Immortals.

[12] Six Vital Organs: heart, lungs, liver, kidneys, spleen, and gallbladder.

[The Old Man, Qingyun said:] "The Mountain Man, White Yang[13] said, 'If one has nothing to do, one should sit in meditation. Then, living for one day becomes two days. So a person originally destined to live for 70 years, will live for a 140 years.' These sentences are all about keeping the mind calm and to see the truth of your Nature. We should set this as a standard, and follow the rules indefatigably for our lifetime."

[The Old Man, Qingyun said:] "'To stretch and massage bones and muscles can keep one's body strong. To cut emotions and desires can make one's mind calm and quiet. To speak softly and cautiously can make one happy. If you can do all these, you are a sage.'

"This paragraph is from *The Immortal Spiritual Grotto Scripture* [洞靈經, *Dong Ling Jing*]. What does it mean to 'stretch muscles and bones?' It is exercising muscles and bones, so the physical body will be healthy. What does it mean 'to cut the emotions and desires'? It is to control emotions and desires, then one can keep spirited. What does it mean 'to speak softly and cautiously'? It means do not speak unnecessary words; you can then avoid getting into trouble and feel happy. So everyone should know about these things."

[The Old Man, Qingyun said:] "As for the Five Organs[14] of the body, they all follow the Five Phases,[15] which mutually reinforce and neutralize each other. So we must take good care of them. Remain indifferent when being favored or humiliated,

---

13   Mountain Man White Yang (白陽山人, Bai Yang Shan Ren).

14   Heart, liver, spleen, lungs, and kidneys.

15   Wood, Fire, Earth, Metal, and Water.

then liver and wood would calm itself. Respecting one's own self, so moving or sitting, then the heart and fire will keep stable by itself. Control diet, then spleen and earth would not leak. Adjust breathing and talk less, then the lungs and mental health will be good. With quiet and lessened desires, the kidneys and water will be sufficient. To understand all of this you can protect your organs."

[The Old Man, Qingyun said:] *"The Three Reeds Scripture* [三茅經, *San Mao Jing]* said, 'When the valley is empty, the sound echoes.' When the mind is empty, it responds [echoes] positively with the Shen. When the Spirit is empty, it responds [echoes] positively with the Qi. When the Qi is empty, it responds [echoes] positively with the Essence [Jing]. At the extreme of emptiness, it is bright. At the extreme of brightness, it will be crystal clear. This is to go beyond the level of the spirit, and life and death no longer mean anything. The Essence is kept inside, and the Qi is born from the outside. Knowing how to use the Qi to get to the Essence, then one can have longevity."

The Old Man, Qingyun said, "The ears are the orifices of Essence. If the ears follow the voice, then Essence begins consumption. When you concentrate on the voice, the Essence will flow out and not remain intact. The eyes are the orifices of the Spirit [Shen]. If the eyes are wandering because of desires, then Spirit follows the desires. It will then be lost and have no cohesion. The mouth is the orifice of Qi. If the mouth talks too much, the Qi will follow the speech and leave, and will not unite [with the Essence or Spirit]. If people want longevity, but do not pay attention to these three key points, and do not tidy up the body and mind, then there will be no benefit."

[The Old Man, Qingyun said:] "To forget our own bodies and focus on raising our own Qi; to forget about our own Qi and concentrate on nourishing the spirit; to forget about our own spirit and developing the emptiness. 'Forget' is the key word, then we will finally arrive into the realm of emptiness and achieve the highest doctrines. The Sixth Patriarch said, 'As there is originally nothing, where then does the collected dust come from?' This is really the highest level of 'forgetting.'"

[The Old Man, Qingyun said:] "For food taboos, Buddhism and Daoism have the same religious discipline of what is called the Five Dirty Foods. Buddhism's Five Dirty Foods are Chinese scallion, shallot, chive, garlic, and asafoetida. Daoism's Five Dirty Foods are chive, garlic, Rapeseed, Chinese scallion, coriander. The Physician's Five Dirty Foods are onions, garlic, chive, knotgrass [polygonum], and mustard. The Five Dirty Foods are also known as the Five Spices, as these are all smelly and spicy foods. Eating these foods will confuse the spirit, hurt the Qi, and encourage immoral thoughts. So those who are cultivating should abstain from them. Confusing the spirit and hurting the Qi is a mark of shortening one's life, so those who want to have longevity should avoid [the Five Dirty Foods]. As for poultry and other kinds of meats, these will not bring as much harm."

[The Old Man, Qingyun said:] "Liquor makes the spirit chaotic, meat confuses people's minds, so the Buddhist admonishes against them. Fascination with them is like smoke and so it deceives [or clouds] our mind. Greed is fire and it burns our bodies, so the Daoist admonishes against being greedy. These are the Ways of Longevity, keeping our spirit peaceful and the Nature of our mind calm."

[The Old Man, Qingyun said:] "The mind can be dragged into all kinds of affairs, and the fire ignites inside when dragged into them. Once the fire of heart [mind] is ignited, the Essence, Qi, and Spirit will follow and be shaken into restlessness, and this will lead to a short life. So some say, 'The mind kills our Nature.' Otherwise, people could have longevity.'"

[The Old Man, Qingyun said:] "The moods [of the mind] are affected by our surrounding environment, and the mood will then directly affect one's perception of the surrounding environment. In order to settle the mind, 'with things people like, and I don't like; with things people do, and I don't do.' The affairs of the mundane world cannot tempt my mind. So that my mind is calm naturally. This is why when the mind is calm, people behave wisely; when the mind is in a restless environment, people behave with confusion."

[The Old Man, Qingyun said:] "The Dao of breathing are the knacks [techniques] for longevity. The Heaven's Gate[16] should constantly remain open, and the Earth's Door[17] should constantly remain closed. Keep the breath smooth and continuous, and not interrupted. When inhaling, go all the way down to the root; and when exhaling, go all the way up to the pedicel. If the Spirit is the son, then the Qi is the mother. Therefore, there is a poem that reads, 'The Shen is the Nature [性, Xing] and the Qi is the Life [命, Ming]. When the Spirit does not run out, then the Qi will be stable automatically. The Spirit and Qi are the most intimate. Lose one is losing both.' Li Jing[18] said, 'The mind returns to the Void and tranquility. The body goes into a non-action status. Forget about both movement and tranquility. The inner and outer will blend into one.' When these are achieved, the Essence converts to the Qi naturally, the Qi converts to the Spirit naturally, and the Spirit returns to the Void naturally."

[The Old Man, Qingyun said:] "The Six Qi are 1) Blowing [吹, Chui]. 2) Exhaling [呼, Hu]. 3) Giggling [嘻, Xi]. 4) Expelling [呵, He]. 5) Hushing [噓, Xu]. 6) Resting [呬, Xi]. These are the Buddhist way of curing internal diseases. There is a chant that reads, 'Expelling breath controls the heart [心, Xin]; blowing controls the kidneys [腎, Shen]; exhaling controls the spleen [脾, Pi]; resting controls the lungs [肺, Fei]; hushing controls the liver

---

16   Heaven's Gate (天門, Tian Men), also called Hall of Heaven
      (天堂, Tian Tang) and One Hundred Returnings (百會, Bai Hui),
      is the Muddy Pellet (泥丸, Ni Wan).

17   Earth's Door (地戶, Di Hu) refers to the Assembly of Yin (會陰,
      Hui Yin) or Collecting Yin.

18   Li Jing (李靖, 571–649 CE).

368

[肝, Gan]; and giggling controls the Triple Warmer [三焦, San Jiao].' Everyone who wants to know about the secrets for treating visceral diseases and longevity can listen to me to explain. Human viscera are the easiest to get sick. If not treating them right away, one would die. The Six Words of 'Chui,' 'Hu,' 'Xi,' 'He,' 'Xu,' and 'Xi' can treat all kinds of internal organ diseases and cure them. If there is no disease, also use these six words to extinguish irrational thoughts and keep demons away. The method for self treatment is: every day between 11:00 a.m. and 3:00 p.m., close the eyes, sit quietly, knock teeth, swallow saliva, and read these six words softly.

"Heart disease patients should cross their hands and place them on the head, then intone *He* [呵, pronounced 'ho,' the Expelling Breath] thirty-six times softly.

"Kidney disease patients should place their hands to surround the knees and intone *Chui* [吹, pronounced 'chway,' Blowing Breath] thirty-six times softly.

"Liver disease patients should cross their hands and put them over the Jade Pillow [玉枕, Yu Zhen, the occiput], close the eyes, and intone *Xu* [嘘, pronounced 'shue,' Hushing Breath] thirty-six times softly.

"Lung disease patients should overturn their hands, place them on the back, and intone *Xi* [呬, pronounced 'shee,' Resting Breath] thirty-six times softly.

"Spleen problem patients should put their hands over the abdomen, bite their lips, and intone *Hu* [呼, pronounced who, Exhaling Breath] thirty-six times softly.

"For Triple Warmer problems, lay down, close the eyes, and intone *Xi* [嘻, pronounced 'she-hee,' Giggling Breath] thirty-six times softly.

"These are the best ways to treat visceral diseases. Only people who have done them can understand thoroughly and know the effects. Before I was thirty years old, I received these chants and did them every day. It took me a total of about 110 years before I became a Daoist, and I never stopped [reciting them]."

[The Old Man, Qingyun said:] "Everyone should keep in mind firmly that greed, anger, confusion, and affections are what most likely steal our bodies and minds. Keeping away from these are the Great Dao of Longevity. These are what the True Person Controller of Horses[19] said, 'When people keep to silence, the Spirit will not be injured. Thinking less will feel good, like candlelight in the mind. Not getting angry, the Qi and Spirit will go smoothly. Not worrying, the mind will be calm and pure. With no desire, flattery and pride will end. Not being stubborn, everything then can be flexible. Not being greedy, you will feel wealthy. Being conscientious, then why should we be afraid of monarchs? Lightly tasting will bring about the sweetness of food. Stabilizing the Qi, the breathing will then naturally become thin and lingering.'"

[The Old Man, Qingyun said:] "When the mental and physical are blinded to specific things, the human body will react and the Spirit will run out. When someone is always thinking about some specific thing, it is just like daydreaming, and the body will become like a zombie and the Qi will run out. The body will then become incomplete and the person will die, and the Spirit will depart and die too. The mind must have no desire so the Primordial Spirit can be resurrected again. When the Mortal Spirit [魄, Po] is eliminated from the body, the Immortal Spirit [魂, Hun] can be strengthened. The transformation between these

---

19   True Person Controller of Horses (司馬眞人, Si Ma Zhen Ren).

two does not go beyond the subtle laws of nature. The changes in the world are all guided by True Nature."

[The Old Man, Qingyun said:] "The most exquisite thing is being concealed in trance [an abstract mind], and the greatest picture is when things of an uncertain nature are mixed in [abstract imagery]. The Nature doesn't know specific rules. Even the ghosts and gods could not predict where he is heading. He doesn't drink nor eat, and he does not sleep. This is called, a True Person Sitting and Forgetting [真人坐忘, Zhen Ren Zuo Wang]. It is a more advanced level than abstaining from grains [辟穀, Bi Gu] in Daoist practice."

[The Old Man, Qingyun said:] "Grief, joy, hate, and anger, these are the root-power [天機 Tian Ji] of death. Any one of these can cause agonies to fill the whole body, and shorten life. What can be feared? Tan Jingsheng[20] had said, 'When someone feels grief, there is crying and tears; smelling spices causes the nose to run; hate causes goiters; and anger causes jaundice. The mind wants to express any of its desires and so will gather the corresponding movements of Qi. This movement of Qi will then breed corresponding things, and so the evil influences and the Qi become in opposition of each other. So people, through deep moral behavior, attempt to control their grief and to not eat spicy food, always warning themselves to prevent anger in their mind, and to enter the door of great Qi, so the Qi can return to its root. Knowing where the Original Spirit [元氣, Yuan Qi] resides and keeping an attitude of humility improves the internal. Just like a clam keeping a pearl inside its shell or

---

20   Tan Jingsheng (譚景升), a poet of the five dynasties forming the interregnum period between the Tang and Song, 936–947 CE.

precious jade concealed inside an ordinary stone. The clam and stone are called "the houses of the pearl and jade." Do you all know the subtleties of these? You should explore them carefully!'"

[The Old Man, Qingyun said:] "Nowadays, people's Essence is flowing out from the bottom, and the Qi is dispersing out from the top. The water and fire fight against each other and do not get along together. These are all caused by the mind. If the idea of attachment does not arise, then the Essence would not flow out from the bottom; if the idea of anger does not arise, then the Qi would not burn upwards. With no single harmful thought in the mind, then all kinds of worries will be cleared. Thus, the water and fire will be in harmony."

[The Old Man, Qingyun said:] "Someone in the past asked Gaoshangzi [高尚子], 'Are there any secrets for longevity? I would love to hear it from you.' Shangzi replied, 'Everything has its secrets, but the only secret for longevity is that the body is the house of life, Qi is the mainstay of life, and Spirit is the controller of life.' The body needs to be filled with Qi, but if the Qi is insufficient, then the body will get sick. The spirit depends on the Qi to function. When Qi is harmonized, then the Spirit will be saved. People who are cultivating and seeking the Dao, they follow the laws of Yin and Yang of the natural world, based on the correct methods of health care and exercise. They are full of Essence and are good at controlling the use of their Spirit, and blend the Essence and Qi into one. Utilize the Spirit as the cart, and the Qi as the horse, making Spirit and Qi work together, then people can have longevity."

The Old Man, Qingyun said, "It is not hard to seek for the Dao, but it is hard to understand the knowledge of it completely. If we could understand the knowledge fully, then we would comprehend the Dao all on our own. Someone had said,[21] 'Completely understand the universe, then there is nothing that we could not contain; completely understanding time [infinite, from birth and beyond], then there is nothing we would feel insufficient about; completely understanding ethics, then there is nothing that can make us feel uneasy; completely understanding the Dao, then there is nothing we could not realize; or completely understanding the laws of Nature, then there is nothing we don't know about. How is this so? Only seeing one side of a thing, we do not understand the full picture of the thing, and this is not the complete understanding of the Dao.'"

[The Old Man, Qingyun said:] "'Before seeking for something, yet not knowing where it has been, and still going off to seek it, then we will be confused. To pursue things and not knowing its image, but just seeking for things that seem to look alike, then we won't be able to get it.' This all means that we won't get confused if we understand the truth. People who do not know the truth only think based on their own interpretation. They live in their house and do not know what they should do. They go out and do not know where they should go. If there were no worthies or sages figuring out that people are heading the wrong way, how would they get rescued?"

---

21   This quote is paraphrased from the *Heguanzi* (鶡 冠 子), a book on Daoism and military strategy.

373

[The Old Man, Qingyun said:] "The feeling of ambiguousness is most fascinating. However, if we do not judge things carefully, we will go astray. The thing that confuses people, is in wanting certain items, yet people will confuse very similar items with the real item. So what the jade businessmen worries about most is that they may buy some rocks that look like real jade. What sword collectors worry about most is that they may buy a counterfeit sword that looks like the Ganjian.[22] For the people seeking for the Dao, what they worry the most is that they are not learning the right way, but entering heterodoxy. When it is ambiguous, immortals and mortals are different. Those who do not have a good foundation and wisdom, it is difficult for them to determine the real or fake in a short time."

[The Old Man, Qingyun said:] "There are a lot of people in the world who like to talk about right and wrong. However, there is no real right or wrong. There is no standard for the right and wrong in the world. Actually people have their own standard for it. The thing they like is right. The thing they do not like is wrong. These people seem to look for the right, but they do not really look for the truth; rather, they are just looking for something to meet their own will. People seem like they are looking to remove the wrong, but they do not really want to remove the bad. They just want to remove something that is against their own will. Such kind of right and wrong, how can they be the real right and wrong? So I think in such cases, it is better not to define the right and wrong. Pay no attention to people's so-called 'rights' and 'wrongs.' This way we can remove the likes and dislikes of the mind."

---

22   *Ganjian* (干 劍) is the name of a famous ancient sword.

Someone asked the Old Man, Qingyun about the chicken and the egg, "The egg is laid by the chicken and the chicken is hatched from the egg. These two things are interrelated with each other in cycles. When all things begin, which one comes first, the egg or the chicken? If it was the egg that came first, then there was no chicken, so where did the egg come from? If it was the chicken that came first, then there was no egg, so where was the chicken from? Which one is the truth? I would like to hear from you."

The Old Man, Qingyun smiled and replied, "You have not understood the truth of things completely, and you still have perception of right and wrong. These deeply linger in your mind. Actually, the evolution of all beings and things are similar. So why do you care so much about chicken and egg things? Before Heaven and Earth separated, the world was chaotic and Wuji [無極, the Illimitable] was complete and indivisible. The Yin and Yang were not yet separated and all things and beings had not begun yet. Until Taiji [太極, Supreme Ultimate] generated Liangyi [兩儀, Two Powers of Yin and Yang], and Liangyi generated Four Directions,[23] then began Heaven, Earth, and Humanity, and all things and beings. Do you know how and where Heaven and Earth separate from? Do you know how and where the human and all things and beings were born from? Isn't it a subtle effect of evolution and transformation of Yin and Yang? You disregarded the question of where your own self came from, and only worry and trouble yourself about the chicken and egg. This is like thinking, 'if I am on this side, then you must be at the opposite side; if I am at the other side, you must be on this side.' If we have this perception of what must be

---

23   *Four Directions* (四方, Si Fang), other books refer to this as the Four Seasons (四時, Si Shi).

right or wrong, or things must have their right or wrong lingering in our mind, then it is difficult for us to understand the truth thoroughly."

The Old Man, Qingyun said, "People know fake gain comes with a real loss. However, they do not know that even the real gain comes with a real loss, too. They only know in the fake truth comes with a real deception. However, they do not know that the real truth comes with a real deception, too. So sages do not talk about right and wrong. Maggots eat snakes, snakes eat frogs, and frogs eat maggots, it is an endless cycle, so there is no definite right and wrong. If we use our right and wrong to argue with someone else's right and wrong, then there will be more and more argument about right and wrong in the world. If we put these down and do not listen and don't ask about it, do not discuss and do not argue about it, then the argument about the right and wrong in the world will be subsided naturally. This is why I said there is no right and no wrong. This is also a big key point of prolonging life. Everyone should keep it in mind firmly."

[The Old Man, Qingyun said:] "Likes and dislikes are similar to rights and wrongs. If we could leave the right and wrong, then we will have no likes and dislikes. When we have no likes and dislikes, the dust cannot stick onto us. Then we can enter the Dao."

[The Old Man, Qingyun said:] "No one can expect when praise or criticism will come. To be angry because of another's criticism or to be happy because of another's praises, both affect the mood. The mood will thus be uneasy. The sensible persons would grin and bear criticism, and refuse praise politely. Then the mind will be calm and clear like a mirror. Those who have this secret of longevity should treasure it. The Physicians' statement said, 'Anger hurts the liver, extreme happiness hurts the waist, too much grief hurts the lungs, fear hurts the kidneys.' This shows that the emotions and feelings will hurt our body, but most people do not understand this. So if we would like to have longevity, we have to get rid of these extreme emotions and feelings."

The Old Man, Qingyun said, "The way of the breath is the element for health and life. I have talked about this several times before. When the movement of Qi is consistent, it will move naturally, just like the spring fish floating in the water to breathe out slowly. When the movement of Qi is active, it will become static naturally, just like winter insects hibernating. When spring fishes get Qi they then move, even though the movement is only slight. The winter insects amass Qi then hibernate, and in their hibernation there is no sign [of Qi]. Breathing should be like this: fine, cautious, and slight. When exhaling, the air should move throughout all sensory organs. When inhaling, we should take back all the air and direct it throughout all the sensory organs.

"When adjusting the breath, we should not interrupt it, then the genuine Qi will arise spontaneously. People's birth, aging, sickness, and death are all related to the True Qi."

[The Old Man, Qingyun said:] "The world of desire, the world of form, and the world of formlessness are Three Realms.[24] When the mind forgets about missing and worry, it is beyond the world of desires. When the mind forgets about the fate and the

---

24   *Three Realms* (三界, San Jie). *Trailokya* in Sanskrit.

borders, it is beyond the world of form. When the mind does not attach to the things outside the Void, it is beyond the world of formlessness. If people can come out from these three worlds, they then can enter the land of immortals, and the nature of mind will be in the realm of freedom and emptiness."

[The Old Man, Qingyun said:] "Abandoning the vision of the eyes, cutting off the hearing of the ears, adjusting the breath of the nose, and sealing the taste of the tongue—these are called *Coordination of the Four Images* [合和四象, He Hu Si Xiang]. When eyes are shut, then the Immortal Spirit [Hun] will be in the liver; when ears are turned to be deafened, then the Essence will be in the kidneys; when the tongue does not talk, then the Spirit will be in the heart; when the nose does not deliberately smell scents, then the Mortal Spirit [Po] will be in the lungs; when the four limbs do not move, then the Mind-Intent [Yi] will be in the spleen—these are called *The Original Courts of the Five Qi* [五氣朝元, Wu Qi Chao Yuan]. The Essence turns into the Qi, the Qi turns into Spirit, the Spirit turns into the Void—these are called *Three Flowers Gathering in the Head* [三花聚頂, San Hua Ju Ding]."

[The Old Man, Qingyun said:] "The True Man Sun's [孫眞人, Sun Zhen Ren] verse on entering Dao said, 'Furiousness hurts the Qi of liver; thinking too much hurts the Spirit.' When the spirit is tired, the mind gets weary easily. When Qi is weak, it's easy to get sick. Don't be too sad or too joyful, eat balanced diets, and never get drunk. The first thing not to do is to get angry in the morning. Knock teeth before sleeping [9:00 p.m. to 11:00 p.m.]. Stir and rinse the tongue in the mouth before getting up in the morning [3:00 a.m. to 5:00 a.m.], then diseases find it difficult to invade you. The Vital Energy [Qi] fills up the body. If you want to avoid getting sick, restrain [eating the] Five Dirties. Keep the mind calm and pleasant, so to preserve spirit and energy. The length of human life is not decided by fate. It is decided by ourselves. If you follow these rules, you can have longevity and be healthy. Although True Man Sun's advice is kind of rustic, it has very deep meaning. If you see through it, there is an exquisite truth inside."

[The Old Man, Qingyun said:] "Zhuangzi said, 'A drunk man crashed his cart and fell out. Although his body was injured, he was not dead. His bones and joints are like everyone else's, but the damage is different than others. This is because his spirit was highly centralized, and did not know while sitting in the cart that it even crashed. Death, birth, being scared, and fearful all could not enter his mind. So when he encountered the dangers from outside things he did not feel afraid. He was able to keep his life, and was saved by being drunk. But more so, who is it that saves and keeps their life through nature? Sages hide within nature, so there is nothing that can hurt them.' This statement does not mean that getting drunk can save and keep your life. It means to follow nature to keep living longer."

[The Old Man, Qingyun said:] "An ancient person said, 'If people want to have longevity, they should augment their Qi by learning Tu Na.'[25] A Daoist internal regime making use of swallowing and refining saliva, combined with specific breathing methods and sounds of drawing in the good Qi [air] and expeling out the old Qi. The Heavenly Circuits [周天, Zhou Tian] they

---

25   *Tu Na* (吐 呐) literally means "to spit out and shout out."

begin and last for a day, a year, and a Jie, [26] which is only the capturing of the Qi. [27] Capturing the Qi for the Lesser Heavenly Circuit [小周天, Xiao Zhou Tian], or capturing the Qi for a Greater Heavenly Circuit [大周天, Da Zhou Tian], capturing the Qi for a day, capturing the Qi for a year or even longer—the period of capturing the Qi can take a very long time or a very short time. People who can capture their Qi are true and sensible persons. When the Qi is in great stableness, we cannot see when it started to be caputured, nor can we know when it will end. No beginning and no ending, even through an aeon there is not even a single breath. The shape and spirit are quiet and empty. It is the exquisite realm for both the shape and spirit.

"The human's life and death is decided by the Qi. The difference between sages and mortals is decided by who can capture the Qi. People who can conceal their Qi, would conceal the Qi deep in the root of Primordial Vitality [元氣, Yuan Qi] People who can capture their Qi would monitor it closely and would not allow it to run out. These two ways should be thought over carefully to prevent danger."

[The Old Man, Qingyun said:] "People who want to cultivate themselves should remove misbehaviors and worldly affairs out of their mind first. Then to look into the true nature of reality, if finding out there is an irrational thought arising, they should get rid of it right away. These thoughts can arise at any time, and they can be eliminated anytime. Be sure to make the mind calm. Although some of them are not greedy thoughts, wanton

---

26 *Jie* (劫) generally refers to an immense period of time, a kalpa in Buddhism.

27 *Capturing the Qi* (伏氣, Fu Qi) is also a reference to this Daoist practice of Tu Na.

imaginations also need to be eliminated. Maintain the effort from day to night and do not slack off even for a moment. Only eliminate the noisy mind and keep the wisdom mind. To retain empty mind, remove the mind that attaches to things. Do not feel the need to rely on one thing to practice, and keep the mind calm constantly. This method is very subtle and has profound benefits. We should be very careful about the diet and daily life. I would list some taboos and good points to admonish my students, 'Rub face frequently, blink eyes frequently, flick ears frequently, knock teeth frequently, keep back warm, keep chest protected, massage abdomen frequently, knead feet frequently, swallow saliva frequently, rub the waist frequently.' These are good things we can do."

[The Old Man, Qingyun said:] "There are some taboos that we should be careful of, 'Combing the hair in the morning, seeking coolness in a shady room, sitting on the wet ground for too long, wearing wet clothes when cold, wearing long drying clothes, fanning when sweating, sleeping with a light on, having sexual intercourse between 11:00 p.m. and 1:00 a.m., using cold water to wash the body, and hot fire to burn skin.'

"There are some other things we need to pay extra attention to, and eight out of ten people will be injured by, which are, 'Staring for too long injures the Jing [Essence], lying down for too long injures the Qi, sitting for too long injures blood circulation, standing for too long injures the bones, walking for too long injures the muscles. Anger harms the liver, anxiety harms the spleen, thinking too much harms the heart. Sorrow in extreme harms the lungs, eating too much harms the stomach, fearing too much harms the kidneys, laughing too much harms the waist, talking too much harms the Vitality [Qi]. Spitting too much harms the saliva, sweating too much harms the Yang [energy], tearing too much harms the blood, sexual intercourse too frequently harms the marrow.' We should be very careful at all times to not be against one of the taboos, otherwise you could get sick and have to use the Buddhist's Six Qi to treat it."[28]

> *Editor's Note:* The statement "do not comb hair in the morning" is probably because ancient people had long hair and it took a longer time to comb. So, when waking up early and then combing the hair first, this could hurt the scalp and possibly cause one to catch a cold. This shouldn't be a concern, though, as modern people normally have shorter hair.[29]

---

28   The Six Qi (六氣) refers to the sounds of Chui (吹), Hu (呼), Xi (嘻), He (呵), Xu (嘘), and Xi (呬).

29   Li's Qingyun's taboo of *"Do not comb hair in the morning"* (忌早起梳頭, Ji Zao Qi Shu Tou) is actually connected to the *Yellow Court Scripture* (黃庭經, *Huang Ting Jing),* chapter 7 of the *Internal Illumination,* wherein there is a comment about the "Spirit of the Hair" and how it is connected to the Muddy Pellet (泥丸, Ni Wan) on top of the head. So upon waking, one should not disturb the Muddy Pellet, allowing some time for the Hun Spirit (which roams during sleep) to reconnect with the body. Most Daoists had long hair and would do their combing before bed, and in the morning after their meditation.

Appendix

Questions About Li Qingyun's Age

By Yan Lingfeng

Today, I received *Zhong Wai Magazine's* issue 4 of volume 7. I read the masterpiece by Li Huan: "Replies to the queries regarding the 250-Year-Old man." I think I need to explain about what Mr. Li said.

1. The title of my article in the last issue was: "Do You Believe That Human Beings Can Live for 250 Years?" Obviously, what I questioned was "can humans live to 250 years old?" I mean, was Li Qingyun really "250 years old" at that time?

2. I did not deny that Li Qingyun was a real person, and did not doubt that the photos published by *North China Daily News* were real.

3. The purpose why I pointed out those several questions was just to see if we can get more information, such as more photos, relatives, his disciples, and any record which can fully prove the authenticity of various statements that Li Qingyun said and described.

Because, after all, every record in history could only have the "relative" authenticity. In Sima Qian's *Historical Records*, there are many contradictory descriptions. We cannot dig up the ancient people and ask them questions. At times, we can only tentatively believe them. Mencius said, "When we read a book we should analyze it on our own, we cannot blindly trust what the book says." This is the same as my opinion regarding historical records. Especially, nowadays, the so-called "Biographical Literature" is very popular. It's not that there aren't those who come out to talk about their own experience. Some people even make up "glorious stories" on their own. Even though Li Qingyun was an honest person, a person's memory deteriorates in later years, so it was possible that he might forget something or remember something incorrectly. If Li Qingyun really lived more than one hundred years old, then I think we cannot believe his memory ability and what he said unconditionally. Not to mention that he passed away many years ago and we cannot verify things with him personally. Do we have no right to doubt?

I Had Seen Li Qingyun

By Liu Guiyun

To whom it may concern: I have read your magazine since the opening issue and thanks for the valuable information. I am an old man from Wanxian, Sichuan province. I left my hometown for more than thirty years when I read the article by General Yang Zihui [Yang Sen], and I feel very homesick. Especially, Mr. Wang Chengsheng's article of "250 years old man Li Qingyun," that was a true story. Because I was there and saw Mr. Li Qingyun's primness and sagelike features. It was a big event in east Sichuan in 1927. There are a lot of old people in east Sichuan who knew about this. I saw Mr. Yan Lingfeng's queries, and also Mr. Li Huan's methodical answers to each of those queries. General Yang and Mr. Li Huan were military and political directorates of Sichuan. Of course, what they said has credibility. I have an irrefutable evidence that I treasured for many years, which is *The Secrets of Li Qingyun's Immortality,* compiled by Li Qingyun's disciple, Master Yang Hexuan. This book was published by Shanghai Dazhong Bookstore. I heard it sold very well. The book is enclosed with this letter. If you would like to excerpt or publish it in your magazine, please do so, and return it to me when you are done.

Sincerely,
Your reader, Liu Guiyun

I Had Seen Li Qingyun, Too

By Wang Liankui

In 1927, Republic of China 16th year, I joined the political warfare school of the 20th army group of National Revolutionary Army in Wanxian, and became the student of Mr. Yang Huigong [Yang Sen]. At that time, I was assigned to the 13th sub unit and served as the captain of the sub unit. My major was "military sports," and could be distributed to the troops as a military sports instructor after graduation. I remembered it was not long after the event that happened in 1926, soldiers and people in Wanxian, they were very resentful to the British's arbitrary and unreasonableness. Because the British sunk civilian ships first and then bombarded Wanxian.

When I was in training, I got to know General Xia Jiong [夏炯] who was the brigade commander of the 13th mixed brigade and also a Wushu [武術, Chinese martial artist] instructor. He was under Yang Huigong's command to fight against British warships. He once took his shirt off, grabbed a saber in his hands and rushed onto a British warship, killing the British captain and many sailors. He was regarded as a hero among the students in our Political Warfare School.

The Political Warfare School of the 20th army group of National Revolutionary Army had twenty-something subunits. Every morning before sunrise, Yang Huigong would assemble all of the teachers and students on the drill grounds. He would admonish earnestly and boost our morale to stimulate our patriotic ambition. At the same time, he also encouraged us not to forget the national humiliation, and to exercise our bodies in preparation of fighting for our country. One day, during his exhortation, he mentioned that he was hosting Li Qingyun, the 250-year-old

389

man in Wanxian. He said he had asked Li Qingyun about his method of longevity, but personally, he thought what Li Qingyun said was not scientific. However, Yang Huigong also said meaningfully,

> Li Qingyun used his unscientific longevity methods and could live to 250 years old. If we could use scientific methods to exercise our body, then maybe we could go beyond him and live more than 250 years old?

These few sentences of Yang Huigong actually made us think deeply and feel refreshed. Later, the teachers and students in Political Warfare School requested Yang Huigong to allow us to choose a representative to meet this 250-year-old man, Li Qingyun. Yang Huigong agreed, then all the teachers and students chose me to go with General Xia Jiong to make a formal visit. This was the origin when I met Li Qingyun.

I remember during that time Li Qingyun received General Xia Jiong and me, when we asked him about methods of longevity, his answer was just plain and simple with three key points:

1. Be optimistic when encountering challenges. Don't let the gains and losses tangle your mind.
2. Do not play schemes, treat people sincerely, tell the truth in your lifetime.
3. Sleep early and get up early. Do not worry about tomorrow, tonight.

Now, in retrospect of what he said, these things that he mentioned I have followed for most of my life. This is not that I want to live to 250 years old so I obeyed these rules. But rather, having an open mind, not seeking fame and wealth, being honest, keeping a regular life, not scheming, and rarely thinking about fame and fortune, these were natural to my personality. If people's personality can control their behaviors, affect their health and life, then, I am 68 years old now, and I still can hear and see well, my hair is not fully white yet, my teeth are not fully loose, I can run and climb mountains. I do think my spirit and energy are not different from the thirty-, forty-year-old, middle-aged people. My teacher Yang Huigong is twenty years older than me, his health and physical conditions are even better than mine. The three simple points that Li Qingyun told us forty-two years ago seemed to be very reasonable. And, of course, people say that "the life span is less than a hundred years, but we often think about worries of a thousand years." Why should we even bother?

At all times in all countries quite a few people have longevity. I read Mr. Yan Lingfeng's masterpiece. He used well-documented and extensive evidence, listed dozens of domestic and overseas [long-lived] people. For example, he excerpted a newspaper report of the Republic of China 53rd year [1964], September 18. In that year, on September 17, in Turkey, a 127-year-old man and his 99-year-old wife actually gave birth to twins, and mother and babies were all safe. This was really an anecdote of the world. From this, we know that people have limited horizons of knowledge, that, in fact, people are limited by themselves. The wider world is full of wonders. When we see or hear thing beyond our knowledge, we feel amazed and think it's unbelievable. I was lucky to see Li Qingyun, and thanks to his regard and willingness to talk with me, he taught me these points. That was one of the adventures in my life. At least, this adventure had broadened my mind and horizons.

Afterword

by Stuart Alve Olson

Despite all the controversy and astounding details of a man in our times to have possibly lived to be over 250 years of age, this is actually not the most important aspect of the book. The real importance is found in the advice for living a healthy and long life. This book should not be read as merely a testimony to Li's long life, but as a guide for attaining your own longevity.

Many years ago, someone asked my Buddhist teacher, Chan Master Xuan Hua, if he was enlightened. He responded, "The question isn't if I am enlightened, the question is why aren't you?" This response can equally be applied here, questioning our own state of health and longevity, not so much about Li Qingyun's. We can easily expend all our energy on the questions validating or doubting Li's age, but this will not bring us health and longevity. Applying his teachings will.

Three excellent examples of this include my teacher, Master Liang, who lived to be 102; Da Liu, who made it to 96; and Yang Sen, who was 93 when he passed away. These three, and many others, followed, in whole or in part, the teachings of Li Qingyun.

So, in my opinion, the teachings contained in this book are far more important than the controversies over Li's age.

Valley Spirit Arts offers books and DVDs on Daoism, Taijiquan, and meditation practices primarily from author Stuart Alve Olson, longtime student of Master T.T. Liang and translator of many Daoist related works.

Its website provides teachings on meditation and internal alchemy, Taijiquan, Qigong, and Kung Fu through workshops, private and group classes, and online courses and consulting.

For more information as well as updates on Stuart Alve Olson's upcoming projects and events, please visit:

www.valleyspiritarts.com

16250075R00249

Made in the USA
San Bernardino, CA
24 October 2014